# The Future of the Book in the Digital Age

# The Future of the Book in the Digital Age

EDITED BY
BILL COPE
AND
ANGUS PHILLIPS

**Chandos Publishing**
*Oxford • England*

Chandos Publishing (Oxford) Limited
Chandos House
5 & 6 Steadys Lane
Stanton Harcourt
Oxford OX29 5RL
UK
Tel: +44 (0) 1865 884447 Fax: +44 (0) 1865 884448
Email: info@chandospublishing.com
**www.chandospublishing.com**

First published in Great Britain in 2006

ISBN:
1 84334 240 5 (paperback)
1 84334 241 3 (hardback)
978 1 84334 240 3 (paperback)
978 1 84334 241 0 (hardback)

© Bill Cope and Angus Phillips, 2006

Printed in the UK by 4edge Limited - www.4edge.co.uk

# Contents

# List of figures and tables

## Figures

## Tables

# Preface

In September 2005, delegates from around the world gathered in Oxford, England for the Third International Conference on the Book, hosted by the Oxford International Centre for Publishing Studies. This was an opportunity to discuss a range of important themes relating to the book – including the past, present and future of publishing, libraries, literacy and learning in the information society. The present book is based on papers given at the conference, and the selection has been made around the overall theme of the Future of the Book in the Digital Age. What place does the book have alongside a rich media environment of TV, radio, the Internet, computer games and the mobile phone? What developments are helping to sustain or disrupt the book's place in our world?

In the context of today's rapid developments in information technologies, the book is indeed an old medium of expression. Do the new media (the Internet, multimedia texts and new delivery formats) represent a threat or an opportunity? What is the book's future as a creature of, and conduit for, human creativity? These were the key questions addressed at the conference. Its provocative central proposition was that, rather than being eclipsed by the new media, the book will thrive as a cultural and commercial artefact. More than this, the information architecture of the book, embodying as it does thousands of years experience with recorded knowledge, may well prove critical to the success of the new media.

Whether by the measure of the East or the West, the book is an old medium of representation. In China, paper was invented in the year 105, wood block printing in the late sixth century, book binding in about 1000 and movable type by Bi Sheng in 1041. In Western Europe, the codex, or bound manuscript, emerged in the fourth century, and metal type and the printing press were invented by Johannes Gutenberg in 1450. Within fifty years of Gutenberg's creation, print shops were to be found in every major city and town in Europe and 23,000 titles and eight million volumes had been printed.

The consequence was a new way of representing the world. Contents pages and indexes ordered textual and visual content analytically. A tradition of bibliography and citation arose in which a distinction was made between the author's voice and ideas, and the voices and ideas of other authors. Copyright and intellectual properties were invented. And the widely-used modern written languages we know today, along with their standardised spellings and alphabetically ordered dictionaries, rose to dominance and stabilised, displacing a myriad of small spoken languages and local dialects.

The impact was enormous: modern education and mass literacy; the rationalism of scientific knowledge; the idea that there could be factual knowledge of the social and historical world; the nation state of interchangeable individuals; the persona of the creative individual author. All these are in part consequences of the rise of book culture, and give modern consciousness much of its characteristic shape.

We are, today, on the cusp of another revolutionary transition, or at least the numbers tell us that we are. Within a decade of its invention, ten per cent of the world's population had become connected to the Internet. There is almost no place on earth where it is not possible to connect to the Internet. Billions upon billions of pages have been published.

And so we find ourselves thrust into a new universe of textual media. In one moment, the commentators supply us with utopian readings; in the next, apocalyptic. Leaving behind the linear world of the book, they speak of hypertext and non-linear readings, of formerly passive book readers whose wilful navigation choices have turned them into active users of texts; and of the representation of virtual worlds in which the distant is brought so close, instantly and palpably. In moments of gloom, they also speak of a new inequality – the information inequality that is the result of the 'digital divide'. And they speak of a world of reduced human interaction, as sedentary persons increasingly find themselves tethered to machines.

Do the new electronic media foretell the death of the book? This is one of the key questions addressed by this book. To answer this question, we need to reflect on the history and form of the book, as well as the electronic texts which, it is alleged, pose a threat. And our conclusion may well be that, rather than being eclipsed by the new media, the book will thrive as a cultural and commercial artefact.

Here are three possibilities for the book in the digital age:

*Access:* As well as the conventional printed book (and there is little doubt that people will always be taking that old printed and bound artefact to the beach or to bed, for the foreseeable future at least), the same text may also be available in a range of alternative media. It could also be available on computer screen or printed to paper on the spot, as there is hardly a computer now without an accompanying printer. It could be something that is read on an e-book reading device. It could be rendered to audio via speech synthesis. Or it could find itself coming to life through new electronic media currently in development, such as the paper-like plastic substrates that can be read from reflected light. The result will be greater and easier access to books, and new markets: the student who needs to have a chapter of a book tonight for an assignment due in tomorrow; the person who is visually impaired and wants the voice synthesised version, or another person who wants to listen to the text while driving their car; the traveller who instantly needs just one piece of information from a travel guide and for whom a small piece of text on their mobile phone, about a particular monument or the nearby restaurant, is sufficient; or the teacher who wants to use some textual material as a 'learning object' in an electronic learning environment.

*Diversity:* The traditional book business ran on economies of scale. There was a magic number, somewhere around the 3,000 mark, which made a book viable – worth the trouble to write, print and distribute. Of course, the longer the print run, the better it was, according to the underlying logic of mass production. Costs reduced the longer the run, and access was at the cost of diversity. Mass production made for mass culture. Supporting this was a cumbersome infrastructure of slow moving inventory, large scale warehousing, expensive distribution systems and heavily stocked retail outlets – bad business in every respect, and providing little return for anyone who made books their livelihood, least of all authors. It is not only the electronic reading devices that change the economies of manufacturing scale. Variable digital print does the same thing. One thousand different books can be printed in one run, and this entails no more cost than printing one thousand copies of the same book. Small communities with niche markets now play on the same field as large communities with mass markets. Book printing machines the size of a one hour photo lab will be located in schools, in libraries and in bookstores, all of which will now be able to 'stock' any or even every book in the world.

*Democracy:* These developments will favour small communities of interest and practice. They will lower the entry point to the world of publishing. Museums, research centres, libraries, professional associations and schools might all become publishers. They will be more than happy if a title sells a few hundred copies, or is even provided to the world for free – options that were not previously possible. As for quality, publishing decisions will be made by communities who feel deeply for their domain of content, for that is their domain of interest and expertise. It has never been the case that quantity, the traditional mass market measure of success, equates with quality. This equation will prove even less tenable in the future.

Thousands of publishers and millions of new titles need not add up to information overload. There is already more than any one person can digest, yet we manage to find ways to locate what suits our particular needs and interests. The result of expanded publishing opportunities can only be good – a healthier democracy, a place of genuine diversity. Digital print will also provide a means to cross the digital divide. If you cannot afford a computer for every person in a readership (a school in a developing country, for instance, or a new literature in a small, historically oral language), proximity to computers and digital print will still allow cheap printed materials to be produced locally. There will be no need to buy someone else's language and culture to fill a local knowledge gap. This could be a world where small languages and cultures could flourish, and even, as machine translation improves, find that smallness does not mean isolation.

So what is the book's future, as a creature of and conduit for human invention? The digital media represent an opportunity for the book more than a threat.

For that matter, on closer examination, what's supposed to be new in the digital media is not so new at all. Hypertext's contribution is mechanical: it automates the information apparatuses that the printed book managed by page numbering, contents pages, indexing, citation and bibliography. And as for the virtual, what more did the written word and the printed image do than refer, often with striking verisimilitude, to things that are not immediately present? Indeed, the information architecture of the book, embodying as it does thousands of years' experience with recorded knowledge, provides a solid grounding for every adventure we might take in the new world of digital media.

These are just a few of the principal concerns of this book. Discussions range from the reflective (history, theory and reporting on research) to the highly practical (examining technologies, business models and new practices of writing, publishing and reading).

Articles have been chosen that reflect on the different aspects of the book and its future. The authors provide an international perspective on the issues that affect publishing, bookselling, authorship, readership and librarianship. What kind of spaces have physical bookstores become and how do book consumers respond to them? What kind of value do publishers add when self-publishing is becoming easier and more accepted? How are the economics of book production altered by print on demand? Is diversity being stifled or encouraged by the increasingly commercial outlook of publishers and the growth of bookselling online? What are the implications of the popularity of audio books and their acceptance as part of mainstream publishing? In a world overflowing with information, how can the librarian assist users to assess and evaluate the wide range of data available? As this volume shows, the future of the book continues to provoke both debate and enquiry.

The digital media have arrived. Let's hold them to their promise of access, diversity and democracy. Long live the book!

Bill Cope, Melbourne, Australia
Angus Phillips, Oxford, England

May 2006

# About the authors

**Mark Perlman** has a PhD in Philosophy from the University of Arizona. He taught at Arizona State University from 1993 to 1998, and since 1998 has been in the Department Of Philosophy And Religious Studies at Western Oregon University. He is the author of *Conceptual Flux: Mental Representation, Misrepresentation, and Concept Change* (Kluwer Academic Publishers, 2000) and co-editor (with Robert Cummins and André Ariew) of *Functions: New Essays in the Philosophy of Psychology and Biology* (Oxford University Press, 2002). His philosophical specialties are philosophy of mind, cognitive science, metaphysics, philosophy of law, and aesthetics (particularly philosophy of music).

**Manfred Breede** started his career in the printing industry as an apprentice in Hamburg, Germany. He worked as a journeyman press operator for ten years in several European countries and in Canada before embarking on a career in education 39 years ago. Since that time he has taught technology subjects at the secondary school and university levels. At Ryerson University where he has worked for the past 19 years, he teaches printing processes, quality control and bindery courses. Breede is a graduate of McGill University. He is the author of the book *Handbook of Graphic Arts Equations*, now in its 2nd edition, and numerous academic papers and articles in professional journals. Manfred is also a software developer and industry consultant, specializing in print, print finishing, quality and efficiency. In 2002 he was recognized by the readers of the Canadian graphic arts journal PRINT*ACTION* as one of the '50 Most Influential People in the Graphic Arts'.

**Angus Phillips** is Director of the Oxford International Centre for Publishing Studies and Head of the Publishing Department at Oxford Brookes University. Angus Phillips joined Oxford Brookes University in 2003. He has an MBA from Warwick University, an MA from Oxford University, and many years experience in the publishing industry including running a trade and reference list at Oxford University Press. He has acted as consultant to a variety of publishing companies, and trained publishing professionals from the UK and overseas in editorial, marketing and management.

Angus is a member of the International Advisory Committee for the International Conference on the Book (held at Oxford Brookes in 2005) and a member of the Editorial Advisory Board for the *International Journal of the Book*. He has written book chapters and journal articles in the areas of the Internet, book covers, and the role of the publishing editor. With Giles Clark he is the author of the new edition of *Inside Book Publishing* (2007). He is a contributor to the forthcoming *Blackwell Companion to the History of Books*, and the *Oxford Companion to the Book*.

**Asst. Prof. Christopher Kular** was born in Toronto, Canada. He has a Bachelor of Technology degree in Graphic Communications Management, and currently teaches print media and management of electronic imaging at Ryerson University.

**Mihael Kovac** PhD is associate professor at the Department of Library and Information Science and Book Studies at the University of Ljubljana, Slovenia. He started his professional career in 1986 as Editor-in-Chief of *Mladina*, the only opposition weekly in then-socialist Slovenia. After 1988, he moved into book publishing and in 1996 became editorial director of Mladinska Knjiga, the largest Slovenian publishing house. In 1995, he started to investigate the Slovenian book industry in order to write his PhD. In 2000, he started to lecture at University of Ljubljana. He is author of numerous articles on book studies. In 2001, together with a group of researchers, he won a grant for a three-year research project on textbook publishing in European Union and former Communist countries. The results of the research were published in a book in 2005. In 2004, together with Kelvin Smith, he co-edited a special edition of *The Public* on book publishing in Europe.

**Mojca Kovac Sebart** PhD is Associate Professor of Sociology of Education at the Department of Pedagogy, Faculty of Arts, University of Ljubljana. Her main field of research is the Theory of Educational Reform, which was also the main topic of her doctoral thesis. Between 1993 and 1999, she played an active role in Slovene school reform. Since 2000, she has been a member of the National Evaluation Council. In 2002, she published a book on the sociology of school reforms in Slovenia. In 2004 and 2003, together with Miha Kovac, she published a series of articles on textbook publishing in both Slovene and international journals. She also publishes in several other fields of research: pre-school education, childhood socialisation, values, multiculturalism and education, authority, classroom and school culture, equal opportunities and differentiation of pupils, assessment in education, and citizenship education.

**Professor Hillel Nossek** is the academic director of the Teaching and Research Authority of the College of Management Academic Studies Tel-Aviv, Israel and a professor of communication at the School of Media Studies of the College. His research and teaching interests are in the implications of new and old media consumptions, and use in social construction of identities, and news in general and media and political violence in particular. *Media and Political Violence*, the book he edited with Annabelle Sreberny and Prasun Sunwalker, is being published by Hampton Press.

**Professor Hanna Adoni**, Hebrew University of Jerusalem and the Academic College of Emek Yezreel. Since the year 2000, Hanna has been the incumbent of the Danny Arnold Chair in Communication at the Hebrew University of Jerusalem. Her research interests are in the area of mass communication and cultural behavior, with special emphasis on literacy, reading and the new media technologies. She is a co-author of *Social Conflict and Television News* (1990), *Twenty Years of Communication and Culture in Israel* (2000), and *Media Minorities and Hybrid Identities* (2006). Hanna co-authored *Readers' Voices: Reading as a Cultural Behavior in a Multi-Media Environment* (2006, in Hebrew) with Hillel Nossek.

**Audrey Laing** is a PhD research student and ad hoc lecturer within the Publishing Department at The Robert Gordon University in Aberdeen. Her thesis is entitled 'Bookselling culture and consumer behaviour: Marketing strategies and responses, in traditional and online environments' and examines how consumers respond to the marketing techniques used by UK chain bookstores. Audrey's interest in this area of research grew out of the 12 years she spent working in chain bookstores, and the many changes that took place in the book trade over that period. Audrey has also published in the *International Journal of Retail and Distribution Management* and *Publishing Research Quarterly*.

**Jo Royle** is Senior Lecturer and Subject Leader for Communication and Publishing within the Aberdeen Business School at the Robert Gordon University and is Undergraduate Programme Manager in the field. She lectures on Electronic Publishing and Consumer Publishing at both undergraduate and postgraduate levels; and has supervised and carried out research in these areas, and gained related external funding from sources including the Arts and Humanities Research Board and British National Bibliography Research Fund. In particular, this research has focused on the role of branding for consumer publishers on the Internet and change management issues associated with multimedia publishing for children. She recently gained internal funding from the RGU Research Development Initiative and it is from this that the research on branding and the community in bookselling is progressing. She was previously Editorial Manager of an independent consumer publishing house.

**Ann Steiner** teaches in comparative literature at Lund University in Sweden. She has written a book on Swedish book trade in the 1970s, *In the Literary Mainstream: the Book-of-the-month Club and Swedish Book Trade in the 1970s*, focusing on the consequences of a complete deregulation of the trade at the time, the growth of subscription book clubs, and the nature of mainstream fiction. Her ongoing research includes studies of the impact of technology, and particularly the Internet, on how literature is distributed, evaluated, and consumed in contemporary society, globally as well as locally. She is also writing an historical overview of the Swedish book trade between 1945 and 1970, discussing matters of mass-market, commercial publishing, and the reading public in the economic boom after the second World War.

**David H. Lynn** has been the editor of 'The Kenyon Review' since 1994, and is the editor of 'The Best of the Kenyon Review'. A new collection of his short stories, 'Year of Fire', will be published by Harcourt in December 2005. He is also the author of the novel *Wrestling with Gabriel, Fortune Telling*, a collection of stories, and *The Hero's Tale: Narrators in the Early Modern Novel*, a critical study. His stories and essays have appeared in magazines and journals in America, England, India, and Australia. David Lynn lives in Gambier, Ohio with his wife, Wendy Singer, and their two children, Aaron and Elizabeth. He is a Professor of English at Kenyon College.

**Jennifer Cavender** is currently an Adjunct English Professor at Marshall University in Huntington, West Virginia. She received her BA in English from West Virginia University in 1999, and in 2005, she graduated with an MA in English from Marshall University. She has worked as a journalist and a librarian, as well as a physical education teacher and a waitress –

all of which serve as great, creative fodder. She is currently working on a novel. She plans to continue research on audiobooks and editorial theory, and to pursue doctoral studies.

**Lisa Stuchell** is currently an Adjunct English Professor at Marshall University in Huntington, West Virginia. In 2001, she received her BA in English and Media Arts from the University of South Carolina. She recently graduated from Marshall University with an MA in English, concentrating in editorial theory, as well as receiving a certificate in Medieval and Renaissance Studies. Her thesis 'Malory's Maladies: Determining Intention and Influence Through Editorial Theory in Sir Thomas Malory's Le Morte D'Arthur' discusses the impact of versions and variants upon the readers of medieval literature. Lisa plans to continue her studies in editorial theory and to pursue a PhD in Renaissance drama.

**Maureen Brunsdale** is from Illinois State University, United States of America.

**Jennifer Hootman** is from Illinois State University, United States of America.

**John Feather** has been Professor of Library of Information Studies at Loughborough University since 1988. He was educated at Oxford, was a Research Fellow of Darwin College Cambridge, and worked in publishing and librarianship before moving to Loughborough. He has served as Head of Department (1990–94, and since 2003), Dean of Education and Humanities (1994–96) and Pro-Vice Chancellor (1996–2000).

His many publications include *A History of British Publishing* (1987), of which a fully revised edition was published in 2006, and *The Information Society: a Study in Continuity and Change* (4th ed., 2004). With his colleague, James Dearnley, he is editing the *International Encyclopaedia of Publishing*, to be published by Routledge.

**Bill Cope** is a Research Professor in the Department of Educational Policy Studies, University of Illinois, Urbana-Champaign, USA. He is also a director of Common Ground Publishing, currently developing experimental mixed medium print and internet publishing *(http:// www.CGPublisher.com)*. He is a former First Assistant Secretary in the Department of the Prime Minister and Cabinet and Director of the Office of Multicultural Affairs. His academic research and writing crosses a number of disciplines, and examines themes as varied as Australian workplace change, the future of the printing and publishing industries and literacy learning. In recent years, he has worked on a joint Common Ground/RMIT University (Melbourne) research initiative, *Creator to Consumer in a Digital Age: Book Production in Transition,* funded as part of the Infrastructure and Industry Growth Fund (IIGF) of the Book Production Enhanced Printing Industry Competitiveness Scheme (EPICS) of the Australian Government's Department of Industry, Tourism and Resources. The outcome of this work was a series of research reports in book form examining changes in book production technologies and markets, as well as a program of national and international seminars and industry training and tertiary education materials *(http://www.C-2-CProject.com).* He is currently working on a project on the next generation of web technologies, the 'semantic web', jointly with RMIT and Fuji-Xerox.

**Mary Kalantzis** is Dean of the College of Education, University of Illinois, Urbana-Champaign, USA. Until recently, she was Dean of the Faculty of Education, Language and Community Services at RMIT University in Melbourne, Australia and President of the Australian Council of Deans of Education. She has been a Commissioner of the Human Rights and Equal Opportunity Commission, Chair of the Queensland Ethnic Affairs Ministerial Advisory Committee and a member of the Australia Council's Community Cultural Development Board. With Bill Cope, she is co-author of a number of books, including: *The Powers of Literacy,* Falmer Press, London, 1993, *Productive Diversity,* Pluto Press, Sydney, 1997; *A Place in the Sun: Re-Creating the Australian Way of Life,* Harper Collins, Sydney, 2000; and *Multiliteracies: Literacy Learning and the Design of Social Futures,* Routledge, London, 2000.

**Mark Woodhouse,** in addition to other responsibilities, has managed the Mark Twain Collections and the Special Collections of Elmira College, NY, USA, for eighteen years.

# Introduction

*Bill Cope and Angus Phillips*

## The book today

Two recent developments throw an interesting light on the debate about the future of the book. The first was the publication in 2004 of *Reading at Risk*,[1] a report by the US National Endowment of Arts into reading in America. The report, based on a survey of 17,000 adults, presented a 'detailed but bleak assessment of the decline of reading's role in the nation's culture'. Less than half of the US adult population now reads literature (defined as novels, short stories, poetry and plays), reflecting a 20 per cent decline over 20 years. Reading levels are higher amongst those with a higher level of education, but reading has still declined amongst every educational grouping. Whereas previously young adults (18 to 34) read the most, they are now the group least likely to read. The decline in reading correlated with increased use of electronic media, including video games and the Internet. The report was greeted with gloom and some despondency about the future of reading when faced with competition from different media.

The second was the awarding in 2006 of the first Blooker prize to *Julie and Julia* (2005) by Julie Powell. The book recounts how in the space of one year, Julie Powell cooked all 524 recipes in Julia Child's *Mastering the Art of French Cooking*. Day 1, recipe 1 is entitled 'The Road to Hell is Paved with Leeks and Potatoes'. The chair of the judging panel, Cory Doctorow, described Powell's book as a 'heartfelt, funny and occasionally obscene tell-all about her journey of self-discovery and cholesterol'. Sales had reached more than 100,000 copies before the book won the prize. What was remarkable about the book is that it had started its life online – it was originally written as a blog. The Blooker Prize was established to celebrate books that had grown out of the phenomenon of blogging. Millions of blogs are now in existence worldwide, as their authors discover this new route to a readership that can number a handful or become a mass audience.

As the *Observer* columnist Robert McCrum remarked, 'writers, publishers and booksellers are living through the biggest change in literary communications since Caxton and Gutenberg'.[2] More books are being published than ever before (160,000 new books and new editions were published in the UK in 2004), and at the same time the evidence is that people are reading less and doing other things. New technology may be diverting us away from reading yet it is making it easier to write and publish, whether online or in print form. Getting published by a mainstream publisher may be difficult, but there are other means available to the budding author, and e-books and print on demand are fuelling a boom in self-publishing.

# A longer view

Dante's decision seven hundred years ago to write his great poem not in Latin but in what he called vulgar eloquence – Italian, the language of his people – and the innovation in the following century of printing from moveable type are landmarks in the secularisation of literacy, and the liberalization of society, as well as an affront to the hegemony of priests and tyrants. The impact of today's emerging technologies promises to be no less revolutionary, perhaps more so. The technology of the printing press enhanced the value of literacy, encouraged widespread learning, and became the sine qua non of modern civilization. New technologies will have an even greater effect, narrowing the notorious gap between the educated rich and the unlettered poor ... That these technologies have emerged just as the publishing industry has fallen into terminal decrepitude is providential, one might even say miraculous.   (Epstein, 2001)

Jason Epstein is one of the truly important people of modern publishing (and thus modern reading and so, modern democracy). He is a man who has helped invent one of the most revolutionary of modern technologies – the paperback book. Epstein founded the Anchor imprint at Doubleday, and in so doing, brought to a huge number of people for just $1.25 per book, works of literature, works of reflection, works of pleasure. Here is a man who for his whole life has stood faithful to the tradition of Gutenberg.

In his recent book about books, *Book Business: Publishing past, present, and future*, Epstein sees us on the brink of another technological revolution, angered that the world of books which he helped to create has fallen into desuetude, yet surprisingly optimistic about the future of the book. The cause for his optimism lies in another wave of technologies, far more significant in his view than the coming of the paperback. In fact, he says that this wave of innovation will be as significant as the revolution that was begun by Gutenberg himself.

The wave of innovation to which Epstein is referring is not centred on a single technology, but a mix of technologies: print on demand, the Internet and electronic book readers. These technologies are in some respects quite different to each other. They do different things and do them in different ways. But at their heart is a common logic – the logic of digitization. And it is this common logic which can tie these otherwise divergent technologies together into an easier and quicker and cheaper way of making books, thus expanding the market for books, and increasing the cultural impact of books.

This is another book about books, written by a group of thinkers and researchers who are equally committed to the culture of the book, and who are trying in a modest way to imagine, and in part create, the new world to which Epstein is alluding. Unlike Epstein, this particular group has not rubbed shoulders with W.H. Auden or Dr Seuss – for Epstein has spent his working life in the towers of cultural influence which dominate the world's English language publishing in the few blocks around Times Square in New York. And, working as we do in universities, we are a long way from the Xerox Laboratories and Apple Computer in California, or the Microsoft complex in Seattle, organizations which have not only invented today's world, but who, for their trouble, now own a substantial slice of it.

In this book, we have set ourselves the task of thinking about the future of the book, inspired to be sure by the Jason Epsteins and the Steve Jobses, but knowing full well that, at the nether reaches of the system of text which we inhabit, we have to think simply and practically. Our task is to consider the ways in which the common platform of digitization will integrate the new technologies of print, the Internet and electronic books into a single publishing ecosystem – one which is easier to access and in some respects enhancing, rather than displacing, traditional publishing. It is our view that if we have the imagination to consider new and hybrid alternatives, the book will prosper, in new forms as well as old, and as an expression of our multifarious cultures as well as a business where authors, publishers, printers and booksellers can earn a good living.

This is a book about books. It describes the relationships of new technologies to the daily lives and changing work practices of players all along the book production supply chain, from creators (authors, in the case of books), to publishers, to bookstores and libraries and finally to consumers. It is about changes in commerce, in technology and in culture – culture understood here as the way we live, as well as the culture business itself as exemplified by the creation, manufacture and dissemination of cultural contents through the book trade.

Needless to say, everything in the book trade is changing. These changes are very much influenced by the technologies of the Internet, digital printing, e-text reading devices, digital rights management, digital design tools, digital content capture and archiving systems, and the many other elements of technological change which impacts on the production of today's books and book-like texts.

## Technologies for making books and the book as technology

This book is about recent changes in the ways in which books are made, as well as possible or even likely changes in the ways in which books might be made in the near future. In part, our focus is on technological actuality, centred mostly on the digitization of text and its consequences. Our focus is also in part on the realm of possibility. Where might these technological shifts lead us? What are the commercial and cultural conditions in which technological possibility might bear fruits?

So what is a book? And what are print and e-text?

Until recently, the question 'what is a book?' would have seemed as ephemeral as the philosopher's question, 'what is a table?' Unless this were a question intended to take us into some fraught metaphysical territory, the answer would have been a relatively simple and direct one – a volume of text, printed on fifty or more paper pages, bound between stiff covers, with certain generic features including a title page, contents, the sectioning of text around chapters and the like. In this definition, the printed book is itself a technology, a means for rendering extended passages of text and images. It is the peculiar generic features of a book that make it immediately distinguishable from other renderings of text or images, such as shopping lists or envelopes full of holiday snaps.

Notwithstanding the stability of this definition, the technology of the traditional book has not been static. In the second half of the twentieth century, more and more books were bound using less expensive paperback covers and using 'perfect binding' processes that depend on strong but flexible modern glues. The commercial and cultural impact of this simple development was enormous, vastly expanding the size of the purchasing public and the number of books produced. And, in another significant development from the late 1960s, what made something a 'real book' (as opposed to a manuscript, or a draft, or a report) was official listing through the registration of an international standard book number (ISBN). As well as being a highly practical tool, this number was a critical sign that the book had officially entered the real world of bookstores, libraries and searchable listings of bibliographical data.

However, technological developments since the beginning of the 1990s have thrown into considerable question this definition of a book. Since then, we have faced two powerful and seemingly contradictory ways of thought.

Some commentators predict that the traditional form and function of books will be replaced by the Internet and various electronic reading devices, from computer screens, to dedicated electronic book reading devices and later by imminent technologies such as 'electronic ink'. To some extent, current trends bear this out. Children writing school assignments used to have to borrow the relevant books from their school library. Now, they can get the information they need from the Internet. More and more of the written material we need and want can be found on the Internet. The direct competition between books and increasingly book-like Internet formats is manifest. e-Book reading tablets may have been of limited success, but probably billions of PDF e-book format texts have been downloaded since the format was invented in the 1990s. And some traditional forms of printed matter have been all but replaced by non-printed media. For instance the encyclopaedia and many technical manuals have virtually been replaced by electronic formats. As a technology, the Internet has a number of distinct advantages over traditional books:

- all its available information is instantaneously available;

- it is more hugely expansive than any library or bookstore;

- it is mostly free;

■ and it doesn't involve chopping down trees.

Surely, say the pundits who predict the end of the book, this is a superior technology for the transmission of text and images? And so, sooner or later, the book is doomed to extinction.

However, in an alternative view, the book is now everywhere. Despite predictions of the imminent demise of the book at the hands of the Internet and electronic book reading devices, the book is now ubiquitous, in three senses:

In the case of conventionally printed books, more are being produced than ever before. To draw a parallel, television and video did not replace cinema. Rather, they extended the cultural and commercial range of cinema. So it is with books. People may be reading more text and images delivered through the Internet, but at the same time, more books are being printed than ever before. The history of communications media tells us that new media often do not replace old. At most, they redefine the purposes and functions of older media. Often they even extend the reach and the power of older media.

Not only is the total number of volumes of conventionally printed books on the increase, cheaper digital printing technologies mean that many texts that could not previously have been viably produced can now become a printed book.

Finally, the book is everywhere in another pervasive sense: its textual forms and communicative apparatuses are to be found throughout the new electronic formats. Computer renditions of text and images are looking more and more like books. Contrast, for instance, older word-processing systems with newer ones, and html files in the first generation of Internet development with proliferation of PDF files. Much of the on-screen rendering of text and images is based on systems of representation derived from the book, including 'pages' of text, headings, systems for listing contents (buttons and menus), referencing (links), cross-referencing (hypertext) and indexing (searching). The technology may differ, but these basic structures and functions are derived from the book, and were developed within the technology of the book over a five hundred year period.

Here's a peculiarly modern story. Having been told of an interesting programme on Australia's ABC Radio, you might go to the ABC website where the programme could be found, not only as audio which could be downloaded and replayed, but as text with images which could be printed out in a variety of 'printer friendly formats'. Radio in this instance had not quite become a book, but it was now more like a book than radio. Oral text had been transcribed, and edited. Images had been added and pages designed to be printed. And the material was available at any time, not just at the time of transmission of the program. In this task, ABC Radio had taken on many of the tasks of a traditional publisher, things that used to make a publisher palpably different from a radio station. Still, the text was not quite a book – in its length and structure, and as a text able to be initiated into the world of ISBNs, and made available in bookstores and libraries. Radio had nevertheless taken on some of the core features of books. It is only one small step to put together a series of radio programmes, and make them a book. In fact, as the growth and success of the ABC Shops attests, more and more television and radio series are being successfully translated into book format. And so, the distinction between radio and books is being blurred. Books and book-like products are to be found in places where they were rarely found before. Content is being developed and designed for multiple renderings, to suit a diverse range of market and cultural needs.

So, what is a book? Our old definition was focused on an object. Our new definition needs to focus on a function.

A book is no longer a physical thing. A book is what a book does. And what does a book do?

A book is a structured rendition of text and possibly also images, which:

- Displays certain generic features: it is an extended text (of say, more than twenty thousand words and/or twenty images), whose size means that for practical purposes, the text needs to be structured around generic features, principally including cover, blurb, title, author, copyright statement, ISBN, table of contents, chapter headings, body text/images and also, sometimes, a referencing apparatus, index, acknowledgements, foreword, author bio-note and introduction.

- Is recognizable in the world of books as a book, either by official allocation of an ISBN and registration as a book, or by equivalent emerging forms of definition, such as registration as a book within the Digital Object Identifier (DOI) framework.

These, then, are the two things books do:

1. They have a characteristic textual, and thus, communicative, structure.

2. They have book-like functions because they are defined, registered and recognised as books. This means that, when we need to 'do books', they can be found in bibliographical listings, they are acquired

through bookstores and libraries; and they can be referenced as books.

However, unlike the traditional definition, a book in this definition does not have to be printed. It can be rendered in many ways, including electronic-visual and audio (talking books). A book is not a thing. It is a textual form, a way of communicating. A book is not a product. It is an information architecture.

So what of those other key terms – print and e-text? In the case of books, 'print' would seem to be a self-evident concept, perhaps timeless. However, what we do when we print – who does it, and how we do it – is radically changing. Once, printing books was something that book printers did. Now, there is a 'printer' in most homes and offices alongside the personal computer, and it is capable of printing (even if not binding) books or fragments of books, to the same quality as a book printer's printing press. Books are everywhere. Printing is everywhere. And this has changed forever books and printing.

As for e-text, this is something quite new, digitally manufactured text and images which end up on our computer screens, or e-book readers, or one day perhaps on pages printed with e-ink. The letters and the images are put together on computers, bit-by-bit, pixel-by-pixel, byte-by-byte. e-Text is a new way of creating books, and leads us inexorably towards the proliferation of e-books.

However, digitization has been making its way progressively into the manufacture of text for some twenty-five years. Today, virtually every printed book would have been e-text at some point in the production process, from word processing, to desktop publishing, to digital imaging of film and plates. The rise of fully digital print radically extends this process. For the first time with fully digital print, the final rendering to print is digitally generated for every page, and every impression. This is the case both for the desktop printer and the digital presses that manufacture a complete book.

This is where print and e-text dramatically converge. Not only are they both manifestations of the same thing – electronically constructed and stored text – they are increasingly becoming versions of the same thing. In the case of the book, print and e-text both do what a book does. They simply render that book using different media. The convergence is so great, in fact, that electronic texts and texts printed to paper can be rendered from the same file. e-Text can be rendered electronically, or it can be rendered direct to paper, or 'printed' to screen. e-Text is everywhere. Print is everywhere. The distinctions in form, function and construction are blurring. This book examines the shape and consequences of this development.

## The book now, and its near future

... But then what will you do ... when you have driven so many independent bookstores out of existence with your discount policies favouring the big chains, and there isn't any shelf space in the mega stores and the mall spaces that you have encouraged to count on a rapid turnover of an insipid inventory of over hyped brand-name commodities in order to amortise their escalating real estate costs, and meanwhile you find that you've wildly overpaid millions of dollars in advance of royalties to some disgraced politician or coked-up child molester for a memoir no one will ever want to read even if it actually gets ghost-written? Here's what you do. You go to those divisions of your conglomerate that were independent publishers once upon a time themselves before you gobbled them up – those 'ghostly imprints of by-gone firms' dating back to when literature, issues, and ideas were the priority instead of 'sales thresholds,' before decency and common sense were asked to lick the hand of 'synergy' – and you tell them to maximise profit by maximising everything else: cut overhead, trim editorial staff, get rid of the marginal and the midlist, win the lottery.' (Leonard, 2001)

Leonard is writing a review of Jason Epstein's book in a magazine which Epstein founded, the *New York Review of Books*, and he's agreeing with him. Here Leonard is adding to the loud complaints which can be heard all the way up and down the book production supply chain.[4]

**Authors:** It seems to be becoming increasingly more difficult to get your work published – and whether this is because publishers are sticking to fewer, low risk, high margin, mass production items, or because there are more titles out there, and more authors are wanting to be published, there is no denying that there are genuine 'push factors' on the supply side. Authors are also angry at the service they get from publishers – how much attention publishers are paying to editing, how much marketing they are doing and how well they distribute the book. And authors are angry about the kinds of royalties publishers pay – rarely above ten per cent, and in many cases, such as academic publishing, nothing or virtually nothing for books sold at sometimes exorbitant prices. For the majority of authors, writing a book is simply not a smart business proposition.

**Publishers:** For all publishers, and particularly small publishers, the margins seem to be dropping. Yet the risks are as high as ever – large up-front investment in working capital, high distribution costs and retailing margins, as well as the unpredictable element of luck with any title.

**Printers:** Always a highly competitive business, printing is a bad mix of capital intensive as well as labour intensive manufacturing. Now, online file transfer protocols, cheaper and faster transportation and an open import regime make printing a more challenging business than ever. Once a localised business, printers are increasingly being subjected to the rigours of global markets.

**Bookstores:** Today's bookstores are the most capital intensive of all retail outlets. No other retail outlet would tolerate the amount of stock that is required, nor the average amount of time it sits on the shelf before it is sold. Even then, although the bookstore is a retail outlet which works well for browsers, in all but the very largest bookshops it is a notoriously frustrating place when you are looking for something specific. Even the largest bookstore can only stock a small fraction of all the books in print.

**Readers:** In some countries books seem to be getting dearer all the time, and in many areas of knowledge and culture, dating more quickly. And in a world which seems to be fragmenting into ever more finely-defined subcultures, specialisms, knowledge areas, fad and fetishes, the general bookstore is becoming less useful to readers' interests and needs. The selection of titles available from the large chains is impressive, but the concentration is often on bestsellers.

In one sense, this all adds up to bad business. But being bad business also means that it is a business ripe for change.

It is too easy to say that imminent changes in the book production workflow from the creator to the consumer will solve all these problems. But they will go part of the way, and in so doing, are sure to change the very nature of the business: the kind of work which is done, and even the kinds of entities which do the work.

One term which is regularly used to describe the direction of change in the supply chain is disintermediation: the collapse of one element of the process into another, or the disappearance of one step. Where have the typesetters, the lithographers and the platemakers gone in the digital printing process? The answer is just that they've gone, never to return except in museums of industrial history. But it's not just a matter of collapsing some of the steps in the process; it's also a matter of creating new kinds of work, doing new things, things that were inconceivable in the old ecology of book production.

These are some of the promises of the new world of digitised book production.

**Authors**: Digital publishing ecologies are about content capture, in which the author does a greater proportion of the total work of the book production supply chain, yet does it with very little additional effort. Authors do two main things – first, they typeset the text into fully designed book templates. This is not such a large request, as there is barely an author who does not work on a word processor these days. And second, through a series of online forms, they build all the metadata required for resource discovery on the Internet and automatic insertion of the book into the world of e-commerce, so that once it is published, it can be effortlessly ordered by any physical bookstore, and automatically put on sale in online bookstores like Amazon. Of course, publishers and reviewers and referees check and refine this metadata as well as the developing text, from proposal to final publication, but they do all of this online and whilst relating to a single, evolving source file stored on a web server mounted relational database. As the process is increasingly automated, productivity through the supply chain improves. The author becomes the primary risk taker (the largest investment in the whole process is the author's time), and so, a substantial slice of the rewards of automation will go to them. This is the commercial outcome: the possibility of making writing a better business for authors. But there's also a cultural outcome: that more people will be able to write – the poet in Melbourne writing in Chinese who knows there's a small market for her books not just in Melbourne but in Shanghai, Penang and San Diego; the academic educator writing about an obscure aspect of dyslexia, of enormous importance to the several hundred academic experts in this field in the world; the Aboriginal elder who knows that their history of their community will become an important book for the local library and that it will enjoy modest sales at the nearby tourist information bureau; the school teacher who has produced a curriculum unit which they want to distribute to their colleagues and students. Call these niche markets if you like, but to get these works published will also be to create a more healthy democracy, a place of more genuine cultural pluralism, than can ever be offered by the mass market.

**Publishers**: No prepayment for printing and no inventory – this is a publisher's dream. If a book sells in the online environment, so much the better. If it doesn't, all that's lost from the publisher's point of view is the time they've spent reviewing, commenting and editing the author's successive drafts of their metadata and their text. Once they've pressed the 'publish' button, the rest just happens – physical books get printed and dispatched as they are ordered, and electronic books are automatically downloaded by purchasers. What they get back is instant payment, and instant market information. What they are relieved of is the burden of discounting, remaindering and dealing with returns. And so, publishers can stick at what they are good at, their core business. They can focus their energies on finding, refining and placing content, instead of having to spend valuable time and resources managing the back end of an old-fashioned mass manufacturing and warehousing business. This is particularly good for small publishers who don't have the warehousing infrastructure and often pay sixty per cent or more of the book's sale price to outsource distribution. Many more small publishers may emerge in this environment, as smaller print runs become more economical and the entry point to the industry in terms of working capital is reduced. Museums, community organisations, university research centres and associations of hobbyists can all become publishers. Being close to their content and close to their potential readers, they are more likely to know the culture, the market, and the community that they serve, than any publishing conglomerate. In Epstein's words, book publishing 'is by nature a cottage industry, decentralised, improvisational, personal'. It is 'best performed by small groups of like-minded people, devoted to their craft, jealous of their autonomy.' (Epstein, 2001). This is the old ideal of publishing. The nice irony is that the new technologies and business processes will allow this old ideal to be realised, and far more effectively than was ever the case in the past.

**Printers:** The new printing technologies are set to transform physical book production, as well as enhance old technologies. As the price of digital printing machines drop (which it is certain to, being built on mass-market laser and Xeroxography technologies), one of the key negatives of the printing business – high capital costs – will be reduced. It will also be less labour intensive, with just one operator running a machine which does the work of the film stripper, plate maker, printer, offsider, folder, collator and binder. With friendly user interfaces, the skills of this book maker will be generic IT, generic process management and generic art/design/communications industry skills learnt increasingly in a Higher Education setting. Specific interface skills will be learned through online tutorials or at short courses in the training room of the machine manufacturer, or be offered by the manufacturer in a university setting. As the number of steps in the supply chain reduces, the printer will take on new roles, including some tasks previously undertaken within the publisher or distributor's inventory system, such as direct dispatch: B-2-B in the case of online or physical bookstore orders and B-2-C in the case of customer orders. Smart small printers will regain their old location-based competitive advantage, near or even co-located within a bookstore, a library, a university, an airport distribution centre, a publishing organization, or an online bookstore's distribution centre. Large printers might set up their businesses as nationally, or even globally, distributed organizations, with small point of print/point of dispatch/point of sale agencies in local centres. Our assumption in this project is that the market for books in the 500 to 3,000 copies range – barely serviced at the moment – is at least the same, but probably much larger than the market for conventional 3,000+ print runs. But it will have to be serviced in quite new ways. The end result is that the online world will produce more books, and more printing, and this is good news for the industry. The technological changes will also, paradoxically, fit well and even extend the market for books printed using older technologies; offset can be printed as mass production titles using the same files as for digital, which means titles that unexpectedly find a market which justifies long-run offset printing can be produced that would never have seen the light of day had they not been printed digitally first.

**Bookstores:** Amazon.com is but a thin modern veneer on an old economy; an economy of large inventories, of moving products from printer to distribution warehouse to bookstore dispatch. It is a business that discounts to compete but which has created few efficiencies in the supply chain. The fully digitised solution is to build a back-end to Amazon, a book production process which creates efficiencies, improves productivity, reduces costs and creates new products for new markets. So, where to, for that old and much loved institution, the bookstore? Will independent bookstores and community bookstores be gobbled up by mass-market behemoths like Amazon? The answer is not necessarily. In fact, we may well see a revival of the convivial, local, community-based bookstore. This bookstore will provide consumers with a very special experience, around local themes, or a cultural niche, or a specialist area of knowledge, or the bookstore owner's eccentric sense of taste and style. You will visit the bookstore, not because it can ever pretend to be comprehensive, but because you want to enter a space where the bookstore's selectivity has created a niche. Its range will be thorough for what it sets out to do, but with much less stock than the bookstores of the past. And it will turn this stock over more rapidly. Yet it will also have every book in print for sale, with next day delivery through online B-2-B ordering. And, not too far into the future, the shelves in the corner of the store will be removed, to be replaced by a small coffee shop and a book printing kiosk, perhaps the size of the photographic development units in chemist shops, or smaller. And by the time you've finished your coffee, any book, from a choice of every book in the world, will be printed.

**Readers:** The world of reading is also certain to change, and for the better. Some forms of print will disappear. The largest printed item in the average household of a generation ago, the encyclopaedia, has largely disappeared. The reason is because, for what it did, it was an expensive and inefficient information technology, easily and quickly replaced by searchable electronic files. Most pages of most encyclopaedias were never read in most households. Most of the shelf space was wasted. A CD-ROM or an online encyclopaedia is just so much more effective, efficient and appropriate a medium for bite-sized information. Speaking at the first e-Book World Conference in New York, Microsoft's Vice President of Technology Development, Dick Brass, even predicted the end of bulky newspapers like the *New York Times*, and for similar reasons – most people don't read most classified advertisements, which are far more easily searched online. Yet, as certainly as the new technologies will reduce the market for certain kinds of print, they will also open up new markets, and the short-run book is sure to be one of these markets. In fact, rather than eliminate books, the online environment has the potential to make the books a more useful and attractive product. With product numbers extended to individual copies (ISBN plus), readers might be granted an extended copyright licence, under which terms possession of a printed copy (bought from a bookstore, lent by a library or borrowed from a friend) allows access to the online version with full search/index functions, access to new editions or postscripts, referencing built on live hypertext, illustrations that move, full colour images where the book can only be economically printed in black and white, and so on. In return for this new book-as-extended information service, the rights of the reader would need to be accurately specified. Too much searching from too many different computers in too short a length of time would indicate that the individual book number was being shared too far from the point of view of the interests of the author and the publisher.

For every agent in today's supply chain this adds up to a new business case, a new technological and cultural case for the book – a case for doing things differently, and by doing them differently, doing them better. Even the business case has a frame of reference which is bigger than bottom lines and financial years, and bigger than supply and demand.

It's also a case about new kinds of text creation, and new forms of production, which will create new markets and at the same time invigorate old cultures and nourish new.

That's what this book is about.

# Chapter overview

The aim of this volume is to provide a selection of articles that represent some of the central issues around the book and its future. The book's scope is international, with authors from a variety of countries, and many of the articles are based on primary research.

Mark Perlman writes of a world in which books now sit alongside other information sources. He argues that it is not a question of the Internet replacing books but of having made them irrelevant. For the students to whom he teaches philosophy, books are just not part of their lives any more. If it isn't on the Internet, it doesn't exist.

Manfred Breede looks at the new opportunities that digital technology provides for producing books to order, much as what happened in the early days of the book. Print on demand is changing the economics of book production, making it easier for books to be published in limited numbers and for them to stay in print. Digital printing processes enable publishers to adopt the business model practised by medieval books printers and booksellers.

Angus Phillips looks at the value publishers can add in a world where it is feasible for anyone to publish their own work. As pointed out by Christopher Kular, companies such as Lulu offer authors the opportunity to self-publish in both print and e-book formats. The Internet enables authors to publish themselves but also provides publishers with the means to add value in a variety of ways, such as functionality, updating and confidence in the quality of the texts provided.

In their paper, Mihael Kovac and Mojca Kovac Sebart examine questions around reading in Europe. What can comparative data tell us about the connection between the educational level of a society and its reading habits? What happens to reading in the economies that are the most successful and competitive? They compare usage of books with both the efficiency of the education systems in those countries and the general level of competitiveness.

The theme of reading and its interchangeability with other media is covered by Hillel Nossek and Hanna Adoni from Israel, who find that reading books is unlikely to be displaced by other media in the foreseeable future. Rather than reading less, users of the Internet and computers continue to read books, newspapers and periodicals and in greater numbers than those without access to new technologies. Whilst the Web may be displacing television, there is little interchangeability between watching television and reading books. (A 2006 survey conducted on behalf of the search engine Google found that the average Briton spends around 164 minutes online every day, compared with 148 minutes watching television.) As one respondent commented: 'I can watch television and films with a friend. But I have to read a book by myself.'

Bookselling has seen big changes in the UK since the disappearance of fixed prices in the 1990s. Audrey Laing and Jo Royle look at consumer responses to discounting of titles, the appearance of coffee shops within bookshops, and the role of bookshops in the community. Their research found that whilst discounting was viewed positively, the choice found in many offers was regarded as bland and homogenous. Coffee shops received a mixed response also, with buyers evenly divided as to their benefits. The lack of social interaction found in shops contradicts the suggestion put forward by some that the bookshop can form the role of a vital community institution.

Ann Steiner writes of the growth of bookselling on the Internet in Sweden, and whether this has increased or diminished diversity. She suggests that the emphasis in physical stores on recent 'hits' is a threat to the range of titles that are stocked. By contrast the Internet enables the user within only a few clicks to reach titles at the end of the 'long tail' of books in print. The idea of the long tail was first put forward by Chris Anderson in *Wired* magazine, who suggested that if all the sales of slow-selling titles are put together they constitute a large part of the overall market.

The theme of diversity continues in the contribution from David Lynn, who edits the *Kenyon Review*, a journal that seeks out new authors. In a world that values insights that are rare and particular, he views this as an advantage for writers from less traditional backgrounds. Precisely because these communities have lacked a public voice, what they bring now is vitality, discovery and freshness.

The growth of portable MP3 players, such as the iPod, brings great possibilities for digital audio books. In their chapter on audiobooks, Jennifer Cavender and Lisa Stuchell examine the different authorial intentions between the versions for a reading audience and a reading audience. With abridged versions of the text, the text changes so much from the original work that it becomes an adaptation of the book.

Maureen Brunsdale and Jennifer Hootman write of the future for librarianship. The overabundance of information readily available to the library user means that the librarian has to teach users how to find the information they need and how to evaluate it. John Feather points out that the university library is no longer the only point of access to research literature – desktop access from the researcher's office is now the norm. The library could become no more than a book storage depot and a working space for students. As publishers and librarians wrestle with different business models, which include free or open access to journals, he makes a plea for public libraries not to be forgotten if the scholarly research community takes greater control of how research is disseminated.

In the penultimate chapter, Bill Cope and Mary Kalantzis address the changing nature of book production technologies, and their cultural consequences. They highlight one paradoxical consequence in an era where everything seems to be affected by globalization, not the least of which is the book trade. This consequence is the enormous potential for a future of publishing in which linguistic and cultural diversity can flourish – not to be drowned by the big international publishers and the English language.

In 2005 Steven Johnson published his book *Everything Bad is Good for You*, which put forward the argument that popular culture, such as computer games and television, is actually making us smarter. He called this the Sleeper Curve, after the sequence in Woody Allen's film where a team of scientists in the twenty-second century is astonished that twentieth-century society did not grasp the nutritional benefits of cream pies and hot fudge. In a coda to the present volume, Mark Woodhouse agrees that we may be getting benefits from our immersion in popular media, but argues we are missing something – the 'soul of things'. Woodhouse makes a plea for authenticity in our digital, networked world. Coming into contact with the real thing, which can include handling a printed book, gives us a sense of what is genuine as opposed to our growing dependence on a virtual reality.

# Notes

1. National Endowment for the Arts (2004) *Reading at Risk: A Survey of Literary Reading in America*. Washington: National Endowment for the Arts.

2. McCrum, Robert (2006) Reinventing the wheel, pt 94. *Observer* 30 April 2006.
3. Epstein, James (2001) *Book Business: Publishing past, present, and future.* New York: Norton.
4. Leonard, John (2001) Cri de Coeur. *New York Review of Books* XLVIII: 14–7.

# If it isn't on the Internet, it doesn't exist
## How the new generation view books as archaic relics

*Mark Perlman*

In the early 1990s a joke e-mail went around the world that purported to sell a new-fangled device for storing and retrieving information, called 'BOOK 1.0'. The e-mail went on to boast that BOOK 1.0 was environmentally friendly, needing no battery or power source other than one's own hand to turn specialised information storage files called 'PAGES' from one to the next. It also extolled the virtue of being able to use the inexpensive Manual Graphite Input Device, 'PENCIL 2.0', to make notes directly on the BOOK 1.0 itself, right next to the text one wanted to mark or notate.

Back then this joke was so amusing partly because it was still absurd to think that 'books' would be so unfamiliar as to need to be introduced to people, and to be done so with such imitation-hi-tech advertising. Books were the primary medium containing and disseminating detailed information, and everyone knew (or thought they knew) that books would remain indispensable into the foreseeable future. Books are bought, read, and collected throughout much of the world, and huge buildings are built specifically to house them. They are part of everyday life and have been doing the job for over five hundred years. So there seemed no reason to think they would not remain so for a long time to come.

Yet, just a few years later, as I teach philosophy to college undergraduate students in the United States, this old joke is less funny and more alarmingly accurate than I had ever imagined it could be. The majority of my students not only don't really read books – they do not accept books as a valuable or even valid object to seek out to obtain information. For most of them, if it isn't on the Internet, it doesn't exist.

I do not want to give the impression that I myself am hostile to the Internet – far from it. It is a fantastic tool, great for searching for obscure information and for buying and selling things. (My eBay feedback is 307, and 100 per cent positive!!) When I want to find out about someone, I *Google* them.[1] I buy plane tickets and concert tickets online, and do research online. How could I be hostile to the Internet? But I also recognise that for serious scholarship in many academic areas, the information on the Web is mostly superficial, sketchy, and sometimes bizarre and disastrously mistaken. In my own field of philosophy, serious, detailed, rigorous treatments of complex arguments and subtle views remain firmly rooted in those old-fashioned information-storage devices we old-timers call 'books'.

But now the generation of people who grew up using the internet is rejecting books as irrelevant and inconvenient, and simply ignoring them. The short-attention-span fans of Xbox and MTV simply have no patience for having to actually touch the actual pages of an actual book to find what they need. Actually reading, or even skimming, large numbers of books to find a mention of an elusive idea is too time-consuming to even be considered. The question then becomes: What should we do about it?

## Assigning research

In my classes, I normally have students write term papers every term. These are philosophical argument papers, not research papers *per se*, so in the past I simply left it to the students to do whatever amount of research was needed to write a decent paper. Many did sufficient research, and some did not, but that is just normal behavior among college students. But in the last few years I noticed a trend – instead of having a list of books cited, I began to have works cited lists contain merely a number of supposedly authorless web page URL addresses. Of course, these pages really do have authors, and some authors are even listed at the bottom of the page, but it would be a lot of trouble to scroll *all the way* down to the bottom of the page, especially after having found a tidbit of information a mere four inches down from the top. So the students conceive of all these web pages as just handed to them from the Iinternet ether, like manna from heaven. And once they have looked at about six websites, they declare the research finished. At no time need they venture into the stacks of the library and get their hands dirty touching those archaic documents that those dinosaurish professors call 'books'.

So I have changed my assignment. The students are now required to use at least three books and five journal articles relevant to their topics. But that's not all! They are required to bring the books and articles to class in a collegiate show-and-tell.[2] I require that they physically demonstrate to me that they have actually gone to the library and taken books out of it. I can't force them to read the books, but having gone to all the trouble of carrying them out of the library and around the campus, I figure maybe there is a chance that between websurfing sessions they'll crack open a book or two, out of guilt if nothing else.

It is true that many journal articles can now be printed directly from websites, and my students are adept at finding these. (More adept, in fact, than I am.) But I was astonished when one student recently lamented that the articles he needed to look at were not on the Web – like a sad helpless puppy he looked up at me and asked: 'How can I get them if they're not on the Web?'

I was momentarily speechless (a rare event) as it struck me that he was serious – it had simply never occurred to him that one could go to the stacks, find the very physical copy of the *Journal of the History of Philosophy* or other such journal, photocopy the article, and take it home and read it. This is when I knew there was a serious generational and techno-cultural phenomenon in progress.

## Computers and change

We all knew computers would change the world, and they have. They were predicted to create paperless offices and an abundance of information free for the taking. In fact they created more paper than ever, with computers and printers making it easier to revise and revise and print and print and kill more trees than ever before. And while much information is indeed free online, the newest trend (since the dot-com bust of the late 1990s) is to entice websurfers with a few bits and then charge them money for the detailed information they seek.

I am told that one interesting change that the Internet has brought is a distinct slowdown of the market for first-editions and moderately rare books. This is initially puzzling, but becomes less so after a little reflection.

There is only a small number of book collectors who desperately want a copy of any particular first edition book title. In the past their problem always was finding a copy. Those book dealers who had them could patiently hold onto them, and when the desperate collector, having searched for years for a fine specimen of the much-sought first edition, finally grasped his or her prize, the seller could charge a handsome price, and the long-on-the-quest collector would pay it. But then many bookstores started cataloging their stock and putting it for sale to the world via the Internet. Collectors began surfing for the titles they sought, and it became trivially easy to find virtually anything. Collectors could take their pick from many copies in many places. Once the few dedicated searchers had acquired their treasures, the market dried up, and prices fell significantly. The supply hadn't increased, but the technology to link demand to the supply had. So the market for such books was altered forever. I have to admit that this same phenomenon has significantly reduced my own 'thrill of the hunt' in trolling through bookstores. There is not a lot of thrill in clicking the computer mouse on *BUY IT NOW*.

Another technological change was a move to put texts of whole books in so-called 'e-books'. In his 1989 novel *Cyberbooks*,[3] Ben Bova describes the possibility of all books being replaced by data files on digital text pads, eliminating the printing and stocking of books, and making bookstores obsolete. That kind of development has not yet occurred – e-books never really took off. But a lesser successor is that one can sync up one's *Palm Pilot* with the Internet and read the day's newspaper on a 3″ LCD screen instead of getting newsprint on one's hands. But have computers and the Internet replaced books? It seems the answer is NO. e-Books faded with the dot-com bust, and I don't know anyone who is reading the latest bestseller novel on their *Palm Pilot* or *Blackberry* or *Clié*. But the danger is that, in the case of my students, the Internet has done far worse than replace books. It has made them irrelevant, and unworthy of being replaced. My students don't have anything comparable to books in their myriad of web pages, and many of them don't know or care. Books are just not part of their lives.

# Education

It was recently widely reported in the US that a certain high school in Arizona was eliminating textbooks from their curriculum, and having their students use notebook computers to read their school material online.[4] Of course, they are quick to point out that this isn't just an elaborate use of Internet search engines. They have programs and resources specifically designed to present information to their students on their screens. And I am sure that the students will indeed learn things, and that these programs have been carefully designed by people with grant money. Officials at this high school boast that this strategy will allow students to get numerous different sources and points of view on each topic, and this will tie in with a style of information-processing that the students are already familiar with, from websurfing.

But their alleged virtue shows exactly what the main downfall is of this trend toward cyber-everything. The students will indeed get twenty different viewpoints, but each will be one twentieth of the detail and analysis and sustained examination that a topic would have received in a traditional book. Getting multiple viewpoints isn't so difficult. What's difficult is really understanding the details of even one. It is the in-depth sustained pursuit of a line of analysis or argumentation that we often see in books and rarely see on web pages. The result is a growing number of students who cannot engage in serious study and serious scholarship, and whose ideas and writing have become as superficial as the web pages that are their only source of knowledge. They don't *read* texts anymore, they *access* pages and *skim* snapshots on a screen. Such cyber-scanning of words just doesn't convey depth of meaning.

Of course all of these claims are generalizations, and we can all cite examples of students who are as devoted to books as any old-timer could wish for. Even children are still reading – 8 million copies of the latest *Harry Potter* book, and climbing. But even here there is a trend away from past habits. Yes they devour *Harry Potter*, but what else do they read? Bookstores are seeing a trend of buyers toward coming in to the stores already focused on buying exactly the title they have heard about.[5] They get that book, buy it, and leave. Some stores report a trend of customers phoning them to have the desired title sitting at the checkout waiting for them, so that they can double park their cars while they rush in to grab the hit of the month. This way buyers need not have their single-minded pursuit of this month's bestseller or Oprah recommendation impeded by any other pesky titles. The notion of browsing to find a book less advertised and publicised is waning. Most people are in too much of a hurry to browse through the stacks.

# Local or global?

Having begun thinking about this phenomenon, I began to wonder if it is a global issue, or a localised problem specific to mediocre American students. Soon afterwards I traveled to St Petersburg, Russia, and was struck by the prominent place of literature and books there – half the statues in the city are of famous writers like Pushkin and Gogol. Russians with low salaries living in meagre apartments still have an admirable number of books on their shelves at home. Then I visited London for a week, and I enjoyed searching through the great number and variety of bookstores. London is a world center of publishing, and an amazing number of new titles continue to appear every year. And having seen old churches, old monuments, old homes, old buildings, guards with large fuzzy hats, and attended the *Last Night of the Proms* concert, I was struck by the extent to which the British retain their enthusiasm for their traditions. It is difficult to imagine Britons turning their backs on books. Perhaps the place of books is safer in Europe than in short-attention-span America.

However, travelling and thinking about the global scope of the popularity of books has not undone my view that books are in danger of losing a place in modern culture. After all, for all their adherence to tradition, the British also gave us the Beatles and punk rock, and London's historic skyline features many ultramodern buildings, from the irregular egg-shaped new London City Hall to the tall new building resembling a giant cucumber. Technology is changing the UK as much as anywhere else. Russia is vigorously plunging forward into capitalism and technological advancement, as are India and China. Japan is more gadget-crazed and high-tech than anywhere. Cellphones and the Internet are everywhere in the modern world, and those same forces moving my American students toward exclusive reliance on the internet are at work worldwide. In the discussion after my presentation of this idea at the Third International Conference on the Book (in Oxford in 2005), conference attendees from around the world helpfully confirmed my view that this is a worldwide phenomenon, wherever people have access to the Internet.

# Conclusion

It may well be that this kind of grousing is the same as one might have heard 100 years ago from grumpy fans of horse-drawn carriages – 'These newfangled automobiles are too loud and too fast. Everyone is in such a hurry these days.' The refrain 'Kids these days are no damn good' has echoed in every generation. But I think this is different.

The information explosion has made it difficult to wade through the maze and find the bits that are really important, and people are becoming satisfied with a multiplicity of viewpoints even if each view must be made to fit on a hyperlinked web page. I do not deny that electronic texts and the technology of their delivery may soon evolve so as to present information in the same detailed manner that books do. It is just that the Internet as it exists now, snapshots of text read off of computer screens, simply does not yet contain the same level of rich, detailed, and thorough information that we find in books.

So I find myself at a crossroads in pedagogy – should I stick to the traditional ways of teaching, or should I cave in to fad and technology and begin using glitzy new methods of teaching and communicating? Even if those methods are not always as good as what they threaten to replace? If what I have described here is indeed a genuine phenomenon of learning in the internet age, and the Web has created a whole new conception of where to find information and a new mode of reading it, or, rather, accessing it, this doesn't mean that teachers must automatically bow to the new learning style of the students. It might mean that we now have more things to teach our students – how to learn, and where to find detailed information and thorough analysis and arguments. We have to show them the difference between different sources of information, and teach them that books are not archaic relics. Even in the twenty-first century cyber-age, books are still valuable and irreplaceable containers of knowledge.

# Notes

1. For the uninitiated, to 'Google' someone means look for information about that person on the Internet, typically using the website *http://www.google.com*, though it can also mean using any website to do research on someone. Google is simply the best one.

2. 'Show-and-Tell' is an activity in early grades of elementary school in which students bring to class objects of interest, and explain to the other children what they are.

3. Bova, Ben (1989) *Cyberbooks*. New York: Tor Books.

4. *http://www.dailystar.com/dailystar/dailystar/83469.php*. See? Even I am doing it now! I never had a physical copy of this story in my hands. I read the Tucson, Arizona newspaper story in my Monmouth, Oregon office on the internet. The article 'All-laptop high school to open in Vail' was by reporter Daniel Scarpinato in the July 10, 2005 *Arizona Daily Star*, and the story was picked up by The Associated Press and appeared nationally in the United States.

5. Hillel, Italie (2005) Booksellers Seeing Changes in Customers – At Annual Convention, Booksellers Say Customers Are More Focused, Less Interested in Browsing. Associated Press: *http://abcnews.go.com/Business/wireStory?id=821466*.

# 3

# Plus ça change...
## Print on demand reverts book publishing to its pre-industrial beginnings

*Manfred Breede*

## Books before the invention of printing

Perhaps nothing illustrates the value of books in the pre-printing era better than the princely sum of 400 to 500 Crowns charged for the manuscript of a Bible in medieval Strasbourg.[1] To put this into perspective, in H.J. Grimmelhausen's 'The Adventurous Simplicissimus', which takes place at about the time of the incunabula period, the protagonist of the story finds himself penniless, save for a gold ring with a diamond worth some 20 Crowns.[2] In other words, in the 1600s a manuscript's value was roughly equivalent to 25 gold rings studded with diamonds. It goes without saying that the majority of the population could not hope to own a book, let alone assemble a very modest library of books. In fact, even a renowned library such as Cambridge in 1442, had only 122 volumes in its collection.[3] It is said 'that it was the dream of Chaucer's Clerk of Oxenford to own 20 (books), but Chaucer certainly does not suggest that his clerk's dream was likely to be fulfilled.'[4]

In keeping with the 'sell and produce vs. produce and sell' thesis of this paper it is likewise quite improbable that books, given their considerable value, would have been commissioned in large stockpile quantities or in any quantity beyond one at a time for that matter. In all likelihood the most probable scenario of book production and transactions would have been the request (sell) and subsequent copying (produce) of a single book. We have some interesting evidence of such a transaction when Cardinal Giuliano della Rovere (later Pope Julius II) requested a printed copy of Appian's 'Civil Wars' to be copied by a master scribe in 1479.[5] Not only do we witness here the reproduction of a single copy being requested, but also a contempt for the perceived inferior quality of mechanically produced books, for why otherwise would the Cardinal have commissioned the reproduction of an already existing book using a method that was infinitely less productive and considerably more expensive? We also have some knowledge about the price differential between scripted and printed books; the aforementioned manuscript of a Bible costing about 500 Crowns, whereas a printed version of a Bible is said to have been sold for as little as 40 Crowns.[6] This was still a considerable sum for average citizens of that time, but nevertheless at a vast 1250 per cent price reduction, it brought average people within reach of book possession.

By way of parenthesis, and to the extent it is possible to compare contemporary items and prices to the medieval market place, it may be noted that in 2005 in Toronto, Canada the most inexpensive gold ring with a single diamond is sold by a major Canadian jewellery chain store for CAN $200, while the most expensive Bible sold by a big box bookstore in Toronto costs CAN $50.

This short history of the book before the invention of printing would be incomplete without some snapshot of the prevailing medieval mindset and attitude about the intrinsic value of books. An overriding concern, or at least a major preoccupation, was the aesthetic appearance of books, as the beautiful and richly illuminated medieval texts bear witness to. However, this was often achieved to the detriment of textual accuracy. It was not uncommon for manuscripts to suffer from whole missing lines, word repetitions and other careless mistakes, because correcting these flaws would have ruined the visual beauty of the manuscript, thereby diminishing its value as an object d'art, which was more important to the medieval reader than textual accuracy.[7] In fact, so taken was medieval man by the beauty of manuscripts, that when it became possible to produce books by means of mechanical methods, their quality was still judged by how closely they resembled their hand-written counterparts.[8] This apparent lack of confidence in printed books is further exemplified by the long coexistence of both hand-written and printed books.

## The invention of movable type

In the year 1450 Johannes Gutenberg perfected an invention that we now consider to be an epoch making event.[9] Often this invention is superficially called printing, however, printing was practised long before Gutenberg's invention using woodblocks, an art perfected by medieval masters like Hans Holbein and Albrecht Düerer. Though printing books from woodblocks was also done, it was a slow and cumbersome method that always bore the risk of an entire page being ruined with the slightest slip of a woodcarver's chisel. Moreover, a page so carved could not be used for any other purpose but printing that very page.

Gutenberg thus invented a method by which individual letters could be cast in metal by means of an adjustable mould. These letters could then be assembled into words and pages, and could just as easily be disassembled to produce new pages. In retrospect this invention of 'movable type' seems to be very simple, but it had a profound effect on mass communication and is seen by many historians as the most influential event of the last millennium.

It is important we remind ourselves that although there are now much more efficient methods of printing that take advantage of computer technology, the conventional printing methods used today still have the same capabilities and inherent limitations as Gutenberg's method – namely the multiple reproduction of identical images or text.

Plenty of evidence exists of early printers incorporating most facets of book production, including the selling of books in one and the same location, but perhaps none better than the oldest depiction of a printing office, 'The Dance of Death' as seen in Figure 3.1.[10]

Clearly seen in this depiction of a medieval printing office are the typesetting, printing and selling of books over the counter. Noticeably absent in this picture are papermaking and bookbinding activities. The crafts of papermaking and bookbinding predate the invention of printing by several hundred years, requiring technical skills, experiences and investments not easily mastered or obtained by printers.

One of the first printers in the English-speaking world, William Caxton, is perhaps the best example of a printer and bookseller.[11] Not only did he print books, he was also involved in the import and export of books on a fairly large scale, in addition to his contributions to typography, design and English literature in general.

# Printing books in large quantities

The obvious advantage of printed books over manuscript books is the increased speed of production of the former, resulting in tremendous

**Figure 3.1**
Typesetting, printing and selling of books. 'The Dance of Death', woodcut by Matthias Huss, of Lyons, France, 1499.

cost savings to the producers, and subsequently the book buyer. Whereas the production of manuscripts was largely a 'one-up' undertaking, the printing of books became one of the earliest forms of mass production.

Inherent in mass production is the concept of the economy of scale, which means that the unit price of a product decreases as the number of products manufactured increases. This volume-to-price ratio has decreased ever since the invention of printing and continues unabated to the present time.

In the fifteenth century the average edition of books was around 200. The Venetian publisher Aldus, who set up a press about 1490, was the first publisher to print a series of books with 1,000 copies per edition, when the hitherto number of copies per edition was at most 500.[12]

Leapfrogging to modern times, in the late 1960s McGraw-Hill Publishing Company kept 7,000 different titles and a million books in their warehouse.[13] In 1979, on a nationwide scale the estimated number of books consumed in the United States was 1,640,930,000 units, which represented a retail value of $7,249,300,000.[14]

With the economic advantage of scale, however, comes also the risk of not selling all or even the majority of books produced. This has always been a problematic aspect of the book publishing market place, which in some product categories such as mass paperbacks results in 'approximately half of all books shipped to wholesalers not being sold, and while some are returned to the publisher whole, most are discarded after the covers have been torn off and submitted for credit'.[15]

With staggering returns of this magnitude it is no wonder that many publishers now generally refuse returns for credit when at one time this was a universal practice. The onus of unsold books now increasingly rests with booksellers and has forced them to be more sensitive to customer preferences, but has also had the unfortunate consequence of reduced selections of less popular, esoteric or niche titles.

One method of dealing with unsold books is to sell them as remainders at a considerable discount. Frequently, when a book fails to sell at the original price, it may sell at a lower price allowing the publishers to at least recoup their printing costs.

# The economics of book production is driven by technology

If we differentiate between extreme high volume titles with mass appeal to tens of thousands or even millions of readers and niche titles that find a limited readership of no more than 2,000, then we must also discuss the most appropriate reproduction technologies for each of these product categories.

As recently as twenty years ago, we did not need to contemplate these differences because the technological choices were limited to conventional printing processes. By conventional it is meant printing processes that are capable only of reproducing a static image, albeit at extremely high productivity rates. The static image limitation is an inherent limitation ever since Gutenberg's invention and is explainable by the fact that these printing processes all require a 'fixed image' image carrier, which transfers the image to the substrate. Every time image content has to be changed, such as is the case when printing multiple signatures of books (see Figure 3.2), the image carrier also has to be changed. The two inherent implications are: 1. the material and image carrier processing costs; and 2. the manufacturing costs every time an image carrier is changed.

**Figure 3.2**  Book manufacturing workflow with conventional printing processes.

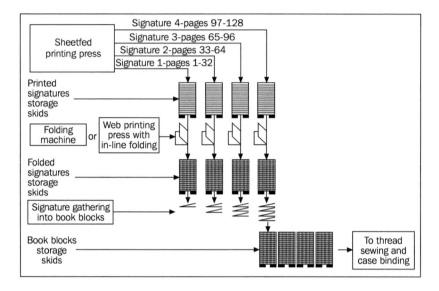

Conventional printing processes suitable for book printing are letterpress, flexography, rotogravure and offset lithography. While the underlying principles of each of these printing processes are quite different, they are all afflicted by the same 'fixed image' limitation.

Image carrier material and processing costs can range from a high of $2,000 for a rotogravure cylinder to a low of $100 for an offset lithographic plate. Image carrier change costs are based on the manufacturing overhead and out of pocket variable charges on the basis of which hourly budgeted rates are calculated. If we consider an hourly budgeted rates for high volume printing presses with inline finishing capabilities of $300, which is not unusually high, then it would cost $150 every time an image carrier is changed because it takes on average about 30 minutes to make the change.

As rudimentary as these cost estimates are, it nevertheless demonstrates that the cost of printing books is closely related to manufacturing and labour charges that are not easily absorbed, especially if the run lengths are small.

The introduction of what now is called digital printing processes in the mid-1980s represents a paradigm shift in printing technology and has increased the complexity of printing economics. Depending on the type of printing project and its run length, one or the other printing process category will be more economically viable.

The term digital printing is a bit unfortunate, because both conventional and digital printing processes require extensive digital preparations. The difference between conventional and digital printing processes is that, in the former process digital-electronic methods are used to create a physical 'fixed image' image carrier, while the latter uses digital-electronic methods to image the substrate.

In fact, some digital printing processes such as ink jet printing do not require any image carrier at all, but the colourant (ink) is directly targeted onto the substrate according to an electronic charge previously calculated by digital information.

Where digital printing systems have an image carrier, they are an integral part of the printing engine, which does not have to be changed even as the image content changes. At the most fundamental level, the difference between the conventional and the digital printing process is that conventional printing processes require a 'fixed image' image carrier and digital printing processes don't. This has significant productivity implications for many types of printing projects but none more so than books. Books consist of many pages and as conventional printing process can only print a limited number of pages at a time (depending on the maximum press sheet size and the size of the book pages, 16, 32, but almost never more than 64 pages), the image carrier, it will be recalled, has to be changed frequently at considerable cost to the printer. Although digital printing can also be used to print multiple pages per press sheet, the most common book printing configuration is to print one leaf or two pages back to back at a time, or to print two pages on each side followed by a single fold and in some cases an additional right angle fold is possible, resulting in a maximum of four or eight page signatures respectively. That is so, because unlike conventional processes, which print identical multiple pages on one press sheet that in subsequent stages are folded and gathered, digital printing processes print the pages in sequence until all pages for one book have been completed, at which time the same cycle repeats itself for the next book and so forth (see Figure 3.3). Note also that digital printing's inherent ability to print different pages in sequence eliminates the gathering phase of book manufacturing and does not preclude the possibility of printing entirely different books in succession without sacrificing the maximum rated speed of the device. This is also the reason why digital printing devices are capable of finishing saleable books in-line, which is possible only when complete book blocks have been produced.

The possibility for printing multiple pages on one press sheet exists for digital printing as well, but these devices typically have no or limited

**Figure 3.3** Book manufacturing workflow with digital printing processes.

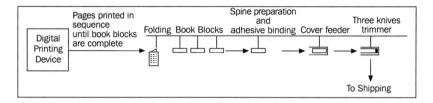

in-line book finishing capabilities. If these devices become available in the future, then the productivity of digital printing devices will increase equal to the multiple of additional of pages printed per press sheet.

Currently, electrophotography, better known by the popular term laser printing, has the largest digital printing market share[16], but ink jet printing is also in wide use. Other processes include electrography, ionography, magnetography, thermal transfer printing and elcography.

# Advantages and disadvantages of conventional and digital printing processes for book printing

Until about 10 years ago when the maximum resolution of digital printing devices was not much higher than 400 dots per inch (dpi) there was a noticeable quality difference between conventional and digital printing. Since then, the majority of digital printing devices have 600 dpi, with some reaching resolutions as high as 800 dpi.[17] These resolutions generate text and line drawing quality that are almost indistinguishable from conventional printing processes. Single and process colour halftone reproduction on the other hand will be reproduced at a somewhat reduced but acceptable quality level. Therefore, if we limit the discussion to books containing only text and line drawing it can be categorically stated that both conventional and digital printing processes produce comparable reproduction quality.

If, however, we compare the economic efficiencies of conventional vs. digital printing processes and use cost per unit as a criterion, the conclusions are not quite as definitive.

Conventional printing processes remain unsurpassed in their ability to reproduce large print runs cost effectively, because of two fundamental reasons: 1. the large square area printed per printing cycle; and, 2. the enormous mechanical speed of modern printing presses. Using an offset lithographic, blanket-to-blanket, full-web press that is often used for high volume book printing as an example, the extent of its considerable efficiency will become apparent. The area printed on such a press is the equivalent of 16 letter pages per printing cycle or 800,000 pages per hour. This is in addition to in-line folding of the paper into book signatures for subsequent gathering and binding into books as separate operations.

These impressive productivity rates beg the question why digital printing devices have their place in book printing. The determining factor is closely related to the run length of a book edition. The enormous productivity of a conventional press can only be exploited when the run lengths are long, because the cost to set up and operate such a machine will then be divided by a relatively large number of units produced. It follows that with short run lengths, the cost per unit will be higher to the point where extremely short runs would become prohibitively expensive.

In comparison, the cost per unit of operating a digital printing device is always the same regardless of the run length. This is so because digital printing devices require almost no set-up time, such as mounting the printing plates and changing the plates, to print multiple signatures of a book. Setting up a digital printing device is not significantly different from printing pages on a home computer printer.

This advantage is offset by the inherently lower productivity rates of digital printing devices. For book printing, typically, image areas that are the equivalent of one book leaf or two back-to-back pages are printed. If, for the purpose of simplicity, we assume that a letter sized book is printed at the top speed of 5,400 leafs (2 pages) per hour, which current digital printing devices with in-line book finishing accessories are able to attain, and compare this output to the 8,000,000 pages a web offset press produces in the same amount of time, then the tremendous productivity deficit of digital printing devices becomes apparent.

The combination of relatively low productivity and extremely low set-up times renders digital printing devices suitable for extremely short to moderately short runs, or in other words for run lengths that are not economically feasible on high volume conventional printing presses. The graph in Figure 3.4, proposed by Fenton and Romano, 1998,[18] shows this relationship and also demonstrates that there is an overlap (shown here to be between 1,000 and 6,000 impressions) in run length,

**Figure 3.4** Run length determination graph for conventional printing processes.

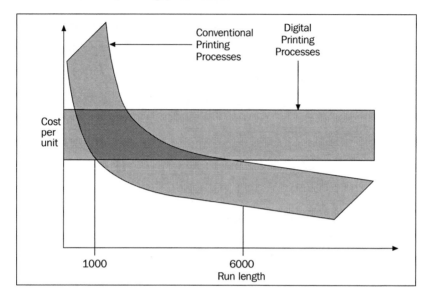

where the decision as to which printing process is more advantageous at given run lengths is uncertain and depends on factors other than run length alone. Accordingly, run lengths below 1,000 units and above 6,000 units are appropriate for digital or conventional printing processes respectively.

Although the absolute accuracy of this graph, especially with view on book printing, may be argued, the general concept is sound, because it is based on the peculiarities of conventional and digital printing processes.

It is for these reasons that no other printing process is as suitable to 'On-Demand-Printing' as digital printing, and consequently, the emergence of these printing processes give rise to predictions that modern book publishing may once again return to the sell and produce business model.

# The economics of book production

While books cannot be produced with greater economic efficiency than by conventional printing processes, this holds true only if large quantities are printed and if the great majority of books are sold. Furthermore, the book publishing supply chain is not limited to the manufacturing of books alone, but also entails inventory maintenance, inventory risk (the cost of unsold inventory), and distribution, which could account for 30 to 50 per cent of the cost of a book.[19]

In an on-demand manufacturing environment printing occurs only if a book or books have actually been sold, thus an inventory is no longer required and likewise the cost of returns are avoided as well.

Distribution costs are also minimised because at least one shipping leg from the printer to the publisher is totally eliminated,[20] simply because orders are so small that direct shipping from the printer to an online seller, wholesaler or directly to the retail customer, is feasible.

A case study called 'A Year in the Life of a POD Title'[21] tracks the production and sales of a Print-On-Demand (POD) book over a period of one year and then makes a comparative cost benefit analysis if the book had been printed conventionally. The 168 page book, a typical niche title on starting ones own computer business, sold 1,623 copies during 2003 through a combination of online book sellers, wholesalers and direct sales from the publisher's website. This project netted them a before expenses (i.e. development and author royalty costs) profit of about $11,000 itemised as follows:

| | |
|---|---|
| Online or other wholesaler sales | |
| Cover price | $14.95 |
| Unit price after 35% discount to wholesalers | $9.72 |
| Printing fees per unit | $3.09 |
| Profit before expense | $6.63 |
| | |
| Direct sales from publisher website | |
| Unit price after 20% discount | $11.96 |
| Delivered cost per unit | $3.74 |
| Profit before expense | $8.22 |
| | |
| Total sales through online or other wholesalers | |
| 1,376 × $6.63 | $9,122.88 |
| | |
| Total sales through publisher website | |
| 247 × $8.22 | $2030.34 |
| | |
| Total profit before expense: | |
| $9,122 + $2030.34 | **$11,153.22** |

Had the book been printed conventionally by offset lithography the following printing fees per unit, not including shipping fees, would have applied (quantity from online print broker):

| Quantity | 200 | 500 | 1,000 | 2,000 | 5,000 | 10,000 |
|---|---|---|---|---|---|---|
| Price per unit | $5.26 | $4.50 | $2.60 | $1.63 | $1.04 | $0.83 |

To match the $3.09 per unit POD printing fee 1,000, 2,000, 5,000, or 10,000 volume-discounted prices have to be used. The cost of printing at these volume discounts is therefore:

| No. of Copies | Price/Unit | Total Cost |
|---|---|---|
| 1,623 | $2.60 | $4219.80 |
| 2,000 | $1.63 | $3,260 |
| 5,000 | $1.04 | $5,200 |
| 10,000 | $0.83 | $8,300 |

If, for simplicity we consider the same discount of 35 per cent as in the POD scenario, then 1,623 copies at a cover price of $14.95 nets the publisher $24,263.85 – $8,482.35 = $15,771.50 before printing costs. Subtracting the above printing fees results in:

| No. of Copies | Profit – Printing Costs | Copy Profit |
|---|---|---|
| 1,623 | $15,771.50-$4,219.8=$11,551.70 | $7.11 |
| 2,000 | $15,771.50-$3,260=$12,511.50 | $7.70 |
| 5,000 | $15,771.50-$5,200=$10,571.50 | $6.51 |
| 10,000 | $15,771.50-$8,300=7,471.50 | $4.60 |

The most profitable volume discount is therefore the 2,000 copies scenario, which with a per unit profit of $7.70 yields $1.07 more than the $6.63 POD per unit profit, but it is not likely that an amount of $1.07 in increased profit per book can finance the previously alluded to inventory maintenance, inventory risk and distribution overheads, which are associated with warehousing and shipping.

As it is difficult to predict how many copies a book will sell, printing it in editions higher than it actually sells is an ever-present probability in conventional book publishing. Printing books by POD avoids this risk, while maintaining a reasonable profit per unit.

# Typical print-on-demand titles

In general, any book that is not expected to sell a huge number of copies has a good print-on-demand potential, and the fewer the copies, the more compelling the reasons for print-on-demand become. Considering that 'the average book in the US sells less than 2,000 copies in its lifetime',[22] it is easy to see why there is no shortage of titles that are suitable for print-on demand production. Beyond this general observation, there are some specific book categories that profit from print-on-demand.

- Various independent alternative or counter-culture publishers specialise in literary, cultural, political, or religious topics that spawn offbeat titles, which often attract a dedicated but limited readership. These could include titles on obscure hobbies, poetry, experimental fiction, new age, radical politics, spirituality, gender politics, and other such topics that have a limited appeal to the middle-of-the-road readership.

- Customised textbooks are ideally suited for on-demand-print because they typically are composites of several textbooks that are specifically selected for a particular College or University course, which may not exceed a few hundred students at the most. Moreover, customised textbooks, or course packets as they are sometimes called, change every year to reflect new and different course contents.

- Self-published books are by definition small editions. Self-publishers often find it impossible to get their books accepted by literary agents or publishers, which leaves them no choice but to go to print directly. Printing self-published books by on-demand and then distributing them via online sellers is to the advantage of self publishers, because the distinction between small publishers and large trade publishers gets blurred when books are sold by online sellers such as Amazon, thus reducing the competitive advantage of name brand recognition.

- Reprints of classics or out of print books that are in the public domain can be converted into POD usable digitised formats by optical character recognition (OCR) technology.[23]

- School yearbooks are well suited for POD from the run length point of view, but customers have to be prepared to accept adhesive bound books as opposed to the more durable thread sewn binding method. Currently this is the only binding method that is possible on digital printing devices with in-line finishing capabilities.

- University presses may be able to print academic dissertations that would otherwise never see the light of day beyond University library shelves.

The ability afforded by POD to print in small editions without the financial risk inherent in conventional printing processes, empowers authors who otherwise would not see their work published and read by the public, and as such democratises print publishing not unlike the democratisation of information exchange that has taken place on the Internet.

# The state of digital printing technology for book printing

On-demand manufacturing in its truest sense implies the initiation of a manufacturing process triggered by the request for a single unit and delivering it to a customer within a very short period of time.

With regard to the manufacture of books, there are numerous digital printing devices that can print the pages of books at considerable speed, but only relatively few were designed and configured to produce saleable books in an integrated on-demand workflow.

The binding method employed on such machines is invariably an adhesive soft cover binding, which requires the milling or roughening of the book block spine edge, application of adhesive to the spine, affixing the softcover, and trimming the books on three sides.

The majority of digital printing devices produce books from individually collated sheets, but now there are also devices available that fold the sheet once to yield four-page signatures. Even eight-page signatures are possible, in which case a second right angle fold must follow the first fold. As has been mentioned earlier, digital printing devices make the gathering of sheets or signatures redundant by virtue of their ability to print consecutive book pages or signatures until a complete book block is produced.

Two companies currently leading in the on-demand book-printing field are Xerox Corporation and Eastman Kodak Co. These companies partnered with traditional finishing machine manufacturers such as C.P. Bourg, Muller Martini and others to build hybrid devices capable of printing and finishing books in one continuous operation.

A good real life example of such a device is the DocuTech 6180 Book Factory by Xerox. It has an electrophotographic print engine that outputs 180 pages per minute at an image resolution of 600 dpi (see Figure 3.5).

The device features a roll to cut sheet feeder that feeds the paper from a roll and cuts the web into sheets prior to printing, a perforating unit, a sheet turning device that reorients the sheets for subsequent folding into 4-page signatures, a spine milling and glue application station where the book blocks receive adhesive to hold the pages together, a cover feeder where pre-printed covers are wrapped around the book blocks and affixed to the spine, and a three-knife trimmer that trims the books to their final size.

Productivity specifications of digital printing devices are somewhat ambiguous, because 180 pages per minute could have a different meaning depending on how the job is configured. The specification of 180 pages per minute indicates 180 sheets are imaged with one page on one side. The same job, if printed on both sides, produces 90 pages on one side and 90 pages on the other side. If however, a sheet is imaged with two pages per side and is printed on both sides, which requires the sheet to be folded in half, then the page count is doubled to 180 pages on one side and 180 pages on the opposite side with a total page productivity of 360 pages per minute.

Supposing a 360-page book, measuring 5.5 × 8.5 inches upright, is printed on 8.5 × 11 inch sheets, then printing the book in four-page signatures would result in a productivity rate of 180 + 180 = 360 pages or one book per minute.

At this rate of productivity it is indeed conceivable for a customer to request a single book and be handed the book within a very reasonable period of time, or in other words digital printing with integrated in-line

**Figure 3.5** Xerox DocuTech 6180 Book Factory. *Xerox Corp. Product Brochure* (Reproduced courtesy of Xerox corporation.)

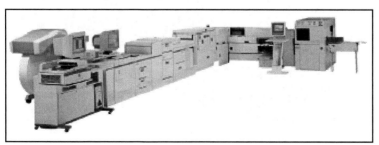

finishing technology makes the sell and produce business model a realistic and attractive possibility.

Printing productivities of 180 pages per minute are currently at the approximate upper limit for electrophotographic devices, but there are no fundamental technical reasons that their productivity cannot be doubled or quadrupled by building larger devices that print more pages per printing cycle. Therefore, in the future we can expect further productivity improvements that may approach productivity rates of conventional printing processes.

In some respects the future has already arrived with digital printing devices, other than those that use electrophotographic principles. For example, Delphax Technologies, a company located in Toronto, Canada, manufactures a digital printing device touted to be 'the world's fastest toner based digital press'.[24] Their CR2000 digital web press is capable of printing at a speed of 3,600 – 6 × 9 inch pages per minute. The CR2000 (see Figure 3.6) is based on a digital printing process called ionography,[25] which is similar to electrophotographic processes in that it also uses toner and produces a 600 dpi image resolution. When this digital press is integrated with in-line finishing capabilities supplied from third-party finishing equipment manufacturers, book manufacturing rates are further increased by an astounding factor of ten.

**Figure 3.6** 'World's fastest toner based digital press', CR2000 by Delphax Technologies (*http://www.delphax.com/printers_100.htm*) (Reproduced courtesy of Delphax Technologies, Bloomington, MN, USA.)

Another high-speed digital printing system not specifically designed for in-line book production is the Kodak Versamark VX5000 digital press. It uses continuous ink jet technology and prints at a speed of 500 feet per minute, yielding 120,000 letter sized pages per hour. While this still falls short of the 800,000 pages a full web-offset press can produce, it narrows the productivity gap between conventional and digital printing processes considerably.

# Conclusion

For the first time since books were sold and produced in small quantities by manual methods, digital printing processes enable publishers to adopt the sell and produce business model practised by medieval book printers/ sellers.

In the past the sell and produce business model was dictated by necessity, whereas today this business model is an opportunity to economically produce small volumes of books at a moment's notice by way of digital reproduction methods.

Conventional printing processes will continue to be used for high volume book production runs because this is where their superior production rates can be economically exploited.

On-demand book manufacturing is a potential godsend for publishers of niche and specialty titles that can often not be produced economically by conventional printing methods because of the small editions that are typically released in this category of books.

The overriding societal implication is that the ability to produce all books economically, regardless of their potential readerships numbers, diversifies the range of titles populating the market place, thus providing the public with a greater variety of books.

In a free market system the communication industries are driven by the economic imperative to keep profit margins at reasonable and attractive levels. Digital printing processes are in part making it possible for the print media, and, by extension, the book publishing industry, to remain profitable. Otherwise, the oldest form of mass communication, the book, will increasingly migrate to non-paper media forms because of their more efficient content delivery.

# Notes

1.  Cave, R. (1983) *The Private Press*, Second Edition. New York: R.R. Bowker Company, p. 4.
2.  Goodrick, A.T.S. (1912) *The Adventurous Simplicissimus*, translation from H.J.C. Grimmelhausen's original. London: Heinemann, Book 4, Chapter 4.
3.  Cave, op. cit., p. 6.
4.  Cave, op. cit., p. 4
5.  Steinberg, S.H. (1959) *Five Hundred Years of Printing*. New York: Criterion Books, p. 38.
6.  Cave, op. cit. p. 6.
7.  Cave, op. cit. p. 5.
8.  Steinberg, op. cit., p. 31.
9.  Steinberg, op. cit., p. 21.
10. Steinberg, op. cit., p. 37.
11. Steinberg, op. cit., p. 79.
12. Steinberg, op. cit., p. 101.
13. Graham, G. (1971) 'Speaking tetrahedrally: the relationship between authors, publishers, booksellers and librarians', *Library Association Record* 70: 58–61, March 1968, in the anthology *Book Publishing: Inside Views*. New Jersey: Jean Spealman Kujoth, p. 77.
14. Dessaur, J.P. (1981) *Book Publishing: What It Is, What It Does*, 2nd edition. New York: R.R Bowker Company, p. 28.
15. Dessaur, op. cit., p. 47.
16. Nothmann, G.A. (1989) *Nonimpact Printing*. Philadelphia: Graphic Arts Technical Foundation, p. 39.
17. Romano, F. (1999) Digital Printing Opens A World of Opportunities. *TechTrends*, Fall 1999, Volume 2, Number 2. New Jersey: National Association of Printing Leadership.
18. Fenton, H.M. and Romano, F.J. (1998) *On-Demand Printing: The Revolution in Digital and Customized Printing*. New Jersey: Prentice Hall PTR, p. 20.
19. Fenton, op cit., p. 55
20. Rosenthal, M. (2004) *Print-On-Demand Book Publishing*. Massachusetts: Foner Books, p. 13.
21. Rosenthal, op. cit., pp. 53–60.
22. Rosenthal, op. cit., p. 65.

23. Ray, W.J. (2000) Large Scale Conversion of Book Backlists for Formatted, Digital Delivery. *TAGA Proceedings*. New York: Technical Association of the Graphic Arts.

24. *http://www.delphax.com/printers_htm*

25. Nothmann, op. cit., pp. 61–5.

# 4

# Where is the value in publishing?
## The Internet and the publishing value chain

*Angus Phillips*

## Introduction

In 2004 I carried out some consultancy work which gave me the opportunity to take the concept of the value chain and apply it to the development of a new publishing company. The environment of the country in which I was working is very different from that in the UK or the USA, and this led me to reflect on the difference that the Internet makes to the thinking and activities of publishers. Where does the value lie in the conventional book model? How does the Internet impact on publishers' activities? In an online world, how can value be created in a context where it is feasible for anyone to publish their own work?

## The value chain

Michael Porter's concept of the value chain[1] provides a model that can be used to map out the set of activities that together form the publishing process. Porter describes the value chain as:

> The set of activities through which a product or service is created and delivered to customers. When a company competes in any industry, it performs a number of discrete but interconnected value-

creating activities ... The value chain is a framework for identifying all these activities and analysing how they affect both a company's costs and the value delivered to buyers.[2]

Value-chain analysis can be applied to the publishing industry by market or sector, or at the level of the individual company. Value is 'the amount that buyers are willing to pay for the product or service that a firm provides. Profits alter when the value created by the firm exceeds the cost of providing it'.[3] The goal of a publisher's activities is to generate a profit, by creating value that exceeds the cost of providing the product to the customer. The raw material in publishing is the author's text, which is taken through a succession of stages before its sale to customers. By adding value to the text, through for example judicious editing and an attractive cover, publishers hope to sell more copies or charge a higher price. Publishing firms make decisions about which activities in the value chain to include in or exclude from their business. Publishers can choose which activities to undertake themselves, and which to outsource to third parties. Taking a part of the value chain in-house adds to the fixed costs of the company. This may enable higher profitability when sales are rising, but can lead to larger losses in poor economic conditions.

The value chain for a publisher is shown in Figure 4.1. Key elements of the value chain are the acquisition of intellectual property, editorial and design, production, marketing and sales. Intellectual property is acquired through the purchasing of copyrights and licences from authors or other publishers. Books then have to be edited and designed, produced, marketed to the book trade and readers, and sold to bookshops or the end purchaser. Other parts of the value chain are the storage of finished books (which begins once the book has been printed), order processing, and distribution. Publishers need to look at each part of the value chain to see where they should be directing resources, or where they can save costs through efficiencies. Competitive advantage can be sought through

**Figure 4.1**   Publishing value chain

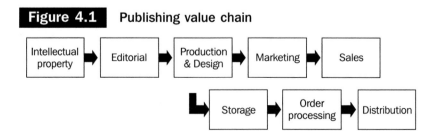

particular activities in the value chain, for example the design expertise of Dorling Kindersley or the print-buying power of a large publisher.

Links between activities may be important, and it may make sense, for example, to combine storage and distribution. Desktop publishing has enabled editorial, design and production to be combined in some companies, where the hybrid post of production editor is common. Editing can take place on nearly finished pages, rather than on the author's typescript, and designers rather than typesetters produce the final version of the text.

# Book publishing model

Under the conventional book publishing model, where does the publisher contribute the most value? For many publishers, the activities of IP acquisition and sales and marketing are regarded as the most important. Selecting and acquiring the most valuable copyrights and licences has to be core to their business, whilst ensuring the rights are exploited to best advantage. The role of the acquisition editor remains important, but greater control is often given to the marketing department, with a power of veto. There are different marketing needs according to which market is served. In consumer publishing, for example, marketing activities are aimed at the end purchaser as well as the different parts of the distribution chain, including distributors and bookshops. Meanwhile the sales department is targeting different sales channels, such as the book trade, book clubs and overseas markets. The last ten years has seen an expansion of the Rights and Marketing departments in many publishing sectors.

Other activities have been regarded as less central to the work of publishers. Publishers no longer try to compete over the distribution of their titles – there are accepted service levels, and third parties who can provide those levels. Wholesalers give a high level of service to smaller publishers. Very few publishers in the UK own their own print facility, as they require the flexibility and cost savings that come from using a range of suppliers. Other activities, such as editing and design, have been outsourced to freelance staff. Authors with some degree of competence have been asked to typeset their own books, for a nominal fee or for free. Agents may work closely with authors to develop their ideas and texts, especially in the area of fiction, taking over the development role from editors. They also perform a selection role as fewer publishers welcome unsolicited typescripts. Despite the emphasis on marketing in publishing, the marketing of many books does not go beyond a catalogue entry, with the publisher relying on the author for promotional efforts, which can range from enclosing a flyer with their Christmas cards to using media contacts to obtain reviews and articles in the press.

The author of *The Oxford Guide to Style*[4] and *The Oxford Dictionary for Writers and Editors*,[5] Robert Ritter, has likened this process to emptying the basket of a hot-air balloon. Just as ballast is jettisoned to make the balloon rise higher, so a publisher's load is lightened to increase output and profitability without the need to expend extra energy. Some books may not be copy-edited at all, and then proofread only by the authors. Authors prepare the index and clear text and illustration permissions. Text design is largely standardised and the insides of many books are not given individual attention. The covers of trade and educational books are still regarded as important, but for academic books the degree of attention paid to the jacket or cover is variable, and can rely on the author providing the image. Publishers will argue that readers either have not noticed or do not care, and that increasing the budget for editorial and design does not justify higher cover prices or result in higher sales.

How does the Internet impact on this process? It has encouraged the lightening of the balloon. Better communication speeds up the processes and enables freelancers to be used in Buckingham or Bangalore. Print prices can be sought from all over the world, and there is a global market in design, typesetting and print. Book files can be sent instantly from author to publisher, publisher to freelancer, freelancer to production department, production department to printer. The Internet has revolutionised picture research and the work of photo shoots (the results can be checked online), just as IT has changed page and cover design work.

This is the first impact of the Internet on the value chain – it has enabled efficiencies in time and money, and aided the outsourcing of activities.

## The second impact

The second impact of the Internet relies on a wired infrastructure of consumers and institutions. Online access to content, readily available to large numbers, opens up the value chain and requires publishers to reconsider linkages and the activities themselves. I should say at this point that I acknowledge that developments in mobile technologies are also important and should not be ignored.

There remains the value in intellectual property, but a greater range of rights is required in order to maximise revenue possibilities. Investing in wholly-owned copyrights becomes more attractive with the possibilities of online as well as print sales. The head of an Oxford-based design company remarked to me that he had noticed that publishers are starting to 'collect' things – for example illustrations and diagrams. Whereas previously publishers largely remained ignorant or apathetic about the rights situation, and did not attempt to clarify who owns what, they are now keen to establish their rights to reuse material and across different formats. In educational publishing, for example, there is a far greater emphasis on digital development, and this has required a new focus on questions of ownership.

There is renewed value to be found in editorial, design and production. Rather than make many, it is more productive to make once, copy many. This requires capturing the structure of a text, the use of a language such as XML, and the archiving of texts so that they can be adapted and reused in different formats. A properly tagged copy of the text can be configured to produce versions in print, for CD-ROM and online. Sample content for marketing websites is readily available. Contrary to recent trends, workflows have to be reconfigured so that editing does not take place on finished pages, but at an earlier stage of the process, as it was a generation ago. With the right work performed on the structure of each text, extra functionality and value can be derived from the electronic versions. New value can be created by databasing texts, aggregating content and linking it together, such as in Oxford Reference Online (*http://oxfordreference.com*). This contains over 100 of the reference books published by OUP, put together online as a searchable database. A search on 'China' returns 175 entries from a variety of reference works, including *The Oxford Dictionary of Dance*, *The Oxford Companion to Shakespeare*, and *A Dictionary of Food and Nutrition*.

The Internet enables a direct dialogue with customers – for many publishers, for the first time. Customer relationships can become very valuable, and e-mail is a straightforward and cheap way of passing on product information and gathering customer reactions. Some companies are seeing the possibilities of the Internet for product development, trialling content at an early stage.

There is renewed value too in the distribution elements of the value chain. Online distribution reduces the costs of printing, storage and distribution in the long term, although there may be a high capital cost of setting up the right database and web solution. Once that investment is made, there are economies of scale to be obtained, as shown by the creation of large media businesses in scientific publishing. For an online journal, the marginal cost of supplying an extra customer is very low. The Morgan Stanley report into scientific publishing, *Scientific Publishing: Knowledge is Power*[6] reported on the boost to profits for journals publishers from online publishing:

> we estimate that the profitability [to a publisher] of a customer improves by 15% as they transfer from paper and online subscriptions (most pay for both currently) and opt for just online access.

There are predictions that just as journals have gone online, academic monographs will follow over the next 15 years.[7]

The Internet also adds value through the level of service that can be provided. Professional online services, such as LexisNexis (*http:// www.lexisnexis.co.uk/*), offer a constant stream of updated material. The degree of service required by the user can vary, and most reference publishers, for example, have found it unnecessary to update on a constant basis, as this is not an expectation of most users. The online version of the *Oxford English Dictionary* (*http://dictionary.oed.com/*) releases new words each quarter; subscribers can compare entries with the previous version, and see how language is changing. Online access gives the user advantages with regard to new editions. For example the library at Oxford Brookes has started buying e-book versions of popular IT texts. This saves the clutter of little-used previous editions on the shelves, and ensures a good degree of access to the most up-to-date edition.

## What value does the author see?

How does the author see the value that publishers can offer? The mathematics publisher Klaus Peters recalled his first meeting with Ferdinand Springer of Springer Verlag, when Springer outlined the *raison d'être* of a publisher:

> ...to facilitate the work of the authors by taking away the burdensome aspects of editing, producing and, most importantly, distributing their work as widely as possible. He made it very clear

that these added values were the justification of a publisher's existence. (Peters and Peters, 2003)[8]

Is there a changed picture today, when publishers have been cutting costs out and simplifying the process of editing and production? When the Internet provides a simple means of global distribution? If authors have the technological expertise to publish their own work online – which on the whole demands less skill than creating a printed page to a publisher's specification – and have the confidence to market themselves, what extra value does a publisher give them? Print publication comes with the risk associated with the investment in the stock. With online production and distribution, there is no charge for shipping, no warehousing charge, no stock to be remaindered or pulped, and no initial investment in the printing of the work. There are lower expectations of print and design quality on the Web, and in any case desktop publishing solutions can create acceptable quality with reduced levels of expertise.

Authors are already experimenting with online publication. Some cannot find a print publisher; others have an eye on a publishing contract or aim to boost their prospects in print. A website such as lulu.com (*http://www.lulu.com*) offers authors the opportunity to publish in both print and e-book formats. Seth Godin, author of *Unleashing the Ideavirus*[9], still has the book free to download on his website, where it is quoted that the book has been downloaded one million times. There is an obvious synergy between a book about viral marketing and the use of the Internet to spread the message about the book. Godin has a number of successful books in print with commercial publishers.

To many authors self-publishing smacks of the vanity press. An established or well-known publisher offers the element of selection, which provides a mark of quality.[10] Associated with that is the value of the publisher's brand, developed through its range of authors and products. Given the variable quality of material available on the Web, these are important influences in the author's mind. In addition there remain the attractiveness of print publication, with the author having a physical object to show for their efforts, and the efforts the publisher puts into promoting the work.

However, as the revenues from online publication continue to grow, authors will increasingly ask themselves why they receive only a small share of the proceeds. If the online publication of journal articles can be highly profitable, this generates the kind of questions presently asked by the movement for Open Access. If publishers mimic the standards of Web publication in print, will authors continue to value the print product more highly? Publishers have to consider their profitability, but they also need to review their approach and decide whether it fits the needs of their market and their base of authors.

# Conclusion

Publishers will always need to question how they can add value in the publication process. Their profit margin, and some would say their existence, depends on these decisions. The Internet has supported the trend towards a concentration on fewer elements of the value chain – the lightening of the balloon's basket. The danger for publishers is that it presents opportunities for other players, whether IT companies or authors, to enter the market and develop suitable products. How do publishers react to an online environment and increasing demand for digital products? Simply putting a text up on the Web may not be enough – where is the extra value in terms of functionality, ease of use, updating and service? In any case the author could post the text in a similar manner, and will wonder why they receive such a low share of any revenues.

The Internet provides not just a ready publication route, but also opportunities to add value that an individual author would find it difficult to match, such as functionality, aggregation and service. Functionality – searching, linking, the addition of images, animation and video – makes the online product more than a simple reproduction of the print text. Aggregation offers a library of texts in one place, giving the user a range of benefits including convenience and confidence in the quality of the product. Online services can provide benefits such as updating, e-mail alerts and community discussions.

The publisher has to re-examine the value chain and adjust their thinking. Up until now have they been jettisoning those elements of the value chain that hold the key to providing extra value? Do they hold the necessary rights to develop the right product? Should they adjust their workflows and invest in the editing and production phases? Do they need to archive their content securely and develop the technology to distribute direct to consumers? How does their brand work in an online environment? Answering these questions appropriately will reap economic benefits but will also help differentiate publishers' products and services from self-published works available on the Internet.

# Notes

1.   Porter, M.E. (1985) *Competitive Advantage: Creating and sustaining superior performance*. New York: Free Press.
2.   Porter, M.E. (2001) 'Strategy and the Internet', *Harvard Business Review* March, 63–78.
3.   Cooper, C.L., and Argyris, C. (1998) *The Concise Blackwell Encyclopedia of Management*. Oxford: Blackwell.
4.   Ritter, R.M. (2002) *The Oxford Guide to Style*. Oxford: Oxford University Press.
5.   Ritter, R.M. (2000) *The Oxford Dictionary for Writers and Editors*, 2nd edn. Oxford: Oxford University Press.
6.   Morgan Stanley (2002) *Scientific Publishing: Knowledge is Power*. Morgan Stanley industry report, 17 September 2002. Available from *http://www.alpsp.org/htp_econ.htm*.
7.   British Library (2005) 'British Library predicts "switch to digital by 2020"'. London: British Library press release, 29 June.
8.   Peters, A. and Peters, K. (2003) 'Small independent publishers: responsible, committed and flourishing', *Logos*, 14 (2): 62–5.
9.   Godin, S. (2000) *Unleashing the Ideavirus*. New York: Do You Zoom. e-Book available from *http://www.sethgodin.com/ideavirus/*.
10.  Hodgkin, A. (2004) 'A topsy turvy e-world', *The Bookseller* 2 April, 24–5.

# 5

# The venues for vanity
## Methods and means of self-published books

*Christopher Kular*

## The desire to publish

Freedom of the press remains a vital fact or aspiration in most societies of the world.[1] For more than five hundred years, authors have sought out viable methods and means of publishing their literary knowledge. In 1455, after Gutenberg could not repay his loans and interest of more than 2,000 gulden, his books and tools were forfeited to satisfy the debt.[2] Traditional book publishing continues to be a highly structured process requiring significant financial investments. In our digital world, newer technologies are available for economical self-publishing. Venues for self-publishing are made available through step-by-step online workflows and low-cost personal investment.

An author's decision to publish his/her work through an Internet service is affected by several factors. Companies researched and referenced for this paper include iUniverse (iUniverse.com), Trafford Publishing (Trafford.com) and Lulu (Lulu.com). These online companies offer similar services for self-publishing workflow applications.

Online publishing companies have utilised the latest digital workflow technologies with Internet applications to create user-friendly tools, which facilitate self-publishing. For many authors, these services provide the only methods and means for creating and converting original content into printed documents or digital downloads for mass distribution. In addition to the streamlined manufacturing workflow, there are many opportunities and pitfalls associated with self-publishing.

Authors creating content for self-published documents, have a personal sense of urgency and lower financial risks compared to traditional publishers, who must meet strict production guidelines, delivery date compliances, and profitable sales targets to satisfy their shareholders. Authors of self-published documents and corporate publishers are subjected to consumer evaluations from their respective audiences, but there are extreme differences in the impact of positive and negative outcomes. Authors who are under contract with corporate publishers receive advance payments and/or smaller royalty percentages based on total book sales. Considering the number of documents that are rejected by corporate publishers or are simply not feasible to produce, authors now have accessible methods and means for self-publishing.

Due to the high preparatory, production and promotional costs associated with commercial publishing, book titles must achieve higher sales targets in order to produce profitable returns. Because of these strict requirements and higher risks, corporate publishers must be certain that the documents they produce are the documents customers are willing to purchase. The low costs and low risks associated with self-publishing makes it easier for authors to publish their own documents. Compared to the user-friendly self-publishing workflow, the traditional publishing marketplace exists as a highly structured environment with strict requirements for publishing protocol. Authors with a desire to be recognised for their expertise in a particular subject area are now able to utilise Internet publishing tools to disseminate their knowledge with mass audiences.

As of September 2005, the Lulu.com site listed four main product segments that authors and consumers could browse for information and/or potential purchasing. The selections are grouped into 38 categories of Books, 42 categories of Images, 17 categories of Music & Audio, and 31 categories of Calendars (see Table 5.1).

Another online publishing service, the Trafford Publishing bookstore (Trafford, 2005) includes 50 categories with over 40,000 titles to choose from. This is a valid testimonial to the rapid growth and acceptance of self-publishing, which could not be possible through traditional publishing venues.

A report in 1998 by KPMG addressing the costs of book distribution in the UK revealed that only 3% of titles accounted for 50% of the total volume of retail sales. The other 50% consisted of thousands of slower moving titles in small quantities. Fewer than 40 of 15,000 publishers were responsible for 56% of bookshop sales, and 4 bookselling chains accounted for 42% of all retail sales. Despite

| Table 5.1 | Popular book categories and titles, *Lulu.com*, 2005. |
|---|---|

| Book categories | Total | Top three choices | Number of titles | % of total |
|---|---|---|---|---|
| Books/novels | 20,656 | Fiction & Literature | 5,164 | 25 |
| | | Children's | 1,263 | 6 |
| | | Religion/Spirituality | 1,117 | 5 |
| Image books | 17,274 | Nature | 2,869 | 17 |
| | | Landscape | 1,673 | 10 |
| | | Animals | 1,407 | 8 |
| Music & audio | 7,191 | Alternative | 1,409 | 20 |
| | | Pop & Rock | 1,037 | 14 |
| | | Electronic | 1,008 | 14 |
| Calendar | 2,510 | Children & Family | 371 | 15 |
| | | Photography | 364 | 15 |
| | | Animals | 299 | 12 |

the consolidation of publishers through mergers and acquisitions, no one publisher had a market share of more than 9% at that time. (Clark, 2001)[3]

These statistics reveal the limitations of traditional book publishing and highlight some opportunities for authors who seek innovative venues for self-publishing.

# Protocol and procedures for self-publishing

The process of creating and uploading self-published documents is facilitated through partnership services (Trafford, 2005). Authors have access to approved resources, which can be hired to assist in the creation, production and distribution of their documents. Common services for content creation include editors, translators, researchers, proofreaders, and photographic resources. For some first-time authors, utilization of these services can dramatically improve the probability of success. Authors with adequate writing skills, who lack creative layout skills, can hire professionals to design their document to suit the content and desired audience. The appearance of a book's cover design draws attention to the document and hopefully compels the consumer to purchase the book. From a publishing perspective, this does not guarantee literary quality because poorly written and designed documents will still be published. This is one of the main caveats associated with purchasing self-published books. Consumers may be enticed by a book's colourful designs and virtual abstract, but may be disappointed by the overall content. To maintain integrity and professionalism in academic publishing, University presses are expanding their 'gatekeeping' function in society.[4]

# Copyright, censorship, licensing and legalities

To avoid copyright litigation issues, online publishing providers require authors to sign publication agreements that clearly describe the legalities of self-publishing. In essence, these contracts state that the 'publishing company' has been hired by the author to provide a publishing service. Trafford's Publishing Agreement states, 'The author guarantees that he or she has copyright to the 'Book' (book, manuscript, work of art or other document) by virtue of being the creator and/or having license from the copyright owner, and will retain copyright to the Book for the duration of this agreement (Trafford, 2005).' The agreement also states that the author 'assumes any and all liability for content and holds Trafford harmless from any liability arising from content provided by the author and that either party may terminate the agreement at any time (Trafford, 2005).' The Lulu.com website provides additional information and policies relating to copyright and censorship issues. A document published through this venue requires a copyright notice, which is 'a combination of the copyright year and author's copyright information (Lulu, 2005)', which is created and entered during the file submission process. This information is displayed on the product detail page on the bookseller's website ensuring full compliance with self-publishing protocol.

Trafford Publishing's approach to censorship issues focuses on a positive reinforcement of an author's work, by stating 'when an author devotes years of work to writing a book, we believe that person has a right to make it available to the public, within the limits of the law (Trafford, 2005).' Trafford also states that they won't touch (publish) anything that appears to constitute hate literature, pornography, obvious libel or slander. To further emphasise their belief in the author's integrity, an introduction or sample chapter is also posted on the Trafford.com site allowing readers to pre-evaluate the nature of the content.

Other book publishing legalities include requirements for ISBN (International Standard Book Number) protocol and the creation and implementation of barcodes. ISBNs are assigned to documents with specific content to enable standardised referencing and worldwide searching. An ISBN identifies the publisher rather than the author, which facilitates ordering procedures and tracking. To assist self-publishing authors, this service is included in the step-by-step formalities when submitting digital files to the publishing provider (Trafford, 2005). Authors and publishers also use the document ISBN and barcode to track work in progress, accounting, and inventory information.

Prior to purchasing any material from the bookseller, consumers have the freedom to browse sample chapters or abstracts to evaluate the content of the document. Consumer's who make purchases from a bookseller's website are assured that the material has met the necessary requirements relating to legal and administrative details (Lulu, 2005).

To comply with website viewing regulations, Lulu.com requires authors to designate audience ratings and suitability of content for their intended readers. Should any consumer feel that the subject matter is abusive in any way, a special 'Report Abuse' link is available, which provides the freedom to express concern over moral issues or cultural values. The ratings range from lowest to highest levels of maturity (Lulu, 2005).

1.  Children: Content is for young children. Contains no material that parents would find objectionable.

2.  Everyone: Content is suitable for people of all ages and tastes.

3.  Teen: Content is suitable for persons ages 13 and older. May contain mild or strong language, mild violence, and/or suggestive themes.

4.  Mature: Content is suitable for persons ages 17 and older. May include intense violence and language and mature sexual themes.

5.  Direct Access: Content is restricted to customers you select. You will receive a web URL at the end of the publishing process. Send this link to the people you want to see and purchase your work. Direct Access content is not searchable.

Online publishing opens the door to consumer purchasing and provides easy access to self-published books, which never go 'out-of-print'. Digitally printed books are never 'out-of-stock' because no physical inventory is required. The only storage space concerns relate to electronic media and security backup protocol. When conventionally published books are no longer 'in-print', all rights revert back to the author. When self-published books are produced through online services, there never needs to be an 'out-of-print' clause. If a traditionally published book is 'out-of-stock' at a bookstore but still 'in-print', an order may be processed and filled from warehouse inventories.

# Book production workflows

Digital printing technologies have a distinct advantage over traditional methods of production in terms of start-up costs and turnaround times. With self-publishing workflows, digital files to be sent directly to the printing press where copies are reproduced on-demand. The length of time to publish a book through traditional workflows from an author's concept to customer delivery can take up to one year or more. A similar project produced through a self-publishing service can be completed in as little as six weeks (Lulu, 2005). The streamlined proofing cycle through online publishing workflow is accomplished via virtual proofing. Because self-published authors are required to submit their work in digital form, the final appearance of the document will be quite similar to the original. The finished product, which will be listed and displayed online, allows consumers to evaluate its appearance and sample virtual abstracts prior to purchase.

To achieve maximum exposure for an author, Internet publishing services offer conversion and distribution of e-books through digital downloads. e-Book downloads are made instantly available after payment has been approved and processed. e-Book versions as PDFs (Portable Document Format) are sold for approximately half the price of the print-on-demand hard-copy price (Lulu, 2005). Because self-published documents are printed or made available as e-books only after they have been ordered, there are no inventory issues relating to storage and unsold copies (Trafford, 2005). The elimination of inventory is one of the most significant differences between traditional publishing and self-publishing through on-demand printing. Traditional publishers produce books in bulk in anticipation of large order sizes to reap the greatest profits and return on investment. However, unsold inventories will often result in greater production costs and lost revenue.

# Royalty considerations

With traditional publishing, generating profit through mass production is one of the most important goals. Corporate publishing companies must risk high initial investments for the potential of high profits. Online publishing services generate price lists based on document parameters and pay royalties to authors based on the profit margin above the cost of production. The royalty percentages paid by Internet publishing services are typically 60 per cent of the profit margin compared to traditional publishing rates ranging from 5 to 20 per cent of the gross margin (Trafford, 2005). Self-published books purchased through online providers are sold 'as is' and are non-returnable unless a processing error has been made by the provider. Traditional booksellers can be faced with subjective returns from their unsatisfied customers, which may result in additional administrative costs. In Table 5.2, sample online book publishing costs

**Table 5.2**    Sample online book publishing costs, *Lulu.com.*

| Book size | Perfect bound | Saddle stitched | Plastic coil |
|---|---|---|---|
| 6' × 9' | | | |
| Binding fee | $4.53 | $4.53 | $4.53 |
| B&W per page | $0.02 | $0.02 | $0.02 |
| Colour per page | $0.15 | $0.15 | $0.15 |
| 8.5' × 11' | | | |
| Binding fee | $4.53 | $4.53 | $4.53 |
| B&W per page | $0.02 | $0.02 | $0.02 |
| Colour per page | $0.15 | $0.15 | $0.15 |
| 9' × 7' | | | |
| Binding fee | $4.53 | $4.53 | $4.53 |
| B&W per page | $0.02 | $0.02 | $0.02 |
| Colour per page | $0.15 | $0.15 | $0.15 |
| 7.5' × 7.5' | | | |
| Binding fee | $4.53 | $4.53 | $4.53 |
| B&W per page | $0.02 | $0.02 | $0.02 |
| Colour per page | $0.15 | $0.15 | $0.15 |

Numbers indicate manufacturing cost per book in US dollars.

(all similar) illustrate the simplicity of calculating manufacturing costs associated with self-publishing.

Authors may have one or more expectations for their self-published document, which may include financial returns, marketplace exposure or personal satisfaction. Because there are no business requirements to generate a profit, self-published authors enjoy greater freedom of expression without conforming to traditional publishing protocols.

Customers who choose to purchase and download e-book versions have the option of printing out an entire document or selected portions on their personal ink-jet or laser printer. The ultimate in environmentally friendliness is achieved when an e-book is consumed and enjoyed as an on-screen document. e-Books can be searched, marked-up, highlighted or modified to improve readability. Computers with access to the Internet can utilise e-book hypertext links to search additional resources. Self-published authors with Internet marketing and promotion abilities can also generate sales through their personal websites.

> The Impulse Buying of Books (1982) survey found that about half the books sold over the counter were on-the-spot impulse buys, and in the confectioner/tobacconist/newsagent (CTN) outlets, about three-quarters were impulse buys. Of possible factors prompting impulse purchase, 30% bought on the name of the author (higher with fiction buyers), 30% liked the look of the book, and only 13% related to the impact of publishers' marketing and recommendations by the bookshop. Over 40% of impulse buys were made without any prior knowledge of the book or author. (Clark, 2001)[6]

The ability to access the Internet at any time creates the greatest exposure for self-published authors. Internet browsing takes place through digital scrolling and clicking rather than physical strolling and flipping pages. Book buying consumers are not confined or restricted by geographic locations, transportation time or fuel costs. The display of documents on a website can be immediately updated and customised to user preferences. Any point of purchase alterations made inside traditional bookstores must be physically changed within each location.

All documents created for online publishing must be submitted into the graphic arts workflow as electronic files, where they remain in digital storage until production orders are received. Should an author desire to make changes to an existing document, he/she pays the publishing service an hourly fee to alter the content (Trafford, 2005). Compared to traditional publishing workflows, an outdated document can remain on bookshelves for a few months to several years.

To assist creators and consumers of online books, the websites provide some very useful tools to make the entire process easy to use. Online publishing providers include web browser links to frequently asked questions, ordering procedures, support forums, instructions prior to publishing, and what to do during and after the publishing process (iUniverse, 2005). This is especially important for authors who are entering the self-publishing marketplace for the first time. Without easy to follow step-by-step procedures, authors may be unaware of the opportunities that exist through online publishing. Due to the complexities and sophisticated regulations associated with corporate publishing, many authors would not consider, or be considered as candidates for traditional publishing venues. In the traditional publishing workflow, an author's role is almost complete after the corrected and edited manuscript has been submitted for print production. Authors who choose self-publishing through on-demand digital technologies, play a much more significant role in all aspects of the publishing workflow. With the exception of a few self-published authors, most writers consider digital print on-demand technologies and Internet applications to be the only viable venue for publishing.

# Benefits of editorial review

Many academic authors appreciate the scrutiny and integrity of a peer-reviewed publication as it validates the content and professionalism of their work. Subject matter may be written for specific or widespread audiences, but a consumer's level of satisfaction is generally based on predetermined expectations. Consumers of peer-reviewed documents tend to have higher expectations of the subject matter and literary professionalism of the author. It has been my observation that consumer's who purchase self-published books, have slightly lower expectations for the quality of content and substrate materials used in producing the document. A well-known exception to this observation is 'The Celestine Prophecy'[7], which was originally 'self-published' (Trafford, 2005). Traditional publishers are more accountable for the books they produce because their reputation is based on the quality of content submitted by individual or co-authored writers. Self-published authors who disseminate their work through Internet publishing services are accountable only to themselves.

# Conclusions

Online book publishing using on-demand printing workflows has opened the door to new opportunities for authors wishing to disseminate their knowledge, skills and personal interests. The ability to self-publish almost any document eliminates restrictions imposed by corporate publishers while allowing greater freedom of expression for any author.

Books published through traditional workflows are subjected to a rigorous proofing cycle and greater editorial scrutiny. With self-published books, the onus of editorial quality, integrity, and moral judgment is placed entirely on the author. In some cases, the lack of professional editorial scrutiny has raised new concerns over the quality of writing and subjective content.

The traditional publishing workflow requires a significant financial investment to produce a marketable book resulting in lengthy print runs to recover costs and maintain corporate profitability. Self-published authors can achieve a sense of accomplishment and recognition through low-cost print on-demand technologies.

Digital printing technologies provide the methods and means to produce books on-demand, thus eliminating bookstore concerns over unsold books, and environmental issues relating to non-recycled inventory.

To maintain cost efficiencies in all aspects of on-demand book printing, the availability of substrate materials and physical book size options are restricted by digital equipment configurations. Authors who have their books published through traditional venues enjoy greater freedom of choices for material substrates and finished book sizes. Authors who have their books published through on-demand venues enjoy greater freedom of expression.

In the future, online and traditional publishing venues will partner with each other to offer both types of services to their clients. A happy medium will be achieved when the expectations of publishers, authors, and consumers are balanced with the capabilities of book printing technologies.

# Web resources

Café Press: *http://www.cafepress.com*
iUniverse: *http://www.iuniverse.com*
Lulu: *http://www.lulu.com*
Trafford Publishing: *http://www.trafford.com*

# Works consulted

Cave, R. (1983) *The Private Press*, 2nd edn. New York: R.R. Bowker.
Dobson, Lyndsay (1983) *The Canadian Private Presses in Print*. Ontario: Lyndsay Dobson Books.

# Notes

1. Chappell, W. and Bringhurst, R. (1999) *A Short History of the Printed Word*. Vancouver: Hartley & Marks, p. 3.
2. Ibid., p. 67.
3. Clark, G. (2001) *Inside Book Publishing*, 3rd edn. New York: Routledge, p. 10.
4. Parsons, B. (1989) *Getting Published: The Acquisition Process at University Presses*. Knoxville, TN University of Tennessee Press.
5. Clark, op. cit.
6. Clark, op. cit., p. 68.
7. Redfield, J. (2005) *The Celestine Prophecy*. New York: Warner Books.

# Towards understanding patterns of book consumption in Europe

*Mihael Kovac and Mojca Kovac Sebart*

## Defining the problem: book usage, competitiveness and efficiency of education

Thanks to data gathered by different agencies and companies, we understand quite well how inhabitants of the European Union use different kinds of media.[1] Similar to Americans, Europeans nowadays devote less time to printed media such as books, magazines and journals than before. In fact, according to data collected by the Parthenon group, college-aged US individuals spent 250 hours reading books in 2004 as compared to 500 in 1984. On the other hand, that same population devoted five times as many hours to playing video games than it had in 1984, while doubling that spent watching TV. Less dramatically, but still revealing a similar trend, the USA National Endowment for Arts Report identifies a fall from 56.9 per cent of American adults reading fiction for pleasure in 1982 to a figure of 46.7 per cent in 2002.[2] On the other side of the Atlantic, research conducted by the Goethe Institute showed that in Germany, the average time spent reading a book each day had fallen from 22 minutes to 18, with the use of other media increasing during that period from 5 hours to 8 hours per day.[3] Consequently, these trends have affected the book trade, such that print-runs have declined and the book-buying base has become more vulnerable to social, cultural and demographic change than before.[4]

These trends seem to be universal. Even so, under this global umbrella, there exist significant differences among countries. In the UK, USA and China, for example, there has been a significant increase of book production as all three countries have more than doubled their annual output of new titles in the last fifteen years: each of them published more than 120,000 new book titles in 2004.[4] At the same time, annual production of new titles remained more or less the same in Germany, and increased by 10 per cent in Japan, France and Italy.[5] Even more dramatic have been the revelations about book-reading habits throughout Europe. In 2002, for example, 67 per cent of the Portuguese population answered 'no' when asked if they had read any books for reasons other than work/study in the last 12 months, while 72 per cent of the Swedish population answered 'yes' to the same question.[6] Similarly, the way people now access books differs significantly. In the Netherlands, for example, in 2002 people budgeted less than 40 euros per capita for purchasing books, while checking out 10 books from public libraries annually. On the other hand, in Austria, they spent around 80 euros per capita on purchasing books, but checked out less than 2 books.[7] Other countries also showed this significant disparity in their overall acquisition of books, with people in Finland annually checking out or buying 24 books per head while those in Spain acquiring only 3 (see below).

What, if anything, do these numbers tell us? What kind of connection exists between the educational level of a given society and book reading habits? What happens to book reading in the most economically successful and competitive countries? Are there any similarities among book reading habits and the level of competitiveness in a given society? And, most importantly, does such data contain any broader significance for understanding contemporary societies as a whole?

In this chapter, we will try to sketch the answers to such questions by comparing annual per capita usage of books in different European countries with the efficiency of their educational systems and their general level of competitiveness.

# How to measure competitiveness, efficiency of education and book usage

Concerning the efficiency[8] of education systems, data comes from well-established international research projects such as PISA, with our notions based on the rankings and achievements of the students as devised in this project. For measuring the competitiveness of countries, there is the equally well-established *Competitiveness Yearbook* that has been prepared by the IMD Institute in Lausanne, Switzerland, including its various set of criteria.

A more difficult task is to gather data about per capita book usage. In the context of this chapter, we understand per capita book usage to be the sum of per head library loans and the per head number of books purchased, analysed with data about non-readers and heavy readers in each country. The reason why we decided on this combination of indicators is the very fact that European countries differ not only in numbers of books purchased/loaned per head, but also in the percentage of population that reads books: we will assume that countries with a similar number of books loaned/purchased per head but with a higher number of readers will have higher and more stable book usage per head than countries with a lower number of readers. In short, the notion 'book usage' combines 'physical' usage of the books per head (measured in number of books loaned/purchased per head) and density of readers in a given country (measured in percentage of non-readers and heavy readers in the reading population in each country). We will use data gathered by Libecon about per head library loans and Eurostat data (as gathered in Publishing Market Watch 2004) about European reading habits.

As data about per head book purchases are not gathered by any international statistical agency or research project, it will have to be estimated on the basis of international surveys or statistical databases, such as Publishing Market Watch, the International Publishing Association, Eurostat and others.[10]

Theoretically, we could get our data on per head book purchases through a simple calculation. Thanks to Eurostat, we know how much money is annually spent per capita on purchasing books in the old EU member states. As the prices of books vary throughout Europe, we consider such book expenditures to be an unreliable indicator, unable to adequately show the differences in book buying habits between countries: obviously, in a country with lower book prices it is possible to buy more books with the same amount of money as in the country with high book prices. Nevertheless, the number of book copies sold per capita can be calculated by dividing per capita book expenditure with the average book price in a given country.

In order to do so, we'll have to make a short digression into European book prices. However, this is easier said than done.

# Book prices in Europe

According to the IPA website, statistics on average book prices can be obtained only for the British, Italian and Finnish book markets. The British Publishers Association (PA) provides regularly updated comparisons among book prices in the UK and USA from 2004 onwards, 'The Book Trade in Finland'[11] research project provides information about average book prices in Finland for the period between 1999–2000,[12] and the Italian Book Market Report provides estimations about book prices in Italy for the years 2001, 2002 and 2003. This means that we have no other choice than to compare data collected in different time periods. As the time differences are not significant and book prices don't vary a lot, we consider such comparisons as accurate enough indicators of trends in book prices throughout Europe.

PA data shows that in 2005, on average, the prices of hardcover books in the UK were around 11.50 GBP and the prices of paperbacks were around 7 GBP. On such a basis, we can estimate that the average book price in the UK is around 9.25 GBP, or 14 euros.[13] Unfortunately, we have no data distinguishing the prices of hard covers and paperbacks in Finland; instead, the estimation deals with a general price of 130 FIM (appr. 22 euros) and a recommended book price of 150 FIM (appr. 25 euros) in 2000.[14] According to the Italian Book Market Report[15] in 2001, the average prices of books geared for the adult market, were similar to those in the UK, varying between 12 and 14.30 euros. In short, average book prices in Finland in 2001 were almost double the average book prices in the UK (2005) and Italy (2001). The book prices in the latter two countries tend to be similar regardless the differences in GDP per capita in both countries (UK 29,600 USD per head and Italy 27,700 USD per head – see CIA World Factbook website[16]).

# Differences in European book prices

Similar differences can be seen if we compare the prices of hardcover editions of bestsellers such as Dan Brown's *Da Vinci Code*. In June 2005, the price varied between Holland (where only the paperback edition was published, but with a similar price as hardbacks in other countries), Italy, Germany and France, ranging from 18.60 euros in Italy to 20.90 euros in France.[17] However, the price of hardcover editions of the *Da Vinci Code* is higher in smaller markets in Nordic countries with approximately 5 mil. inhabitants, such as Finland (32 euros), Norway and Denmark (299 Danish or Norwegian kronas, respectively, or about 40 euros).[18] Meanwhile, the price in the biggest Scandinavian book market (10 million habitants) remains the same as in Western europe: Swedish editions of the *Da Vinci Code* cost around 200 SKR (about 20 euros).

All in all, comparisons among the prices of bestsellers and among the average book prices in Italy, UK and Finland show that in old EU member states that reached similar level of development, book prices tend to be similar in markets with more than 10 million people and are significantly higher in smaller markets.

Unfortunately, at the time when this chapter was written, Eurostat provided no data about per capita book expenditures in new EU applicant and member states.[19] As a consequence, new EU member and applicant states will have to be left out of book usage, competitiveness and efficiency of education comparisons here as it is impossible to estimate the average per head book usage in these countries.

# European book usage per capita

What does all this mean for our purposes, particularly using the average book price in order to calculate the number of books purchased per capita in old EU member states?[20] As stated before, it seems that the data about per capita book purchases is somehow misleading as purchases per head, as measured in euros, does not tell us much about the number of books sold because average book prices differ throughout Europe. In Britain and Italy, for example, one can get more books for the same amount of money than in Finland. Further, we can estimate that in countries with a long and established tradition of cheap paperback publishing, more books per capita will be sold than in book markets dominated by hardback publishing.

As stated in note 10, there is no data for the proportion of paperback and hardcover sales, and average book prices for the majority of old EU member states. What we do know, however, is that in general, book prices tend to be higher in smaller Nordic markets. Therefore, we will assume that the average British, Italian and Finnish book prices could be applied to demographically and economically similar European countries.[21] With such an approach, all numbers below should be considered only as rough approximations. However, we do believe that they show more exact trends and differences in book purchases throughout Europe than Eurostat data (as published in Publishing Market Watch 2004) about per head book expenditure.

| State | Book sales per capita in euros (2002) | Average book price | Book sales per capita |
|---|---|---|---|
| Austria | 80 euros | 14 euros | 5.7 |
| Belgium | 110 euros | 14 euros | 7.9 |
| Denmark | 90 euros | 22 euros | 4.0 |
| Finland | 130 euros | 22 euros | 5.9 |
| France | 50 euros | 14 euros | 3.6 |
| Germany | 80 euros | 14 euros | 5.7 |
| Greece | 20 euros | 14 euros | 1.4 |
| Ireland | 60 euros | 14 euros | 4.3 |
| Italy | No data about per head expenditure | 14 euros | No data |
| Luxembourg | 40 euros | 14 euros | 2.9 |
| Netherlands | 35 euros | 14 euros | 2.5 |
| Portugal | 65 euros | 14 euros | 4. 7 |
| Spain | 40 euros | 14 euros | 2.9 |
| Sweden | 45 euros | 14 euros | 3.1 |
| United Kingdom | 85 euros | 14 euros | 6.0 |

Purchasing, of course, is not the only way to access books. In some countries, library loans are even more important. As the data about public libraries in the UNESCO database[22] was quite outdated when this chapter was written, we used more recent data collected by Libecon in 2001 that covers the old and new EU member states, Romania, Bulgaria, EFTA members the USA and Japan.[23]

Similarly as in case of book prices, due to the difference in data collection periods, we had to merge that dealing with book loans from 2001 with that concerning book sales in 2001 and 2004 in order to get at least a rough picture of book usage in the old European Union member states. Regardless of the fact that the book industry seems to be as similarly dynamic as the rest of the media world, we do believe that these small time differences do not significantly affect the overall picture of trends in book usage amongst old EU members in the first years of the new millennium:

| State | Library loans in public libraries per capita | Total book consumption per capita | Book sales per capita |
|---|---|---|---|
| Austria | 1.8 | 7.5 | 5.7 |
| Belgium | 7.1 | 15.0 | 7.9 |
| Denmark | 13.4 | 17.4 | 4.0 |
| Finland | 19.0 | 24.9 | 5.9 |
| France | 5.2 | 8.8 | 3.6 |
| Germany | 3.7 | 9.4 | 5.7 |
| Greece | 0.2 | 1.6 | 1.4 |
| Ireland | 3.2 | 7.5 | 4.3 |
| Italy | 4.1 | No data | No data |
| Luxemburg | 0.3 | 3.2 | 2.9 |
| Netherlands | 12.1 | 14.6 | 2.5 |
| Portugal | 0.3 | 5.0 | 4.7 |
| Spain | 0.6 | 3.5 | 2.9 |
| Sweden | 9.1 | 12.2 | 3.1 |
| United Kingdom | 6.9 | 12.9 | 6.0 |

As stressed above, we assume that book buying and lending do not necessarily correspond equally with book reading. Therefore, it is worth pondering book consumption data with book reading data, as collected by Eurostat. In the table below we will compare book consumption data (= yearly purchases as estimated by above calculations + loans per head) with that looking at the number of non-readers versus the number of heavy readers (= those that read more than eight books per year) amongst the overall reading population. As the amount of book consumption per capita represents a very rough indication of trends, we will skip the use of decimals in our figures:

| State | Book consumption/ capita | Number of non-readers in population | Number of heavy readers in reading population |
|---|---|---|---|
| Finland | 25 | 24% | 43% |
| Denmark | 17 | 33% | 41% |
| Belgium | 15 | 58% | 27% |
| United Kingdom | 13 | 25% | 52% |
| Netherlands | 12 | 37% | 44% |
| Sweden | 12 | 19% | 44% |
| Germany | 9 | 41% | 23% |
| France | 9 | 43% | 46% |
| Austria | 7 | 38% | 26% |

*Continued*

| State | Book consumption per capita | Number of non-readers in population | Number of heavy readers in reading population |
|---|---|---|---|
| Ireland | 7 | 43% | 44% |
| Luxembourg | 3 | 35% | 37% |
| Portugal | 5 | 67% | 15% |
| Spain | 3 | 53% | 21% |
| Greece | 2 | 54% | 22% |
| Italy | No data | 50% | |

As we can see, there is a rough correspondence among books purchased and borrowed per head and the number of readers and non-readers in a given country, with just three exceptions. In comparison with other EU countries, Belgium has high book consumption per capita, but also a much higher number of non-readers. As well, Luxembourg has a similar number of non-readers as Denmark and Netherlands, yet only a quarter the amount of book consumption per capita. Finally, Portugal has the highest number of non-readers in the European Union, yet at least two countries seem to have lower book consumption per capita. It is also worth noting that countries with the highest numbers of library loans also have the lowest numbers of non-readers in population. This clearly means that libraries are a more important generator of reading habits than the publishing industry.

As stressed above, these tables do not represent the exact hierarchical relationship among European countries in terms of book usage; they only represent trends. In accordance with this fact, we will avoid ranking the countries in a list. Instead, we divide them into three groups: countries with a high usage of books (more than 10 per capita purchased and loaned annually), countries with a medium usage of books (between 5-10 books purchased and loaned per capita annually) and those with a low usage (less than 5 books purchased and loaned per capita annually). Additionally, we consider this data along with that showing the number of book readers in a given country. Due to its very high number of non-readers, we will move Belgium from group one to group two and Portugal from group two to group three. Additionally, considering its low number of non-readers, we will move Luxembourg from group three to group two:

**Group 1.** Countries with a high usage of books per head: Finland, Denmark, Sweden, the United Kingdom and the Netherlands.

**Group 2.** Countries with a medium usage of books per head: Austria, Belgium, Luxembourg, France, Germany and Ireland.

**Group 3.** Countries with a low usage of books per head: Portugal, Greece and Spain.

As we have seen, public libraries play a more important role in the promotion of reading than the publishing industry. It is therefore not surprising that throughout the European Union, there also exists a link between book usage and the quality of library systems: all five old EU member states with a high book usage and one with a medium book usage per head are among the top ten Libecon countries[25] regarded as having the best public library systems. Finland is the first, Denmark the second, the UK the fifth, Sweden the sixth and the Netherlands the tenth. Along with Ireland, they are the only old EU member states on the list. It is worth stressing, as well, that besides Japan (tied for tenth with Ireland and the Netherlands), Iceland (4th) and Norway (6th), we can find three new EU member states in this list: Estonia at third, Slovenia tied for sixth (together with Sweden and Norway) and Lithuania at ninth.[26]

At this point, we can return to the comparison between book usage, efficiency of education and competitiveness of countries.

# Competitiveness, education systems and book usage

The World Competitiveness Yearbook (WCY), created every year by the IMD Institute in Laussane, Switzerland, presents an overall competitiveness ranking for 60 countries and regional economies. The economies are ranked from most to least competitive and their performance is analysed on the basis of a time-series, with four main sets of criteria being used: economic performance (77 criteria), government efficiency (73 criteria), business efficiency (69 criteria) and infrastructure (95 criteria).

The WCY 2005 ranks the old EU member states with the highest book usage per head amongst the twenty most competitive countries in the world (Finland being the sixth, Denmark the seventh, Netherlands the thirteenth and Sweden the fourteenth; the UK is the exemption to this rule, sitting in twenty-second place). Three old EU member states with a medium book usage have successfully penetrated this level (Luxembourg being in ninth place, Ireland twelfth and Austria seventeenth). Significantly, all three old EU member states with the lowest book usage per head can be found at the bottom of the list (Spain being the thirty-eighth, Portugal the forty-fifth and Greece the fiftieth).

We get a similar picture when comparing this data with the results of the PISA project. In general, the Programme for International Students Assessment (PISA) measures reading literacy and mathematics performance and is 'concerned with the capacity of students to apply knowledge and skills and to analyse, reason and communicate effectively as they pose, solve and interpret problems in a variety of situations'.[27] As such, the concept of literacy used in the PISA 'is much broader than the historical notion of the ability to read and write' rather choosing to assess the ability 'to complete tasks relating to real life, depending on a broad understanding of key concepts, rather than limiting the assessment to the possessions of subject-specific knowledge.' In short, the purpose of the PISA is not to measure the ability of students to reproduce curriculum knowledge, but to apply it to a simulation of real-life situations.

The project assessed the performance of well over a quarter of a million students, representing about 23 million 15-year-olds in the schools of the 41 participating countries. All old member states and the majority of new EU member states are among those studied.[28]

As shown in the table below, there exist similarities among PISA mathematics performance and reading literacy, World Competitiveness Yearbook rankings and book usage:

| Country | PISA 2003 mathematics performance | PISA 2003 reading literacy | World Competitiveness Yearbook 2005 | Book usage | Ranking of public libraries |
|---|---|---|---|---|---|
| Finland | 1 | 1 | 6 | HIGH | 1 |
| Netherlands | 2 | 10 | 13 | HIGH | 10 |
| Canada | 3 | 3 | 5 | | |
| Korea | 4 | 2 | 29 | | |
| Hong Kong | 5 | 6 | 2 | | |
| Macao-China | 6 | 12 | – | | |
| Iceland | 7 | 21 | 4 | | 4 |
| Australia | 8 | 5 | 9 | | |
| New Zealand | 9 | 8 | 16 | | |
| Ireland | 10 | 7 | 12 | MEDIUM | 10 |
| Japan | 11 | 15 | 21 | | 10 |
| Liechenstein | 12 | 4 | – | | |
| Denmark | 13 | 18 | 7 | HIGH | 2 |
| Switzerland | 14 | 13 | 8 | | |
| Belgium | 15 | 11 | 24 | MEDIUM | |
| Norway | 16 | 14 | 15 | | 6 |
| Sweden | 17 | 9 | 14 | HIGH | 6 |

*Continued*

| Country | PISA 2003 mathematics performance | PISA 2003 reading literacy | World Competitiveness Yearbook 2005 | Book usage | Ranking of public libraries |
|---|---|---|---|---|---|
| France | 18 | 16 | 30 | MEDIUM | |
| Poland | 19 | 17 | 57 | | |
| Czech Republic | 20 | 24 | 36 | | |
| Spain | 21 | 26 | 38 | LOW | |
| Hungary | 22 | 27 | 37 | | |
| Austria | 23 | 22 | 17 | MEDIUM | |
| Luxembourg | 24 | 25 | 10 | MEDIUM | |
| United States | 25 | 19 | 1 | | |
| Germany | 26 | 20 | 23 | MEDIUM | |
| Latvia | 27 | 23 | – | | |
| Slovak Republic | 28 | 31 | 40 | | |
| Portugal | 29 | 28 | 45 | LOW | |
| Italy | 30 | 29 | 53 | | |
| Greece | 31 | 30 | 50 | LOW | |
| Russia | 32 | 33 | 54 | | |
| Turkey | 33 | 34 | 48 | | |
| Serbia | 34 | 38 | – | | |
| Uruguay | 35 | 32 | – | | |
| Thailand | 36 | 36 | 27 | | |
| Mexico | 37 | 37 | 56 | | |
| Indonesia | 38 | 40 | 59 | | |
| Brazil | 39 | 35 | 51 | | |
| Tunisia | 40 | 39 | – | | |

As we can see, the first 15 countries in the PISA 2003 mathematics performance ranking were also very high in the WCY 2005 scoreboard. Finland, for example, was first on the mathematics performance list and sixth on the competitiveness scoreboard, while Hong Kong was second on the competitiveness scoreboard and fifth in mathematics performance, and Australia was eight on the mathematics performance list and ninth on the Competitiveness scoreboard. In general, a huge majority of the top 15 countries on the mathematics performance list were also amongst the top 16 countries in the competitiveness scoreboard, with the only exemptions being Korea (fourth in the mathematics performance list and twenty-ninth in competitiveness scoreboard), Japan (eleventh in mathematics performance and twenty-first in the competitiveness scoreboard) and Belgium (fifteenth in mathematics performance and twenty-fourth in competitiveness scoreboard). Moreover, amongst the top 15 PISA reading literacy countries, only two (Japan and Korea) were not listed amongst the 16 most competitive countries.

The relations between education and competitiveness are similar in old EU member countries than in countries above. Even more interesting are relations among book usage, competitiveness and efficiency of education. As we have seen the majority of old EU member states (UK being the only exemption) with a high book usage and two with a medium usage were among the top 18 countries on the Competitiveness Scoreboard. Two of them (Finland and the Netherlands) were also among the top 10 PISA countries both in mathematics performance and reading literacy. On the other end, old EU member states with a low book usage were also low on the Competitiveness Scoreboard (Greece fiftieth, Portugal forty-fifth and Spain thirty-eighth), on the PISA mathematics performance list (Greece thirty-first, Portugal twenty-ninth and Spain twenty-first) and on the PISA reading literacy list (Greece thirtieth, Portugal twenty-eighth and Spain twenty-sixth).

In order to better understand these data, it is worth stressing two important facts:

First, another research project dealing with efficiency of education systems, TIMMS (in 1999 it included the majority of PISA 2003 participant countries), has also asked questions about home libraries of the students (unfortunately, PISA never asked such questions). TIMMS 1999 showed that it is the parental context that links high book usage with high performance of students, as there is 'a consistent relationship between number of books in the home and student achievement in both mathematics and science in the 8 grade, and PIRLS 2001 demonstrated a similar relationship with reading literacy at the fourth grade.'[29] In all TIMMS countries, students that have more than 200 books at home perform much better than students that have less than 25 books.

Second, as observed by Skaliotis,[6] people with less than a secondary education are generally low book users. Not surprisingly, countries with a high usage of books tend to have a greater percentage of more highly educated people. In all of the old EU member states with a high or medium book usage, more than 60 per cent of the population aged 25–64 has completed at least an upper-secondary education. On the other hand, in all of the EU member states with a low book usage, less than 60 per cent of the same-aged population has completed at least an upper-secondary education.[30]

This clearly means that family socialization represents an important element in the reproduction of highly-educated book users. In other words, parental context seems to be one of the most important elements in transmitting education, knowledge and book reading as a value from one generation to another.

# Questions for further research

The usage of books seems to be closely related to the level of the formal education of the population and to the competitiveness of respective countries: at least in the European context, comparisons among the PISA 2003 results, book usage and World Competitiveness Yearbook 2005 rankings have shown that, in general, the most competitive countries also have the best educational systems, the highest usage of books and the greatest percentage of upper-secondary educated people. Moreover, as there are no countries with poor education systems and lower book usage among the most competitive ones, we can assume that the latter two elements represent important parts of the social and cultural infrastructure that aids competitiveness.

The findings in this chapter, therefore, seem to confirm the fact that we live in an era of knowledge-based economies in which added value is created through research and innovation and an educated work force represents one of the important pre-conditions for economic growth. In this context, even though it is more than five hundred years old, the printed book remains one of the most important carriers and transmitters of knowledge.

Out of this conclusion, many questions arise that need further research. For example, as the parental context seems to be an important element, does this mean that equal opportunities in education with easy access to knowledge as embodied in books, are not only important in generating a social environment that allows for the growth of the intellectual class beyond existing numbers, but are also a pre-condition for economic growth? If the answer to such questions is yes, what does this mean for countries such as Korea, for example, that achieved such tremendous economic growth, has a good educational system and a fast growing book industry but is not considered as highly competitive at this very moment? On the other end, what to do with the USA, which is the most competitive country in the world according to the WCY 2005 but has poor PISA results? And what about Armenia, with its above average percentage of tertiary-educated people, but no economic growth and results well below the international average in the TIMMS? Furthermore, how should one interpret the fact that Nordic countries are all highly competitive and have a high usage of books, but differ significantly in terms of PISA results and book usage, where Finland is incomparably better than the rest? More precisely, what about Norway, with its above Nordic average investments in education and its higher than European average book usage, but poor PISA results? Similarly, what about the UK, with its relatively low level of competitiveness, a high usage of books and bad results in TIMMS (UK never moved from TIMMS to PISA, as if it was afraid of the likely bad results)?

Most likely, each of these questions would produce their own set of answers. If a country has an ineffective education system, small book production, poor library system and low penetration of computers, even a high percentage of people with formal tertiary education would not greatly change the society, as such a society would not be able to keep pace with intellectual developments and achievements throughout the developed world. Moreover, knowledge-based economies can take root only in societies well beyond a given point of social development; a country with no effective rule of law and no proper institutions to support a market economy will not achieve economic growth, regardless of the level of formal education in its population. On the other hand, we can assume that a high-quality tertiary education system and an inflow of the most talented students from around the world could minimise the inconveniences created by not having a highly successful primary and secondary education system. Therefore, a country without such an influx of talented students from abroad, but with a good education and book infrastructure and high degree of competitiveness, could consider poor educational results as a warning that it is not properly using its resources and risks losing its competitive advantage over the long run.

Without additional statistical and sociological research such questions and answers are only speculations, sketches and educated guesses. Even more, they could not be studied or answered without resolving one more issue concerning the book as a media. Namely, what does the above role of the printed book mean in an era in which all dominant media are visual and when at least in the European Union significant printed media such as daily papers are losing ground to the TV and Internet?[31] What is the meaning of the very fact that attempts to substitute printed books with electronic ones have slowed down in last three years (see Richardson)[4] and the book publishing industry has not faced a serious decline in sales as a consequence of the growth of digital media although the book buying base became more vulnerable than before? In other words, how can we interpret the fact that all five old EU member states with a high book usage are among the twenty countries with the highest number of Internet users in the world?[32] Does this mean that the printed book and digital media have complementary roles in the educational process and in the processes of information preservation and retrieval? Even more, does this mean that the growth of the Internet stimulates the growth of book production and usage and vice versa? Or are these data the first signs that the substitution of print with digital media has already begun but is more or less invisible and will take decades before it is completed? And last but not at all least, what is the cultural meaning of the changes that affect the printed book in the context of digital civilization?

Twenty years ago, in his lucid and foreshadowing book *Amusing Ourselves to Death* (1985), Neil Postman observed that there is always a link between the nature of the media and the content of the message; obviously, one cannot transmit highly sophisticated texts such as Freud's *Interpretation of Dreams* or Joyce's *Ulysses* with smoke signals. Similarly, it is hard to imagine a civilization in which complex products of human mind would be studied, contemplated and analysed by using only media such as Internet and TV: it seems to be in its very nature that the content transmitted by printed books requires a different and more sophisticated approach on the side of the recipient than the majority of messages found in today's dominant media. This leads us to the final and most important question, namely does this mean that we are facing a zero-sum game here: the disappearance of the printed book could mean either a radical change in our civilization, or the emergence of a new media that will allow the reproduction of similarly sophisticated knowledge, given its enormous importance in knowledge-base economies? And what would such substitution of the book mean in the context of the fact that the printed book has been around for more than five hundred years and has become almost a part of our second nature?

As already stressed, the ambition of this chapter was not to look for answers to such complex questions. What we intended to show, however, was that there exist statistically proven links among book usage, competitiveness and efficiency of education throughout European Union that make such questions legitimate. Even more, we firmly believe that such questions open a whole new research field concerning the book as a media. We consider our task as successful if we discovered at least the beginning of the path that leads towards it.

# Notes

1. Eurobarometer (2005) *Eurobarometer Survey on European Participation in Cultural Activities: Basic Tables*. Retrieved on June 2005 from *http://www.europa.eu.int*.

2. Finkelstein, D. and McCleery, A. (2005) *Introduction to Book History*. London and New York: Routledge.

3. European Commission: DG directorate (2004) *Publishing Market Watch Sectoral Report 2: Book Publishing*. Retrieved on June 2005 from *http://www.publishing-watch.org/*, p. 74.

4. Richardson, P. (2005) 1995–2005: World Publishing's Revolutionary Decade. *China Book Business Report*. p. 7 (quoted from English manuscript).

5. International Publishers Association, publishing statistics from various European countries. Retrieved on May 2005 from *http://www.ipa-uie.org/ipa/links_members.html*.

6. Skaliotis, M. (2002) *Statistics in the Wake of Challenges Posed by Cultural Diversity in a Globalization Context. Key Figures on Cultural Participation in the European Union (2002)*. Retrieved on May 2005 from *http://www.readingeurope.org/*.

7. European Commission, op. cit. p. 16 and 37.

8. In the context of PISA, efficiency of education is primarily understood as the ability of schools to reproduce effective work force in congruence with labor market demands. For more on this see Stefanc.[9]

9. Stefanc, D. (2005). Competency Assessment: Critical Consideration. Published at the International on-line scientific conference, 'Measurement and Assessment in Educational and Social Research', University of Ljubljana, July–October 2005, available from *http://www2.arnes.si/~ljzpds1/conf/*.

10. Various (2003) *The EU Publishing Industry: an Assessment of Competitiveness 2003*. Luxembourg: Pira International 2003.

11. Stockmann, D., Bengtsson, N. and Repo, Y. (2002) *The Book Trade in Finland From Author to Reader – Support Measures and Development in the Book Trade*. Ministry of Education, Department for Cultural, Sport and Youth Policy, Arts and Cultural Heritage Division. Series 11/2000, Helsinki. New net version, updated in Autumn 2002. Retrieved on May 2004 from *http://www.minedu.fi/minedu/publications/booktrade.doc*.

12. It is worth mentioning that this data is not absolutely accurate. British estimations are based on bestseller prices and Finnish on average recommended prices for books sent by sample stock.

13. This is of course happy medium between both prices. After this paper was written, *The Bookseller* published a report on BookScan's Total Consumer Market in which it is stated that average price of a book sold in British bookshops was 7.77 GBP in 2004 (or approximately 11 euros); in 2005, such average book price dropped

for an additional 17 pence. Obviously, the PA bestseller prices don't include discounts and 3 for 2 sales. Additionally, trade paperback sales were growing in 2004 and 2005 in the British market; as a consequence, cheaper books were sold in larger quantities than more expensive hardbacks. All in all, this means that in Britain, the average book price was lower and the number of books sold per head was higher than calculated. However, we decided to keep the average book price as we calculated it on the basis of PA data because this discrepancy doesn't change the overall picture of book consumption in UK much. Further, we don't know the influence of discounts on book prices in other EU countries. Obviously, in order to get a clear picture of average book prices of sold books in Europe, we'll have to wait until BookScan or similar organizations start to operate in all EU markets.

14. As already stated in note 13, when this chapter was written, both authors didn't know the exact relation between paperback and hardcover sales in Britain. In the lack of such data, they assumed that this relation was 50:50. Just before this book went to print, Nielsen Bookscan data became available that showed the relation between hardback and paperback sales in UK market is 70:30 in favor of paperbacks. Due to the fact that paperback publishing is more common in big book markets (as the structure of print cost up until the invention of digital printing didn't allow paperback printing in low prin-runs) it is very likely that paperback sales as a proportion of total book sales are traditionally higher in the British than in the Finnish book market. This clearly means that higher number of paperback sales than 50 per cent of total book sales in Britain doesn't change drastically the basic relation between average Finnish and British book prices.

15. Associazione Italiana Editori (AIE) (2004) *The Italian Book Market Report 2004*. Milan: AIE.

16. CIA World Factbook (2005) Retrieved on June 2005 from *http://www.cia.gov/cia/publications/factbook/rankorder/2004rank.html*.

17. Data gathered on Internet bookshops such as amazon.com and bol.com on 14 June 2005.

18. Data gathered on websites gyldendal.dk and gyldendal.no on 14 June 2005. All of these are cover prices that were significantly lowered for Internet sales.

19. The trends in new EU member and applicant states are different than in old ones. The Czech Republic, for example, has a similar GDP to Slovenia and a similar size population to Sweden, but its

book prices tend to be much lower than those in other old EU member countries as well as in Southeast EU member and applicant states. The average book price in the Czech Republic is estimated at around 7 euros, with the price of the hardcover edition of the *Da Vinci Code* at around 10 euros (information provided by Dr Jaroslav Cisar, Czech Publishers' Association). Similar prices can be found also in Slovakia and Poland, most likely courtesy of an old socialist tradition of low book prices. On the other hand, book prices in Southeast European EU applicant and member states are 180 Croatian kunas or around 24 euros in Croatia and 6478 Slovene tolars or approximately 27 euros in Slovenia. Most likely, reasons for these differences are historical, as book prices in former socialist Yugoslavia were traditionally higher than in the rest of communist Eastern Europe.

20. The aim of this paper is not to look for reasons underlying such similarities and differences in European book prices; these calculations and comparisons are just a tool needed to measure the role that books play in different societies. Let us just mention briefly that the determinants for the above-described similarities and differences in book prices include the size of the market, book price traditions and similarities in GDPs, and the percentage of secondary and tertiary educated population that represent majority of book users. Further analysis of these factors is not the topic of this paper.

21. Due to linguistic similarities, we consider the Austrian, Belgian, Luxembourg and Irish book industries as closely related to book industries that operate in much bigger German, French, Dutch and British book markets. As a result, the book prices in these small markets tend to be similar to prices in bigger markets.

22. UNESCO (2005) *UNESCO Library Statistics*. Retrieved on May 2005 from *http://stats.uis.unesco.org/TableViewer/ tableView.aspx?ReportId=14*.

23. For a better understanding of the differences among European public library systems, see Torstensson.[24]

24. Torstensson, M. (1993) Is there a Nordic Public Library System? *Libraries & Culture*, 28 (1).

25. In creating the list of these countries, nine indicators were used: membership in public libraries as percentage of population, visits per head, workstations connected to Internet per population, book additions per head, loans per head, audio and video additions per head, library staff per head, loans per head of staff and spending

per head). As some states achieved equal score there is more than ten states on the list.

26. Fuegi, D. and Jennings, M. (2004) *International library statistics: trends and commentary based on the Libecon data.* Retrieved on May 2005 from *http:/www.libecon.org.*

27. Organization for Economic Co-operation and Development (2004) *Learning for Tomorrow's World. First Results from Pisa 2003.* Paris: Organization for Economic Co-operation and Development, p. 23.

28. Ibid, p. 24.

29. TIMMS & PIRLS International Study Center (2004) *TIMMS 2003 International Science Report. Findings of IEA's Trends in International Mathematics and Science Study at the Fourth and Eighth Grades.* Boston: Lynch School of Education, Boston College, p. 138.

30. European Commission, op. cit., p. 58.

31. European Commission: DG directorate (2005) *Publishing Market Watch Final Report.* Retrieved on May 2005 from *http://www.publishing-watch.org/.*

32. IMD (2005) *IMD World Competitiveness Yearbook 2005.* Lausanne: Institute for Management Development.

# 7

# The future of reading as a cultural behaviour in a multi-channel media environment

*Hillel Nossek and Hanna Adoni*

## Introduction

An article by Hester Lacey titled, 'The Tyranny of Reading', published in the *Guardian*, in 2005[1] opens with the following sentence:

'So Victoria Beckham has never read a book in her life'.

In the article, Lacey, a devoted book reader herself, claimed that reading books is just one of the ways of spending leisure time and consuming mass media. In Lacey's view the choice not to read books is legitimate and does not harm the individual. Responding to this, Michael Handelzalts, a leading Israeli literary critic, wrote an article titled: 'They Have Never Read a Book – What a Shame!',[2] which argues the importance of reading books for enhancing a person's intellectual development and sharpening their critical faculties.

The controversy about reading as a cultural behaviour is not new. Indeed, this subject has appeared on the research and public agenda since the 1960s. Nevertheless, the study of the interaction between reading and other types of media consumption and leisure activities (as cultural behaviour) has been rather limited.

The main premise of this article is that today, at the beginning of the twenty-first century, it is important for us to examine reading as one aspect of a wider multi-channel media communication environment, which offers its public a combined abundance of old and new media.

The present article investigates three important issues regarding the persistence of reading as a cultural behaviour. The first question concerns changes in the size of the reading public and in the frequency of reading over time by individuals defined by different socio-demographics variables. The second question concerns the patterns of interaction between reading and other types of media consumption. The third question addresses the functions of reading in fulfilling psycho-social needs and its degree of interchangeability with the other media. In our view there are three relevant theoretical approaches to the study of these questions: The media technology approach, the sociology of culture, and the functional theory of communication, as elaborated below.

## Literature review and theoretical framework

The dynamics of interaction between different media technologies has engaged communication students since the early 1950s and remains controversial to this day. Innis,[3] who is considered the founding father of the media technology approach, argued that civilizations are shaped by their use of a particular medium of communication over a lengthy period and that the dominant communication medium in any given period will eventually be replaced by a medium better equipped to handle the problems of communicating knowledge across time and space. McLuhan[4] developed the idea of the displacement of one medium by another a step further, and explored the social consequences of the invention of print and the later widespread use of electronic media. His main contention was that, in time, prolonged, persistent use of a dominant medium would affect the organization of social structure, the cultural characteristics of society, and the personality and cognitive processes of individuals in that culture. He argued that the traditional form of literacy, which evolved from the linear nature of print and its consequential nature, affected human cognitive structures and hence the entire societal and cultural system, including the development of nationality, sciences, and a rational, 'linear' way of thinking.[5] McLuhan argued that exposure to television encourages cognitive structures based on oral expression, gestalt perception, and shared experience. He predicted that a new cognitive structure generally more compatible with modern, fragmented experience would ultimately displace the traditional form of literacy based on linear print.

Although in his later works, McLuhan modified his original displacement hypothesis, one of the alternatives for interaction he predicted between the various communication media remained the obsolescence of an older medium and its displacement by a new one.[6] As print is the oldest media technology of the modern era, one prediction of the media technology approach was the displacement of print by television and more recently by the new digital technologies.

Sociological and socio-cultural researchers have implicitly criticised the media technological approach[3,4] claiming it disregarded the dynamics of media interrelations and the idiosyncrasies of different socio-cultural systems and generally failed to corroborate empirically the displacement effect hypothesis. This line of research demonstrated that the patterns of diffusion of print and its functions were by no means universal as they interacted with the unique social and cultural characteristics of different societies.[7-9] It also showed that relations between the various media are far more complex than the simplistic postulate of the media technological approach that the dominant medium makes all others obsolete. Eisenstein,[10,11] for example, has suggested that the advent of print provided the impetus for the spread of new types of images such as lithographs, etchings, caricatures, and cartoons. Print also contributed to the development of modern science by enabling the duplication and dissemination of precise pictorial and mathematical statements such as maps, equations, charts, tables, and graphs, all visual, non-linear aids which help to overcome language barriers.

On the micro-level of the individual consumer of culture, Bourdieu[12,13] suggested that a key function of cultural consumption is the social construction of distinctions between different groups in society. Whereas the contents of reading can be associated with high as well as popular culture, reading in general and book reading in particular is considered an activity requiring a rather high level of cultural capital, and is therefore considered a type of cultural behaviour. Among the reasons for this are, first, reading requires traditional literacy for which rudimentary levels of reading and writing are needed, which are acquired through a long process of study. By comparison, media literacy, associated usually with the comprehension of television content, is based on knowledge of and familiarity with the dominant conventions and genres of the audio-visual media. These are acquired from early childhood through viewing television and without any direct investment by young viewers, parents or caregivers. Second, the reading of complex contents that are part of the canonical culture requires a cultural capital, which is acquired through familial and social status group socialization.[12–16]

The use of the new technologies requires a new type of literacy, integrating the two forms of literacy referred to above with new elements of basic computer expertise and interactive communication skills. The command of this new type of convergent literacy is a sine qua non condition for the use of the digital media.

The functional approach to mass communication has demonstrated that different psycho-social functions linked to various media are based on an ever-changing functional division of labour between them.[17] The consumer-oriented perspective at the core of the 'uses and gratification' approach has defined media consumption as an active process of utilization whereby individuals attempt to satisfy some of their psycho-social needs through selective self-exposure to specific media and contents.[18–24] Empirical studies based on these theories have indicated that each medium specialises in fulfilling certain types of needs for its consumers.

**Figure 7.1**   **Dialectic model of media interactions**

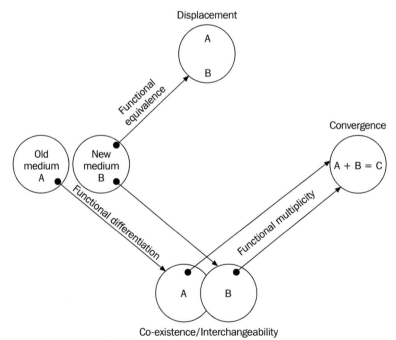

Source: Adoni and Nossek.[25]

A model was constructed based on the three theoretical approaches and new research findings, which dialectically link patterns of media interactions.

The model describes the possible interactions between the media, addressing their production, distribution, and consumption patterns. The interaction between any two media, such as the print media and television, arises from their varying functional equivalence. Where functional equivalence exists, one medium may make another obsolete while creating the optimum circumstances for the substitution or displacement of its predecessor. This can significantly reduce the production of the displaced medium, its distribution channels, and consumption. In contrast, functional differentiation, or a low degree of functional equivalence creates circumstances in which both media may co-exist. This situation will be characterised by stability or even growth in the production and supply of both forms of media and their continued or even increased consumption and use by individual consumers. For example, if reading books and watching television are not functionally equivalent, their functional differentiation enables them to exist side by side. However, the functional differentiation between them might be partial and, consequently, there might be some degree of functional interchangeability between them.

According to the technological approach a decline in size of reading public and frequency of reading could be an indicator of the displacement of the print media, and consequently will cause a significant decrease in the production and distribution of books. However, if such a decline does not occur it might indicate that book reading is not affected by other media consumption and that print media will continue to exist side by side with other media of communication.

Reading as a cultural behaviour and the differences in reading habits between individuals from different social groups could be explicated in the theoretical framework proposed by Bourdieu. As elaborated above, we may assume that reading books, as a component of cultural consumption, will continue to be an indicator of distinctions among groups of different social status. Apparently, notwithstanding the tremendous educational progress in Western societies, the patterns of cultural and media consumption are still formed and crystallised in the individual's habitus.

As for the functional approach, the persistence of reading books might be related to the degree of interchangeability or uniqueness of print media use. If reading books fulfils unique psycho-social needs for the individual reader, then it can be assumed that it will persist as a cultural behaviour even in the multi-media environment.

# Israel as a case study

The above mentioned issues were examined in Israel and provide a case study of a Western society with a large reading public, which is also active in a multi-channel media environment.

The secular reading public in Israel that generally, though not exclusively, reads in modern Hebrew did not exist until a hundred years ago. The revitalization of Hebrew as a spoken, written, and read language did not occur in a vacuum. The tradition of literacy that was essential for prayer and learning religious texts in traditional Jewish society provided a solid foundation for the growth of a Hebrew reading public. In the long process of secularization, the Hebrew language has changed from being a sacred to a secular language, from a language used in prayers and religious rituals to a language of everyday life: a language written and read in order to communicate a wide range of subjects relevant to a secular culture and a modern democratic state. Hebrew has been Israel's official language since the country was founded and is taught in the education system from kindergarten to university as well as to new immigrants who received their formal education in their country of origin.

Israel's print media are comprised of several national dailies and hundreds of local weeklies. In addition, about 5,000 new book titles are published annually. Most of the books published were originally written in Hebrew, though about 25 per cent are translations, mostly from English. In the early 1990s, a multi-channel media system arose very rapidly, to replace a monopolistic system that had existed for decades. At the time of the last data collection presented in this article, in 2001, Israel's new media map had two national television channels (one public and one commercial), cable TV with a wide choice of channels (national and global satellite channels), and channels broadcasting from other countries: Europe, neighbouring Arab countries, and the United States. The national cable channels also offer a domestically produced Russian channel, a channel serving the religious community, and a music channel. Direct broadcast satellite (DBS) is also available, offering subscribers a similar choice of channels.

In 2001, over 80 per cent of Israeli households had a multi-channel television system. Both the cable companies and the satellite company provided home Internet connection; in 2001, over 50 per cent of households owned a PC and over 30 per cent were connected to the Internet. There was also widespread Internet use at work.[25] The new media map also contained 14 commercial regional radio stations as well as dedicated radio stations for the Arab minority and religious community, two national, public radio stations, and some 150 local pirate radio stations.

## Methodology

The findings presented below are based on empirical data collected by the authors during a period stretching from the 1970s until the beginning of the present century. The data were collected by several surveys using both face to face and telephone interviews. The survey questionnaires contained mostly closed, multiple-choice questions. The surveys were conducted among representative samples of the adult (21+) Israeli population at different points in time (1970, 1990, 1997, 2001).

The last research project, conducted in 2001, included, in addition to a survey, nine focus groups, conducted by the authors.

## Long-term changes in the Israeli reading public

The longitudinal reading study shows that reading is still a widespread cultural behaviour. At the beginning of the second millennium the reading public in Israel consisted of 80 per cent of the population.

A comparison based on four time points (1970, 1990, 1997, 2001), shows a slight decline in the book reading public of Jewish adults between 1970 and 1990, with a trend towards stabilization in the last decade (see Table 7.1). In 1970, over three-quarters of the Israeli public reported reading books, while in 1990 a slight decrease (2 per cent) occurred, which appears insignificant. However, the picture changes when we consider the rise in standard of national education. If the educational level is the variable that determines reading frequency then one would

| **Table 7.1** | Readers of print media in 1970, 1990, 1997, and 2001 (% of readers of the jewish population) | | |

|  | 1970 (N = 3,671) | 1990 (N = 2,902) | 1997 (N = 2,424) | 2001 (N = 520) |
|---|---|---|---|---|
| Books | 78 | 76 | 85 | 85 |
| Daily newspapers | 86 | 89 | 91 | 98 |
| Periodicals published in Israel | 53 | 43 |  | 28 |
| Periodicals published Abroad | 21 | 10 | – | 8 |

*Data sources:* Katz and Gurvitch,[26] Katz et al.,[24] Adoni and Nossek,[25] Adoni and Nossek, 2001 survey data.

expect a rise in the population's educational level to be accompanied by a concomitant rise in number of readers. However, an almost equal percentage of readers was found at each of the time points, indicating that despite the rise in national level of education, there was a relative decrease in the size of reading public as a percentage of the whole population. This will be discussed later on.

A slight rise in the number of book readers began to appear in 1997 when it reached 85 per cent, a percentage that was found in 2001, as well. This was apparently caused by a wave of immigration from the former Soviet Union during the 1990s, of which 95 per cent of the adult population were book readers. Slightly more than a third (37 per cent) of the reading public reported reading 1–5 books a year, 22 per cent read 6–10 books a year, and 41 per cent were active readers that read eleven or more books per year. The proportion of daily newspapers readers was already high in the 1970s. Since then there has been a further rise in 2001 when 98 per cent of Israeli adults reported reading newspapers.

# Reading habits in Israel and other countries

Locating social phenomena within a broader perspective requires cross-cultural comparisons with societies similar to Israel in terms of the national educational level. The comparative data presented here (Table 7.2) are based on several surveys which all asked the question about

| Table 7.2 | Readers of books, periodicals and newspapers in Israel and other countries (% of the population) | | |
|---|---|---|---|
| | Books | Periodicals | Newspapers |
| Australia**** | 72 | 63 | 91 |
| Austria* | 72 | 88 | 98 |
| Belgium* | 42 | 84 | 77 |
| Denmark* | 67 | 88 | 95 |
| United Kingdom* | 75 | 76 | 91 |
| Finland* | 76 | 97 | 100 |
| France* | 67 | 83 | 84 |
| Germany* | 59 | 91 | 94 |
| Greece* | 46 | 54 | 70 |
| Netherlands* | 73 | 83 | 90 |
| Ireland* | 66 | 71 | 97 |
| Israel** | 85 | 36 | 98 |
| Italy* | 50 | 83 | 75 |
| Luxembourg* | 75 | 86 | 93 |
| Portugal* | 33 | 63 | 75 |
| Spain* | 47 | 71 | 77 |
| Sweden* | 81 | 91 | 100 |
| United States*** | 50 | 80 | 83 |

* The data are based on a Eurobarometer survey in the fall of 2001 among 16,200 men and women above the age of 15 living in 15 countries of the European Union.[27] The survey studied different patterns of recreation, leisure, and cultural and media consumption including habits of reading books, periodicals and newspapers, television viewing, radio listening, movie attendance, concerts and theatre, use of PC and Internet, arts production, and other activities. The same questionnaire was used in all countries and interviews were conducted face to face.

** The data on reading books and newspapers was gathered via a telephone survey in 2001 of a representative sample (520) of the Jewish urban population above the age of 21. The question regarding reading books was 'Have you read a book recently?' Possible responses were: 1 – yes; 2 – no; 3 – never read books. The question about periodicals was 'Do you regularly read weekly or monthly magazines that are published in Israel?' Response options were: 'yes, I do read'; 'I do not read periodicals'. The question about newspapers was 'Do you read newspapers – if so, how frequently?'

*** The data are based on a 1999 survey by the US Department of Education[28] of a representative sample of adults 25 years or older (no information on sample size). The question asked was 'Have you read any books during the last twelve months?' Response options were: 1 – Yes, for work; 2 – Yes, as required reading for a course; 3 – Yes, for educational purposes (not required); 4 – Yes, for purposes other than work or study; 5 – I did not read any kind of book in the last 12 months.

**** Australian Bureau of Statistics.[29] Based on a 2001 telephone survey of a representative sample of 1,500 men and women above the age of 18. The data are based on a survey accompanying a multi-year project jointly funded by the Department of Communication, Information, Technology and the Arts and the Council of Australia. The project goal was to advance books, especially by Australians, and promote reading

*(Continued)*

*Table footnote (Continued)*
and literacy (principally among children). The survey questioned a representative sample of 1,500 men and women above the age of 18. Interviewees were asked a long list of questions about their reading habits and how they accessed books (purchase, library, borrowing from friends or family, gifts, home library, used book stores, and other sources). The wording of the question on reading was 'Have you read a book for pleasure during the last week?' Response options were: 1 – I read a book for pleasure; 2 – I read a book related to work; 3 – I never read books.

book reading in a different manner, the question was located in a different position in the questionnaire and in different interview contexts (as noted in the body of the table). Also note that although the surveys all used representative samples of the population, we do not have full details regarding the sampling method used and the composition of these samples.

The comparative data shows that the percentage of book readers in the Israeli population (85 per cent) was higher than the US (50 per cent) and similar to several European countries. Sweden was the only country with the same percentage of book readers as Israel and the proportion in the rest of the European Union was lower, ranging from 33 per cent in Portugal to 76 per cent in Finland. Newspaper reading was more popular than reading books for all of the countries compared, and even reached 100 per cent of the population in Sweden and Finland. In Israel too, the proportion of newspaper readers was very high, reaching 98 per cent of the adult population. In contrast to Israel's high ranking for books and newspapers, the proportion of readers of periodicals was relatively low – 51 per cent of the entire population. However, having presented these data it is important to emphasise that such data are problematic and should be treated with great caution. In a detailed position paper published by the Center for Arts and Culture Policy Research at Princeton University, Steven Tepper[30] analysed the lack of consistency in survey findings measuring attitudes of different subjects, among them attitudes and patterns of participation in the cultural consumption of different populations over relatively short periods of time. As we know, a lack of consistency undermines the validity and reliability of the survey method and of findings based on data gathered using this method. Tepper quoted the research findings of John Robinson,[31,32] who studied American leisure by systematically comparing the findings of surveys on cultural consumption. Tepper extended and probed these comparisons further and highlighted various factors that may distort a respondent's answers and undermine the validity and reliability of the survey.[33]

# Frequency of reading among groups defined by demographic and socio-economic variables

Findings of research conducted in Israel and other countries[34] had established that educational level is a principal factor in determining the frequency of book reading. Because of the centrality of education as a variable, we examined the relationship between reading frequency and other background variables when the education variable was held as a constant (i.e. we examined the effect of age, gender, ethnic origin, etc. on reading frequency in groups with identical education).

Analysis of reading patterns of persons classified by education and age revealed that between 1970 and 1990, the period when television became popular in Israel, a decline in frequency of reading began among all readers, especially pronounced among young adults (20–29) with 11+ years of education. The proportion of active readers (that is readers who read at least eleven books a year) in the young adults group in 1970 was 68 per cent compared with 48 per cent in 1990 – a dramatic decline of 20 per cent. Surprisingly, a more moderate decline was found amongst two older adult age groups (30–50 and 50 and above), with both medium and high level of education.

Gender also influenced the frequency of reading. Among people with 13+ years of education, 63 per cent of women and 50 per cent of men regularly read at least one book a month. Nearly half (48 per cent) of all women with a moderate level of education were active readers compared with slightly more than a third (36 per cent) of the men. The only exception to this pattern is the case of people with a low educational background, where the number of active readers was identical for both genders (34 per cent).

The opposite trend existed in relation to reading newspapers, as men read more newspapers in comparison to women. The largest gap was found for those with the lowest educational level where 88 per cent of the men and 75 per cent of all the women occasionally read a daily paper. This gap narrowed with the rise in educational level and nearly disappeared among those with the highest level of education, with 84 per cent of the men and 81 per cent of the women reading a daily newspaper.

Regarding ethnic background, the differences between people with the same number of years of study from different ethnic groups were small and not significant. No differences were found among persons born in Israel of different ethnic origins who had 13+ years of study. A different picture emerged for those of medium educational level. In this case, there was a clear difference between three groups of Israelis: the proportion of active readers among Israelis of European-American origins reached 52 per cent, slightly higher than those whose parents were born in Israel (49 per cent). In contrast, among Israelis of Middle Eastern origin, the proportion of active readers was only 36 per cent. In other words, the effect of ethnicity on reading frequency and the gap between the three ethnic groups almost disappeared only in the group with the highest educational level.

# Influence of socialization on reading habits

The findings suggest that parents' reading habits influenced reading frequency throughout a person's lifetime. People whose parents read books (or who had parents who did so in the past) read more than people whose parents did not read, irrespective of educational level (see Table 7.3). Thus, while education still remained the factor that most strongly determines reading frequency, it did not entirely supersede the importance of early socialization to reading. Regardless of their educational level, adults raised in an environment where their parents read books, tended to read more. This group contained a significantly higher percentage of both people that belong to the reading public in general and active readers in particular.

**Table 7.3** Reading books by education and parental reading habits

| | Readers | % of entire population | Active readers (read more than 11 books per year) | % of reading population |
|---|---|---|---|---|
| Years of schooling | Neither parents customarily read books | Both parents customarily read books | Neither parents customarily read books | Both parents customarily read books |
| 0–8 | 51 (N = 94) | 64 (N = 47) | 28(N = 42) | 37 (N = 27) |
| 9–11 | 53 (N = 122) | 70 N = 76) | 33 (N = 64) | 46 (N = 41) |
| 12 | 75 (N + 162) | 90(N = 195) | 38 (N = 55) | 53 (N = 174) |
| 13+ | 80 (N = 100) | 93 (N = 290) | 49 (N = 80) | 61 (N = 271) |

*Source:* Katz et al.[24]

The data presented in the table indicated that formal education did not completely succeed in overcoming the role of early socialization to reading. The combination of high educational level and socialization to reading at an early age through the family was a better predictor of the amount of reading than educational level alone.

# Frequency of reading and the use of other media

In Israel reading books, newspapers and periodicals is an important component of people's leisure activities and their consumption of communication. Book readers also engage in a long and varied list of leisure activities and media consumption – they listen to the radio, watch television[35] and use the Internet.

In order to study the influence of the new media on reading we examined the differences in reading frequency and exposure to other media for two groups: non-PC owners and PC owners who were connected to the Internet. It was assumed that after controlling for age and educational level, the differences in reading between the two groups would be the result of adopting the new media.

Nearly all those in the research sample regularly viewed television and a similar number listened to the radio. Nearly everyone (91 per cent) read daily newspapers and approximately three-quarters read books, with nearly half (48 per cent) reading at least one book a month. At the same time, nearly half the participants spent an hour a day on the computer with some using it for more than two hours a day. Ten per cent of the sample had a PC at home and access to the Internet from home, and approximately half of them spent at least an hour a day surfing it while others devoted more than two hours a day to the Internet.

PC ownership and Internet connection positively correlated to income and educational level. Frequency of PC use was positively correlated to the respondents' level of education, and use of the Internet was positively correlated to age. There was no significant correlation for gender. Regression analysis indicated that income and years of education were the best predictors of both access to new technologies and their use.[37]

The findings suggest that the displacement effect depends upon the type of media used and that it varies depending on the person's age and education (Tables 7.4 and 7.5). When age was controlled, there was no indication of a decrease in book reading. For all age groups, the proportion of readers was highest among those who owned a PC and were users of the Internet (Table 7.4).

A similar pattern was found for frequency of reading daily newspapers. In other words, across most age groups, the percentage of daily newspaper readers was higher among those with access to the new media. In all age groups, PC owners connected to the Internet watched television for fewer hours per day than those who were not connected. The percentage that listened to the radio was higher for those aged 50+ who were connected to the Internet and lowest for those in the youngest age group who were connected to the Internet.

Examination of the correlation between educational level, rate of media consumption and reading indicates several differences between the two groups (PC owners and non-PC owners). Thus, a higher percentage of active book readers was found for PC owners connected to the Internet (Table 7.5). This was most evident and significant for the medium level of education. Regarding the less well educated, the frequency of reading both newspapers and periodicals was higher for PC owners connected to the Internet than for non-PC owners.

The percentage of 'heavy' television viewers was found higher among non-PC owners than PC-owners with Internet. No difference was found between Internet owners and non-PC owners with regard to 'heavy' television viewing among the lowest educated. Among those with medium and higher education, 'heavy' television viewing was lowest among those who were connected to the Internet, while no significant difference was found between groups regarding radio listening.

# Functions of reading for self and society

Setting aside the differences between high culture and popular culture, book reading fulfilled the most basic personal needs for all readers irrespective of education, age, gender, and ethnicity. Our respondents expressed the following views about reading books: books can be exciting and relaxing at the same time; they help readers to learn about themselves and better understand life (72 per cent). Books allow readers to switch off from the daily realities of life (62 per cent) and return to it rested and more complete; above all, it offers lovers of reading pleasure and a

## Table 7.4 — Percentage of heavy media users by age and new media ownership

| Media & other activities | Group 1: no computer age group | | | | | Group 2: computer & Internet age group | | | | |
|---|---|---|---|---|---|---|---|---|---|---|
| | 20–29 | 30–39 | 40–49 | 50–65 | Total | 20–29 | 30–39 | 40–49 | 50–65 | Total |
| N | 373 | 250 | 203 | 529 | 1355 | 86 | 57 | 62 | 28 | 233 |
| 1. Internet | – | – | – | – | – | 41 | 39 | 61 | 50 | 46 |
| 2. Books | 44$^a$ | 37$^{a,b}$ | 34$^{a,b}$ | 37$^{a,b}$ | 38$^{a,b}$ | 79$^a$ | 77$^{b,c}$ | 66$^{b,c}$ | 82$^{b,c}$ | 76$^{b,c}$ |
| 3. Newspapers | 84$^{a,b}$ | 86$^a$ | 86$^{a,b}$ | 86$^a$ | 85$^{a,b}$ | 94$^b$ | 94$^a$ | 94$^b$ | 100$^{a,b}$ | 95$^{b,c}$ |
| 4. Magazines | 40$^a$ | 39 | 34 | 19$^{a,b}$ | 31$^{a,b}$ | 41 | 28 | 43$^a$ | 43$^b$ | 39$^b$ |
| 5. Television | 35$^a$ | 26$^{a,b}$ | 28$^{a,b}$ | 39$^{a,b}$ | 34$^{a,b}$ | 19$^{a,b}$ | 9$^b$ | 16$^b$ | 8$^{b,c}$ | 14$^{b,c}$ |
| 6. Radio | 36$^a$ | 37 | 34 | 44 | 39 | 33$^b$ | 39 | 43 | 46 | 38 |

Operational definitions of heavy media use:
1. Internet use (at least 2 hours a day)
2. Reading books in the past month
3. Reading newspapers (several times a week)
4. Reading magazines
5. Television (at least 4 hours a day)
6. Listening to radio (at least 4 hours a day)

* Significant differences (p < 0.05) between two or more percentages in similar age groups for different groups of media ownership is shown by $^{a,b,c}$ next to the percentages. Significance was computed using the Z test for testing the difference between two proportions. Single, similar letters (e.g. a,a.) in cells appearing in the same row show the difference between the percentages to be significant. Cells with more than one letter (any combination of a, b, and c) means that significant differences exist between more than one cell in the same row.

**Table 7.5** Percentage of heavy media users by level of education and new media ownership

| Media ownership | Group 1: No computer level of education | | | | Group 2: Computer & Internet level of education | | | |
|---|---|---|---|---|---|---|---|---|
| Media & other activities | Low | Medium | High | Total | Low | Medium | High | Total |
| N | 280 | 882 | 180 | 1342 | 7 | 109 | 115 | 231 |
| 1. Internet | – | – | – | – | 50 | 40 | 49 | 46 |
| 2. Books | 18 | 37[a,b] | 74 | 38[a,b] | 43 | 67[b] | 85 | 75[b,c] |
| 3. Newspapers | 82[a] | 87 | 84 | 85[a,b] | 100[a,b] | 94 | 96 | 95[b,c] |
| 4. Magazines | 19[a] | 35 | 28 | 31[a,b] | 71[a,b] | 39 | 37 | 39[b] |
| 5. Television | 42 | 34 | 22[a,b] | 34[a,b] | 43 | 21 | 6[b] | 14[b,c] |
| 6. Radio | 42 | 39 | 33 | 39 | 33 | 41 | 36 | 38 |

Level of education:
■ Low – up to 10 years
■ Medium – 11–13 years
■ High – Academic degree
Operational definitions of heavy media use and frequent participation in leisure activities:
1.  Internet use (at least 2 hours a day)
2.  Reading books in the past month
3.  Reading newspapers (several times a week)
4.  Reading magazines
5.  Watching television (at least 4 hours a day)
6.  Listening to radio (at least 4 hours a day)
* Significant differences ($p < 0.05$) between two or more percentages in similar age groups for different groups of media ownership is shown by [a,b,c] next to the percentages. Significance was computed using the Z test for testing the difference between two proportions. Single, similar letters (e.g. a.a.) in cells appearing in the same row show the difference between the percentages to be significant. Cells with more than one letter (any combination of a, b, and c) means that significant differences exist between more than one cell in the same row.

unique experience (63 per cent). Books are the most efficient means of communication media for learning, enrichment, and satisfying intellectual curiosity (76 per cent; see Table 7.6).

Books and newspapers also connect between people with similar interests and strengthen relationships with family and friends: people

| Table 7.6 | | Percentage of respondents reporting that media use helped them to fulfil psycho-social needs | | | |
|---|---|---|---|---|---|

| Psycho-social needs | | Reading books | Reading news-papers | Watching television | Surfing the Internet |
|---|---|---|---|---|---|
| Cognitive needs | To learn and enrich myself | 76 | 52 | 55 | 54 |
| | To develop critical faculties | 49 | 57 | 53 | 37 |
| | To know myself and learn about life | 72 | 44 | 51 | 35 |
| Affective needs | To escape from the reality of everyday life | 62 | 43 | 76 | 44 |
| | To experience beauty | 63 | 30 | 55 | 28 |
| Instru-mental needs | To be in touch with people with the same interests | 47 | 45 | 48 | 46 |
| | To spend time with my friends | 31 | 30 | 46 | 31 |
| | To participate in discussions with my friends | 53 | 43 | 46 | 37 |
| | To spend time with my family | 44 | 31 | 55 | 22 |
| | To participate in discussions with my family | 50 | 44 | 50 | 28 |

*Source:* Telephone survey of representative sample (520 interviewees) of adult population 21+, Adoni and Nossek.[25]

revealed a strong need to discuss books they have read and to share their experiences with those close to them. Thus, reading strengthens relationships between friends, couples, children, and parents and even between grandparents and grandchildren.

Besides fulfilling basic personal needs, we found that reading books and using other media contributed to the complex process of construction of an individual's social identity. Watching television, reading newspapers, and reading books contributed significantly to constructing an Israeli identity, whereas Internet and television both help to construct a global identity, as one would expect.[38,39] Nevertheless, television still seems more effective than any other media in constructing a social identity, although there is only a slight difference between television and the other media. Reading newspapers satisfies different needs to those described above; above all, they meet the need for citizenship and political involvement, by providing updates about local events and elected representatives, and by helping people reach decisions at election times.

Functional interchangeability between reading and other media was examined by computing the average correlation between each pair of media (see Table 7.1). The highest degree of interchangeability was found between watching television and reading newspapers; reading books and reading newspapers, and between reading books and the Internet. The least interchangeability was between watching television and reading books. The differences between the levels of interchangeability between

| Table 7.7 | Average pearson correlation between each pair of media use for fulfilling cognitive, affective, and instrumental needs |

| Social needs | Affective needs | Cognitive needs | Overall (with reference to the activity) | Media uses media consumption activity |
|---|---|---|---|---|
| 26 | 12 | 15 | 17 | Reading books and watching television |
| 32 | 17 | 24 | 24 | Reading books and reading newspapers |
| 25 | 17 | 27 | 23 | Reading books and surfing the Internet |
| 33 | 24 | 19 | 25 | Reading newspapers and watching television |
| 22 | 21 | 10 | 18 | Reading newspapers and surfing the Internet |
| 21 | 22 | 16 | 20 | Watching television and surfing the Internet |
| 27 | 19 | 19 | 20 | Overall (with reference to the needs) |

* The average of the Pearson correlations between the 'helpfulness' of each pair of media for every one of the needs was computed as an index of the degree to which each pair of media performs similar functions and therefore might constitute functional alternatives for each other. A high average signifies that the two media are interchangeable, that is, fulfil the same needs. A low average indicates the specificity of the medium, that is, its helpfulness in fulfilling specific needs. This measure of interchangeability was used by Katz and Gurevitch.[40]

the different activities are a function of different types of needs. The low level of interchangeability between book reading and other media is a function of people's affective needs. As for cognitive needs, the lowest average correlation and therefore the least interchangeability was between reading books and watching television. As for the instrumental needs relating to spending time and participating in discussions with family and friends, the pattern is different and there is greater interchangeability between the different media. The highest degree of interchangeability was found between the two print media, books and newspapers.

According to the responses of participants in the focus group, watching television did not appear to be interchangeable for reading books and printed newspapers. Orna (an academic in her 40s) testified that for her the Internet had replaced television news and that she preferred 'to go to YNET on the computer and not to news on television or radio'. She also reported that she still read print newspapers.

Other reasons for preferring books to television were that books were special, and the act of reading is something the reader does alone. People also preferred books because of intellectual challenge they offer. Thus, for example, Morit (an academic in her 20s) reported: 'I can watch television and films with a friend. But I have to read a book by myself. I have to find the time to be alone'. Arnon (51, an academic) reported that 'Books make me independent of time. Television requires me to be on schedule. It shackles me and also gives me what I don't want ... I control my time with a book. It develops my intellectual side'. Alex (27, academic) also related to the ease of television use: 'A book makes you work. With television – the pictures just float by you. Books make my brain work more'.

Furthermore, regular Internet users in the focus group reported that they used the Internet as a resource to find book recommendations. Natalie (25, an academic immigrant who arrived in Israel 12 years ago) explained, for example, that when she read about an interesting author on the Internet she would look for the book.

# Discussion and conclusions

The main finding of this study is that reading books continues to be a cultural behaviour and will not be displaced by any other media in the foreseeable future. The most general conclusion is that the media technology approach, which in its early stages predicted the displacement effect of the television and the disappearance of print, is inapplicable to the dynamic relationship of the multi-channel media environment.

The diffusion of the new technologies – the PC and the Internet – will not lead to the disappearance of print media. PC and Internet users continue to read books, newspapers and periodicals and even appear to do so to a much greater degree than persons of a similar age and with the same level of education who do not have access to the new technologies. Thus, it is possible to conclude that print media are surviving in a period of widespread computer and Internet usage. Moreover as use of the Internet requires a high degree of traditional literacy and involves active reading, it might well trigger greater enthusiasm for reading books. We should remember, however, that the process of adopting new technologies is still in its infancy and there might be more changes ahead.

Though our findings are based on longitudinal comparisons and solid representative samples we must be cautious about making international comparisons based on survey results. We discussed the problem of the validity and the reliability of the survey method overall and its use for studying cultural consumption and reading habits specifically. However, noting our reservations, we do believe that we should not neglect such comparisons as despite their lack of accuracy; they do provide us with information on the approximate size of social phenomena – in this case, the proportion of the reading public in different societies and their reading habits. Furthermore, we believe that we cannot assess and interpret statistical data on Israeli society without comparing them with data from developed societies to which Israel seeks inclusion.

Taking into account the above reservations, the comparative data showed that the percentage of book readers in the Israeli population was significantly higher than in the US, slightly higher than in Australia, and similar to Sweden, the European country with the highest percentage of book readers in its population. This might be the result of combined effect of several factors. The rapid rise in formal education (years of schooling) in Israel in the last decades combined with the socialization for reading in the Israeli family as a trait of the long tradition of literacy and reading in the Jewish history. Nonetheless, with the increase in the size of the reading public in Israel, since the seventies we also witnessed a decrease in the percentage of active readers. The proportion of newspaper readers among the adult population was also very high and was almost similar to the highest proportions of newspaper readers in European countries. This might be due the intensity of the high social and political involvement of the Israeli citizens.

The informal socialization process in the family and the societal habitus also affected reading patterns in adult life. Reading reinforced and intensified distinctions between different status groups, and reproduced social gaps generation after generation. Thus, at an early age, individuals from higher status groups were positioned to access cultural capital essential for active reading and consequently, their reading habits were distinct from members from lower status groups. Moreover, this cultural capital provided access to a much richer reading repertoire for the members of the higher status groups compared to that of readers from lower status groups. Thus, rapid mobility in terms of the number of years of study was not sufficient to ensure the same extent of reading, as did the combination of high educational level and socialization to reading at an early age with strong reading role models in the family and the status group.

The unique functions of reading in fulfilling psycho-social needs and consequently the low functional interchangeability of reading with other media may explain the persistence of book reading as a cultural behaviour and the scale of the reading public in Western democracies. In contrast to the low functional interchangeability between watching television and reading books, we noted the high degree of functional equivalence between television and the Internet that might explain the current process of the displacement of television as an autonomous technical device.

According to the proposed model the non-displacement of reading and the apparent endurance of this pursuit might be due to the centrality of reading in the use of the new media and its distinct role in fulfilling psycho-social needs. This coupled with the low functional interchangeability between reading and other media has caused book reading to retain its unique appeal, a fact indicated by the finding that most, if not all, readers could not find any substitute for book reading.

# Notes

1. Lacey, H. (2005) 'The Tyranny of Reading', *The Guardian*. Accessed October 10, 2005. Available at *http://www.guardian.co.uk/comment/story/0,3604,1550326,00.html* (published 17 August 2005).
2. Handelzalts, M. (2005) Hem lo karue sefer, chaval [They Did Not Read a Book, What a Pity!]. *Ha'aretz* B1 (In Hebrew published 22 August 2005).

3.  Innis, H. (1951) *The Bias of Communication.* Toronto: University of Toronto Press.
4.  McLuhan, M. (1962) *The Gutenbeg Galaxy.* Toronto: University of Toronto Press.
5.  Katz, R. and Katz, E. (1988) 'McLuhan: where did he come from, where did he disappear?', *Canadian Journal of Communication* 23: 307–19.
6.  Levinson, P. (1999) *Digital McLuhan.* New York: Routledge.
7.  Goody, J. and Watt, L.P. (1963) *The consequences of literacy, Comparative Studies in History and Society.* 5: pp. 306–26, 332–45.
8.  Goody, J. (ed.) (1968) *Literacy in traditional societies.* New York: Cambridge University Press.
9.  Havelock, E.L. (1976) *Origins of Western Literacy.* Toronto, Ontario: Institute for Studies in Education, Monograph Series, p. 14.
10. Eisenstein, E.L. (1979) *The Printing Press as an Agent of Change: Communication and Cultural Transformations in Early Modern Europe.* Cambridge: Cambridge University Press.
11. Eisenstein, E.L. (1980) 'The emergence of print culture in the West', *Journal of Communication* 30: 99–107.
12. Bourdieu, P. (1984) *Distinction: A Social Critique of the Judgment of Taste.* Cambridge: Harvard University Press.
13. Bourdieu, P. (1990) Artistic taste and cultural capital. In *Culture and Society,* eds J.C. Alexander and S. Seidman. Cambridge: Cambridge University Press, pp. 205–17.
14. DiMaggio, P. J. (1987) 'Classification in art', *American Sociological Review* 52: 440–55.
15. Gans, H.J. (1974) *Popular Culture and High Culture.* New York: Basic Books.
16. Zolberg, V. (1990) *Constructing a Sociology of Arts.* New York: Cambridge University Press.
17. Adoni, H. (1985) 'Media interchangeability and co-existence: Trends and changes in production distribution and consumption patterns of the print media in the television era', *Libri* 3: 202–17.
18. Rosengren, K.E. and Windahl, S. (1972) Mass media consumption as a functional alternative. In *Sociology of Mass Communications* ed. D. McQuail. Harmondworth, Middlesex: Penguin, pp. 166–94.
19. Katz, E. and Adoni, H. (1973) 'Functions of the book for society and self', *Diogenes* 81: 106–18.

20. Blumler, J. and Katz, E. (eds) (1974) *The Uses of Mass Communications*. London: Sage.

21. Rosengren, K.E., Palmgreen, P. and Wenner, L. (eds) (1985) *Media Gratification Research: Current Perspectives*. Beverly Hills, CA: Sage.

22. Neuman, S.B. (1986) 'Television, reading and the home environment', *Reading Research and Instruction* 25: 173–83.

23. Neuman, S.B. (1991) *Literacy in the Television Age: The Myth of TV Effect*. Norwood, NJ: Ablex.

24. Katz, A., Hass, H., Weitz, S, Adoni, H., Gurevitz, M. and Schiff, M. (2000) *Tarbut ha'pnay be'Israel: Tmurot be'dfusay ha'peilut ha'tarbutit 1970–1990* [*Leisure Patterns In Israel: Changes in patterns of cultural activities 1970–1990*]. Tel Aviv: Open University (in Hebrew).

25. Adoni H. and Nossek H. (2001) 'The new media consumers: Media convergence and the displacement effect', *Communications, The European Journal of Communication Research* 26(1): 59–83.

26. Katz, E. and Gurevitch, M. (1976) *The Secularization of Leisure*. London: Faber & Faber.

27. Skaliotis, M. (2001) *Statistics in the Wake of Challenges Posed by Cultural Diversity in a Globalization Context: Keys Figures on Cultural Participation in the European Union*. Luxemburg: EUROSTAT, Unit E3, Health, Education and Culture.

28. US Department of Education, National Center for Education Statistcs. (2001) *The Condition of Education, 2001*. Washington DC: Government Printing Office.

29. Australian Bureau of Statistics (2003) *2003 Year Book Australia: Culture and Recreation Literature and Print Media*. Accessed November 11, 2003 from *http://www.abs.gov.au/ausstats/abs@.nsf/0/B3FAD3C7217F4D62CA256CAE00.1*.

30. Tepper, J.S. (1998) *Working Paper #4*. Center for Arts and Cultural Policy Studies, Princeton University.

31. Robinson, J. (1989) 'The Polls – a review: survey organization differences in estimating public participation in the arts', *Public Opinion Quarterly* 53: 397–414.

32. Robinson, J. (1993) Arts Participation in America: 1982-1992. *Research Division Report* #27. Washington DC: The National Endowment for the Arts.

33. The first factor, according to Tepper,[30] concerns the question's location in the list of questions. When questions about attitudes to the arts and cultural activity precede the questions about reading,

the interviewees will seek to be consistent with the stances established earlier and will match responses regarding their behaviour.

Different wording of the questions, too, is a factor that weakens the validity and reliability of the replication of the survey as a research tool for data gathering. Tepper further found that even the smallest differences in the question wording can produce different results. Similarly, some of the questions, especially questions about cultural consumption, including reading, can arouse social desirability and therefore biased answers.

A third difficulty can arise from the context of the interview itself, its length and the interview method. Too long an interview can cause interviewee fatigue. Telephone versus face-to-face interviews or completion of the interview as part of a group may also influence the content of responses.

The fourth factor that can be a strong influence is, of course, the sample and sampling method. On comparing the results of two representative samples, Robinson found that one had a slight over-representation of persons with higher education and income and as a result the findings with regard to frequency of cultural consumption were higher. In a number of activities, reading for example, women comprise a large portion of the reading audience, and here, too, over or under-representation of one gender group can influence the data. Related to sampling is the problem of the different degree of response of different groups to the request of the researchers that can cause bias in selection of the sample. It may be the case that persons who agree to requests to provide information about their cultural consumption are those who are more interested in such activities.

The fifth factor, the most illusive of all, relates to cross-cultural differences between the interviewees in different countries. All of the problems of validity and reliability cited above are true for these studies and, in addition, there are the idiosyncrasies of the mentality of each society that, too, can influence the content of the response.

Survey researchers of the European Union whose data are presented in Table 7.2 are aware of the problems of attempting to compare cultures, or as defined by them, the 'challenges of cultural diversity in a global context'. What they are seeking to develop are 'harmonised European cultural statistics'; that is, a uniform method of measurement capable of comparing cultural behaviour in different societies.[27]

34. Kaestle, C. F. (1991) *Literacy in the United States*. New Haven, CT: Yale University Press.

35. According to the same 2001 survey, 72.8 per cent of the Jewish population in Israel regularly watched television during weekday evenings. 46.5 per cent of the respondents reported that they enjoyed viewing television in their spare time. 58 per cent watched television for up to two hours a day, 35 per cent for over two hours daily, and 7 per cent reported not watching television at all. According to the data of the research department of Keshet,[36] the average amount of time spent viewing television daily is three hours; in comparison to four and half hours in the United States, for example, 3.9 hours in England or 2.4 hours in Austria. According to this data, in 2001, the viewing market was divided as follows: 20.5 per cent Channel Two, 15.5 per cent Channel One, 22.2 per cent the 'own produced' cable channels (that is, channels 3, 4, 5, 6, 8 and the Russian channels), and 41.8 per cent viewed the foreign and news channels.

36. Barbash, C. (2002) 'Ha'mesima: Lechanes et ha'mishpacha mul ha'mirka', [The task: To gather the family in front of the screen]. *Ha'aretz*, C7. (In Hebrew).

37. Regarding computer use – education : Beta = .120, T=3.603, Sig. P<.000; income – Beta=.076, T=2.265, Sig. <.02; Internet use – education Beta=.177, T=2.335, Sig. T<.021.

38. Nossek, H. and Adoni, H. (1996) 'The social implications of cable television: restructuring connections with self and social groups', *International Journal of Public Opinion Research* 8(1): 51–69.

39. Nossek, H. and Adoni, H. (in preparation press) The global village, the nation state and the ethnic community: Audiences of communication and boundaries of identity. In *The Toronto School of Communication Theory: International Perspectives*, eds M. Blondheim and R. Watson. Jerusalem: Magnes, Hebrew University Press and Toronto Universitry Press.

40. Katz, E. and Gurevitch, M., op. cit., pp. 232–5.

# 8

# Bookselling culture and consumer behaviour
## Marketing strategies and consumer responses in UK chain bookshops

*Audrey Laing and Jo Royle*

## Introduction and research rationale

UK chain bookshops have gone through a period of dynamic change over the past few years. Intense competition has seen the disappearance of some chains as they have been swallowed by competitors, and the change of others from upmarket bookshops concentrating on 'high-brow' literature, into retail stores where focus is devoted to what might be regarded as mass market literature. Socioeconomic group ABC1 – encompassing the most affluent and highly educated in our society – still forms the main core of book buyers in the UK.[1] Nevertheless, whereas some specialist bookselling chains may formerly have seen themselves as serving primarily this sector of society, many changes have taken place regarding the image of bookshops in the high street over the past few years. Indeed Alan Giles, then managing director of Waterstone's, has acknowledged that in the past the chain may have been 'intellectually intimidating' for some sections of the community.[2]

Most chain bookshops have adopted a discounting-orientated approach to bookselling with tables covered in various promotional offers. In addition to the broad similarity of promotional techniques to be seen across most UK chain booksellers, many have also adopted a US lifestyle approach to bookselling with the introduction of coffee shops, comfortable sofas and browsing areas. However, to date no study has been undertaken analysing the impact of these marketing trends on the bookshop customers.

Despite the prominence of writing, books and bookshops in current cultural life, there is a dearth of scholarly work in this field. Bookselling in particular has no significant body of academic research which investigates either the commercial or cultural implications of the trade. Useful data can be drawn from Mintel and Key Note reports, as well as book trade journal *The Bookseller*[3] and trade researcher BML[4] (Book Marketing Limited). Nevertheless, sources of academic work on this subject crop up only occasionally. While there has been a growing interest in the related field of online bookselling, it is still the case that much of the research carried out within this context uses online bookselling simply as an example of the online phenomenon, rather than studying online bookselling per se.[5-7] In order to underpin research in the field of bookselling with an academic foundation, research carried out in the project described has been examined in the broad context of retailing research and also in the light of related fields such as marketing, branding and consumer behaviour. However, even within the broad field of retailing, there have been calls for further research. Gilbert[8] contends that the whole field of retailing is now 'an accepted area of academic debate'. Further research is also called for by Peterson and Balasubramanian.[9] 'There is an urgent need to develop comprehensive theories to more systematically guide retailing practice, strategies, and empirical research'.

Recent changes within the book trade such as the rise and rise of the market share of the supermarkets[1] and the success of online book selling, especially Amazon, highlight the dynamic, interesting nature of this trade, as a particular facet of retailing which is ripe for research. Consumer spending on books has grown from £2,329 m in 1999 to £3,102 m in 2003.[1] This lends further weight to the need to carry out academic research in this field, providing useful evidence for both the academic and commercial fields of bookselling.

## Focus of the research paper

This paper focuses on key findings emerging from data collection and analysis to date, concentrating in particular on consumer responses to the key issues emerging from the initial interviews carried out with bookshop experts. These key issues emerged from the semi-structured interviews and became more pronounced as the data collection progressed with the questionnaires and focus groups. A consideration of these themes in the context of trade and academic literature clarified the focus of this paper upon three predominant themes. These themes are shown in the following matrix.

> The promotional techniques used by bookshops with particular regard to the predominant use of discount-based approaches.
>
> The cultural role of bookshops as lifestyle destinations and our changing expectations of what a retail outlet, especially a bookshop, should be offering. This is examined in the context of the use of coffee shops within bookshops.
>
> The bookshop as a 'third place' and its potential role as the centre of the community.

It is notable that an analysis of these themes has potential relevance for the wider retail trade.

It became clear from the initial interviews carried out with the bookshop experts (consisting of managers, one marketing manager and one marketing director) that considerable overlap exists among UK chain bookshops regarding both *marketing strategies* as well as the *marketing tools* used to implement these strategies. The more overt marketing tools used by UK chain bookshops can be summarised as follows:

- Considerable use of discounting: including predominantly '3 for 2' offers; two books for £10 and reduced prices on 'book of the month'.

- The introduction of seating and sometimes browsing areas (with seating, newspapers and tables).

- The introduction of coffee shops to a specific in-store area, sometimes a whole floor.

Underlying each of these marketing tools is the fundamental strategy of expanding the market. Intense competition across chains, independents and now supermarkets and online bookshops has made the UK book trade highly competitive and chain bookshops in the UK perceive the need to expand the market as being crucial to their survival and continued development.

## Methodology

Forming part of ongoing doctoral research, the methodological approach adopted for this project has been driven by the emergent research questions rather than adhering to any particular research paradigm. This has resulted in the use of methods both qualitative and quantitative. Creswell comments that quantitative and qualitative research 'are not mutually exclusive. Most research will exist somewhere on the continuum between the two'.[10] Clough and Nutbrown say, 'The issue is not so much a question of which paradigm to work within ... but how to dissolve that distinction in the interests of developing research design which serves the investigation of the questions posed through that research'.[11]

The first step in the data collection process was to carry out in-depth semi-structured interviews with book trade experts at various levels, across three UK chain bookshops. Key themes emerging from these interviews were analysed and fed into the development of the next stage of the research: 100 face to face questionnaires with bookshop users across a range of chain bookshops. Once again, key findings were analysed and investigated in more detail in the forum of focus groups, as focus groups 'typically add to the data that are gathered through other qualitative methods'.[12] Furthermore, Stewart and Shamdasani contend that, 'focus groups ... have been proven useful following the analysis of a large-scale quantitative survey'.[13] They 'produce a very rich body of data expressed in the respondents' own words and context'.[14] Whereas the interviews were used to draw out opinions as well as strategies from the managers, the focus groups were more concerned with drawing out experiences and opinions from groups of customers. The three focus groups allowed complex issues arising from both the initial interviews as well as the questionnaires to be investigated in more detail, as well as addressing issues thought to be too complex to address in the medium of questionnaires (for example, culture of bookshops; sense of community in bookshops). This developmental, evolutionary approach to the research enabled a reflective, holistic attitude to be engendered and opened the way to adopting both qualitative and quantitative methods, as the research questions required.

## Promotional techniques

The strategic thinking behind the discount-based approach from bookshops is based primarily on a desire to expand the existing book market beyond what is predominantly made up of socioeconomic group ABC1.[1] Increasing competition from online bookshops, supermarkets as well as across the chains has led to the cut-price approach in an effort to retain the existing book market, as well as hopefully to expand to a socioeconomic group less traditionally associated with book buying. However, de Chernatony and McDonald[15] note that 'marketers should not regard each consumer in a target segment as being equally attractive and assume that the same brand marketing strategies are appropriate across all the target segment'. In this instance, it is necessary for retailers to know and understand their customers, indeed to embrace the term 'customer relationship management' (CRM). Palmer, however, points out that the term CRM is used widely to describe slightly differing things.[16] This might range from the development of a database to monitor purchasing patterns among clientele, to a more philosophical understanding of this term, where the lifetime needs of the buyer are focussed upon, rather than the products on sale. However one conceives of the term CRM, it is important to understand this term in the context of the book trade and in particular the strategy of chain booksellers to expand the market, using discounting as a technique. It is well documented that it is economically more sensible to retain loyal customers than indulge in the expense required attracting new ones,[17,18] especially if the new customers need not necessarily continue to display loyal behaviour, or economically valuable behaviour. In terms of bookselling, an example might be someone who comes into a bookshop only at Christmas and buys one or two heavily discounted titles. Ryals[19] comments that 'a new customer is treated as though he or she is equally as valuable as a long-term loyal customer'. In fact, information about buying patterns can help retailers assess the long term value of their customers, but this kind of information is by its very essence very complex, and subtle distinctions must be made between valuable customers who should be retained and relatively expensive customers.[19] With this in mind it is clearly crucial that loyal bookshop customers' views and responses to discounting are taken into account.

Overall, responses to discounting were largely positive, although the focus groups provide a forum for more detailed views – and objections – to be expressed. One focus group participant mentioned her resentment at having discounted books 'forced' on her. She was suspicious of what she felt was a financially motivated agenda to promote these books. Indeed, in a recent article in *Publishing News*[20] a small publisher bemoaned the fact that in order to be included in a large UK chain bookseller's summer '3 for 2' promotion they were having to pay £750 per month.[21,22]

This clearly has implications for the ability of small publishers to get the kind of exposure which these offers can give. Many other focus group participants said the choice of discounted books was often 'bland' and that it was necessary to have time to hunt in detail for anything of interest in these kinds of offers (primarily '3 for 2'). However, a significant minority simply passed by these discounted promotions as they felt their particular interests were never catered for in this section of the bookshop. This significant minority tended to be heavy book buyers with specialist subjects of interest. Here, it would seem there is a potential danger of repelling heavy book buyers. Furthermore, each of these heavy book buyers also bought books on the Internet, particularly because their own interests were not satisfied by high street bookshops.

It is also of interest to note that several focus group participants mentioned that they would 'take advantage' of these offers, especially the '3 for 2' offers. For example, some would shop with family members, each selecting one book from the offers in order to get the third book free. Others would 'stock up' on a favourite author. Another participant mentioned shopping with friends and each choosing a book they wanted in order to get the third free. One could potentially see this set of circumstances as 'win-win' given that the bookshops is selling books and the customer is buying books. However, given that the people relating these tales were experienced book buyers who might otherwise have bought books at full price, and that the bookshops are giving away margin on these titles, in order – primarily – to attract new customers (which these people patently are not) it does make one ponder the wisdom of such an approach. Of course, if these offers really do serve to attract new customers then they do indeed make sense. Ongoing research will help to establish the effectiveness of these offers at attracting new bookshop customers.

In addition to the potential for repelling some customers, another key aspect raised when analysing consumer responses to discounted books was the homogeneity of range across many bookshops. This does not only apply to the '3 for 2' offers, but arguably applies to the whole front of store heavily branded part of most chain bookshops. It is hard to think of any branch of a chain which does not have several tables of '3 for 2', a top ten, a book of the month and a recommends section. (Although it is recognised that the recommends section will certainly introduce an element of individuality to this part of the store). It was acknowledged by one manager interviewed that commercial pressures had led to books needing to justify their presence on the shelves in terms of turnover (i.e. they needed to be good sellers), whereas previously books had been on the shelves because it was felt they *ought* (culturally speaking) to be there. Andy Ross, president of Cody's Bookstores in the USA says, 'The chain stores are mass merchants. They are very good at promoting highly commercial titles with huge printings and giant promotional budgets.' However, they are as a result 'formulaic and predictable'.[23] This opinion was underpinned by focus group participants' assessment of many chain bookshops as 'faceless' and 'sterile' and of their '3 for 2' promotions as 'bland'. They were broadly of the opinion that despite chain stores' efforts to develop local identities within chains, it was hard to distinguish amongst them, if one was looking at promotions and stock. As one participant said, 'I did think of (Bookshop x – a large chain) as being a bit more sort of esoteric and hippyish but they aren't now…You could find odd choices on the shelves…you can't really now. It's a shame'. Willie Anderson, deputy chairman of John Smith's Bookshops seems to bring clarity to the problem of choice, quality and the blurring of these in the chains. 'The accusation that the chains have in some way reduced the quality of books is a misconstruction. They could perhaps be accused of confusing quantity with quality, on the ground that they have made far too many books accessible, causing confusion in the readers' choices'.[24] This would seem to be underpinned by the focus group participants, who said that the '3 for 2' offers meant you had to search harder to find anything good, it somehow made browsing more difficult, unless you 'knew to walk past these tables'. Retail analyst Hugh Phillips warns that discounting can be an easy fall-back position for retailers to adopt – sometimes indicative of a lack of thought – but also allows that it can give clarity to a range of choices, if used *discerningly*.[25] Findings from this research would suggest that the wide range of bookshop discounts and offers available has served to confuse rather than clarify.

# The culture of the bookshop

The adoption of coffee shops by UK chain bookshops is part of the overall shift of focus of bookselling towards a 'lifestyle' destination. As Gilbert says, 'The retailer is not simply selling "things"; the sale has to incorporate aspirations, benefits, pleasure and new emotions'.[26] However, Gardiner notes that bookshops' community-building activities have been 'broad brush to say the least'.[27] There has certainly been little in the way of analysis or examination of how bookshop consumers respond to these sorts of initiatives.

With this in mind, details of consumer responses to in-store coffee shops were sought. Findings from this research showed that 50 per cent of the bookshop users questioned in-store used the coffee shops. Further questions concentrated on various qualities or facilities within the coffee shop, such as meeting friends; the quality of the food and being able to drink coffee while reading books. The following graph illustrates frequencies with which respondents said they liked or liked very much the named coffee shop attributes.

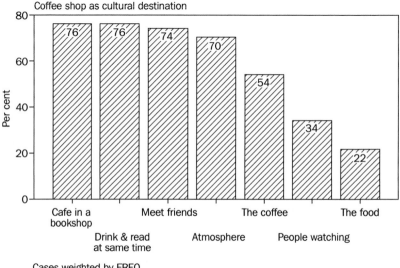

Cases weighted by FREQ

It is interesting to note that while the food and the coffee are at the lower end of the scale, the most popular features amongst users of in-store coffee shops seem to encapsulate the evocative link between coffee and books. The fact that the coffee shop is *within a bookshop*; the fact that it enables the bookshop customer to *read and drink at the same time*; the fact that the bookshop coffee shop enables one to *meet friends* and the *atmosphere* therein are all qualities rated highly among the bookshop/coffee shop user (50 per cent of those questioned). It is, however, important to note comments made about coffee shops within bookshops both in the wider context of the questionnaires as well as the focus groups carried out subsequently in order to investigate the subject in more detail.

Some of the focus group participants were strongly in favour of coffee shops within bookshops, commenting that it added 'value' to the experience of book shopping; it was an 'integral part of book shopping' and that even the smell of coffee enhanced their book shopping experience. However, there were caveats added to the inclusion of coffee shops in book shops. The most significant one was the perceived lack of sufficient space: several focus group participants relayed their own experiences of coffee shops which felt as if they had been crammed in as an afterthought rather than having been planned beforehand. Linked to the need for space was the general opinion that the bookshop and the coffee shop should be clearly demarcated from each other in separate areas.

Another reservation about coffee shops within bookshops was the feeling of an imposition of 'lifestyle' on the book shopper. This seemed to be most prevalent among the heavier book buyers who were very aware of the introduction of coffee shops and special price offers to the bookshop environment. There was a degree of resentment at the 'dumbing down' which they perceived to have taken place. The overall impression from the questionnaires and focus groups was that coffee shops within bookshops enabled a *social aspect* to be added to the book shopping experience – if one so wished. However, given that not everyone wishes to partake in the coffee shop experience, the clear demarcation between bookshop and coffee shop would seem to be an advisable step.

## The bookshop as a 'third place'

It is interesting to consider the role of the coffee shop within bookshops in the context of one of the key themes coming through from the initial interviews with book trade experts: that of the bookshop as a third place. Books have a long history as educator and socialiser.[28] Even before printing was mechanised, public readings by the few people who were literate provided occasions to come together, learn and be with one's neighbours.[29,30] The role of the bookshop in local communities has been studied to some degree in the US[31] where it is recognised that in some cases it has inherited the community role formerly held by the village hall or library as meeting place and socialising environment. Nevertheless, the bookshop as third place is a relatively new concept in the UK.

While the terms 'lifestyle' and 'destination' bookshops have been used by managers in other interviews, and indeed in the book trade for several years[32,33] the term third place was introduced as an extension of these terms, suggesting that bookshops can play a role in the community, serving as a destination for people who need not be in search of a particular book, but could simply go to a bookshop to sit, read, relax or even chat with others in the community.[34,35] Satterthwaite summarises the qualities which can be encapsulated by bookshops aiming to create a 'third place':

> The surprising popularity of bookstores and the increase in the number of stores and the sales of books are partly due to the communal nature of the stores. The bookstore can be a community gathering place, a safe and friendly harbour in an increasingly impersonal world. Amidst automation, sound bites, isolated computer communication, and all the effects of stretched living, the image of a small bookstore with a library ambience, piles of books to explore, helpful clerks to discuss your potential purchases, fellow customers with shared interests, and cosy cafes produces a warm, collegial feeling.[36]

Earlier research in this broad field[37] also found that bookshop users were keen to make suggestions to improve their local store. These ideas included introducing a coffee area; more tables for browsing and social evenings with authors. In this instance, the consumers themselves seem to want to make their bookshops into centres of the community. This potential for the bookshop to be a 'third place' is seen by many chains as the future of bookselling. It sometimes seems as if bookshops can call themselves a 'lifestyle' destination simply by offering customers a cup of coffee and somewhere to sit down[38] but even as far back as 1998, there was recognition from at least one Waterstone's manager that to give oneself that title, a little more commitment was required. Carl Newbrook, then manager of the Sauchiehall Street store in Glasgow defined it as 'the way that a bookshop interacts with the customers who use it'.[38] In more detail it involves not just the sofas and the cafe, but author events; a large range of books and, in his opinion, the sheer scale of the shop. Kreitzman[39] refers to 'the bookshop as a social club', where customers come in the evening 'as though it were an event, an entertainment, rather than just buying a book. They can meet, have a coffee – it is a social thing'.

The potential for bookshops such as this to play a role in the community as a club, a place to meet, or even a third place[34] has huge social implications for the future role of bookshops in society, in particular those chain bookshops which are eager to take on this role and have the floor space to house sofas, cafes and browsing areas. In the case of Borders, Cartwright goes so far as to suggest 'they have provided a sense of community in many suburban areas where community has been missing and where there were often no bookstores'.[40]

One can appreciate that bookstores in the US are serious about their links with the community when 'community relations coordinators' were at one point employed in every Borders store.[41] The fact that the US are rather further ahead of the UK as far as serving the community is concerned is clear when the manager of Borders in Nevada says his clientele includes 'teachers who sit down to grade papers, students working on laptop computers and business people who use the store's café to conduct meetings and interviews'.[41] Selected Borders stores in the UK are currently involved in community outreach programmes such as Reading is Fundamental UK (*http://www.rif.org*). This involves activities such as visiting schools and having school visits to stores where pupils are given vouchers to spend. They are not the only bookshop to provide community benefits however, given that WH Smith were putting £1.5 million into an initiative designed to 'improve literacy, through donations of reading materials, student mentoring and work placements in secondary schools.[42] The altruistic aspect of this kind of bookshop activity may sometime be at odds with the fact that essentially, they are businesses whose goals is to make money, despite the add on effect of being a wholesome addition to and promoter of community.

Miller[31] expounds on these and many other theories related to the community role of the bookshop. She oversees the developing role of the bookshop as it changes from 'retail establishment... [to] a vital community institution'. As the global urban population are gradually being pulled further away from local communities because of lifestyle changes (longer working hours, more women at work, less lifelong relationships, more working at home) we are more prone to belong to multiple communities based on job, interests and lifestyle rather than simply inhabiting a physical place. So, as the village hall, church, community centre are falling into disuse, perhaps this frees the way for bookshops to fill the role of community centre, providing a safe meeting place in which to meet others with similar interests. As Miller notes,

> Theorists of urban and consumer culture have shown, shopping is increasingly seen as an activity which can provide individuals with entertainment, fulfilment and the opportunity for meaningful connections with others.

She points out that 'the current association of the bookshop with the idea of community needs to be understood as the confluence of several different social processes' As chain bookshops became more widespread, more popular and more successful, this had the knock-on effect of making the independents search for a competitive advantage. They began to stress their 'superior selection and service, but gave these familiar retail slogans a particularly moral and political cast'.[31] They became more vocal that their choices of book stock underlined their commitment to communities and rather than the concentration by the chains on the bottom line, the independents claim that 'the right kind of business, nourished by its vital connections to a local community, can rise above profit considerations to provide the community with a multitude of meaningful services'.[31]

The bookshop as community centre has evolved into a setting with seminars, coffee shops, and meeting place. 'In part a marketing ploy, in part a deeply and sincerely felt sentiment, this emphasis on community service and community embeddedness has become integral to the independent bookseller's identity'.[31] Of course, these aspects of the independent bookshops are now common fare in many chain bookshops, who also claim the mantle of community centre. Miller goes on 'Consequently, it is not so clear which (or whose) actions qualify as 'authentic' gestures aimed at community enhancement'. The concept of community is an interesting one in the bookshop particularly when one thinks about the potential for interaction and the generation of new ideas. With the advent of browsing areas and coffee shops and the encouragement to browse for long periods of time, could the bookshop take on the mantle of the new cafe culture; the new Parisian salon, where the exchange of stimulating ideas can take place? Indeed, where else in current society could such a phenomenon occur? Kieron Smith (formerly Internet site manager for Ottakar's) wrote in *The Bookseller* about how the Chelmsford branch hosted political debates. As he points out, 'Society is far more individualised than it was 10 years ago, with the decline in membership of trade unions, churches, and the mass political parties. This, combined with the decline in social space, with multiples owning and controlling what were previously public areas, has weakened a sense of collectivity'.[43] He points out that the benefits of such events are a sense of ownership of the shop for the customers: it is a community space where there can be customer interaction. However, it is interesting to reflect upon these ideas of community within bookshops in the light of current research findings.

While most respondents to the questionnaires regarded bookshop atmosphere as being important and most of them felt more relaxed or even happier while in bookshops, the question of regarding the bookshop as a third place clearly takes this term a step further. Part of the definition of a third place is somewhere to go where entry is cheap or free and where one can relax and *interact with others in the community*. However, when one considers the lack of interaction which takes place in bookshops, according to findings from this research, it is debatable as to whether the bookshop plays such a role yet.

Each of the questionnaire respondents were asked whether they had ever spoken to another bookshop customer and the results are shown in the pie chart below.

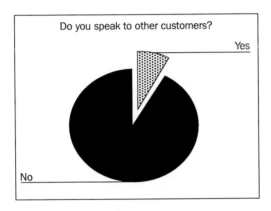

Of the 8 per cent of customers who *had* spoken to another customer, this had only ever happened occasionally or once. It would seem that the bookshop as a third place falls down in this aspect. It is the *interaction* which seems to be absent in the bookshop environment. Indeed focus group correspondents concurred that if they talked to other customers, this was the exception rather than the rule. Comments included, 'The socialising side of it really doesn't apply to me...it's a very anti-social experience.' 'I have to book shop alone.' 'I think book shopping is a really ... isolated thing that you do yourself'. If this community role does exist for bookshops in the UK, it is interesting to note Miller's acknowledgement of Sennett,[47] who opines that communities can be exclusive and not necessarily open to all-comers. As she says,

> People ... constantly scrutinise each other for signs of not being legitimate community members. They also attempt to set up territorial barricades to keep outsiders away (Miller, 1999).

Similarly, Underhill[44] writing on the science of shopping, comments that stores may have 'more than one constituency.' These 'constituencies' may sometimes rub along perfectly happily alongside each other, but at other times may be repelled by each other. In his essay on consumption, Rob Shields says that 'consumption both solidifies the sense of personal self, and confirms it *as social* through common membership in a shopping fraternity'.[45] As one focus group participant said, 'you look for something which is close to your personality and you take it from the shelf and that's almost like acknowledgement to the rest of the world 'Look! This is what I am about'.' This can certainly be said to solidify the sense of personal self and to confirm it as social, but Shields seems also to raise the idea that simply by *being present* in a shopping environment one is potentially participating in a 'shopping fraternity'. Does this therefore mean that despite any talking taking place between bookshop customers, one can still see the bookshop as a 'third place'? Nozzi refers to Oldenburg[34] when defining the qualities of a third place.

> There are essential ingredients to a well-functioning third place. They must be free or quite inexpensive to enter and purchase food and drink within. They must be highly accessible to neighborhoods so that people find it easy to make the place a regular part of their routine – in other words, a lot of people should be able to comfortably walk to the place from their home. They should be a place where a number of people regularly go on a daily basis. It should be a place where the person feels welcome and comfortable, and where it is easy to enter into conversation. And a person who goes there should be able to expect to find both old and new friends each time she or he goes there.

It would seem that entering into conversation is a vital part of what constitutes a third place, and therefore, one would have to say that while the bookshop may satisfy many other social needs of the book shopper, being a third place is not one of them.

However, tempering these focus group comments were further comments that this lone shopping experience might be interspersed with sessions in the coffee shop to meet friends or family. Therefore, might the introduction of the coffee shop into the bookshop enable its transformation into a third place, by dint of introducing a social aspect to the whole experience? Talking overtly about the potential for the bookshop to be a third place met with resistance from the focus group participants who were clear that they were unlikely to go to a bookshop for the sake of it, but would always go with a purchase in mind, or to browse the shelves. However, if one introduced the potential for other leisure activities to be going on in the bookshop at the same time, the reaction was more favourable. Jazz, or poetry readings engendered a positive reaction from focus group participants, so clearly many people seem to recognise the potential role that bookshops can play in the community, particularly with regard to the dearth of other activities in the evening. As one participant said, it is an alternative venue to go to in the evening. This is supported by research findings from Cartwright.[46]

# Conclusions

Analysing consumer response to the key themes of discounting, coffee shops and bookshops as a third place, it is important to take a holistic view and to appreciate that these topics would probably not have arisen in any interviews 20 years ago, perhaps not even ten years ago. Discounting emerged in the wake of the fall of the Net Book Agreement in the UK which occurred in 1995. Even then, it emerged very gradually and only became widespread in a very gradual fashion. Coffee shops may well be the current norm in large chain bookshops but have become widespread in the UK only in the last few years. The bookshop as a third place still seems to be undecided. It is often referred to in the trade press as a destination or a lifestyle shop, but for the bookshop – in particular the chain bookshop – to play a community role, seems to push our conceptions of what a bookshop could, even should, be.

Overall, the discounting approach to bookselling was met by consumers in a positive fashion. Most people liked, or liked very much these offers and found them tempting. The main caveat for these offers was that a significant minority avoided them, as they felt the choices did not cater for their specific interests. This opinion was offered most vocally in the focus groups, where a more concentrated selection of heavy book buyers was present. Also, many people found the choices in these offers to be bland and homogenous across all of the book chains. This opinion was offered both by focus group participants as well as by respondents to the in-store questionnaires.

Coffee shops received a similarly mixed review. While 50 per cent of questionnaire respondents used the in-store coffee shops, this obviously leaves another 50 per cent who do not. Nevertheless, most of the non-users did not object to a coffee shop in-store per se, as long as it did not interfere with their book shopping. Certainly most focus group respondents who did not use coffee shops expressed a preference to have the coffee shop clearly demarcated from the bookshop, and this seemed to be accepted by those who did like the coffee shops. The most important aspects of the bookshop coffee shop seemed to be the social qualities such as meeting friends, the atmosphere and the very fact that the coffee shop was within a bookshop. It would therefore seem that the coffee shop as a cultural destination has potential for further development within the realm of bookshops. Nevertheless a note of caution was sounded by some who felt that the coffee shop was being imposed upon their book shopping habits as a symptom of the 'lifestyle' shopping, without any consultation as to whether they actually wanted this integrated into their shopping experience.

Finally, the bookshop as a third place pulls these threads together and allows us to consider whether the bookshop has such a role to play in the UK. Given the crucial point that overall, there is a lack of socialising within bookshops, one would have to say that the chain bookshop does not yet fulfil this role. However, it is important to bear in mind the findings from the coffee shop setting and that people seemed more inclined to meet friends in that particular environment rather than in the bookshop itself. In other words, perhaps the coffee shop within bookshops has potential for development as a cultural site. Furthermore, it is also important to bear in mind that this particular study examines chain bookshops. Miller has noted that independents can play a key role in the community, certainly within community life in the US.[31]

Therefore, while the preponderance of the themes examined in this paper may be regarded with regret by some, given the implications of lack of range and homogeneity linked to discounting and the homogeneity even of the chains of coffee shops within the chains of bookshops, it is nevertheless important to recognise the dynamic nature of the chain bookshop. While people may not interact with each other in chain bookshops, they are nevertheless spending time in a bookshop. Furthermore, while many research respondents regretted what they perceived as the diminution of range across the chains, they were widely agreed that chain bookshops are more welcoming to the whole of their respective communities than they have ever been before.

# Notes

1. Mintel (2005) *Books, Music and Video Retailing UK*. London: Mintel International Group Limited. Available from: *http://www.reports.mintel.com* [Accessed 14 August 2005].

2. Lottman, H. (1999) The American Invasion of British Bookselling. *Publishers Weekly* 246(8), Feb, 24.

3. *The Bookseller* is available from *http://www.thebookseller.com*

4. Book Marketing Limited is available from *http://www.bookmarketing.co.uk.*

5. Loebbecke, C., Powell, P. and Gallagher, C. (1999) 'Buy the book: electronic commerce in the book trade', *Journal of Information Technology* 14: 295–301.

6. Sanghavi, N. (2000) Customer retention and the implications for the Internet: a case study of the UK book retail market. In: *Marketing Advances in the New Millennium*, Florida: Society for Marketing Advances.

7. Latcovich, S. and Smith, H. (2001) 'Pricing, Sunk Costs and Market Structure Online: Evidence from Book Retailing', *Oxford Review of Economic Policy* 17(2): 217–34.

8. Gilbert, D. (2003) *Retail Marketing Management*. 2$^{nd}$ ed. Essex: Pearson Education Ltd, p. 6.

9. Peterson, R.A. and Balasubramanian, S. (2002) 'Retailing in the 21$^{st}$ century: reflections and prologue to research', *Journal of Retailing* 78(1): 9–16.

10. Creswell, J.W. (2003) *Research Design*. 2$^{nd}$ ed. London: Sage, p. 4.

11. Clough, P., and Nutbrown, C. (2002) *A Student's Guide to Methodology*. London: Sage, p. 19.

12. Morgan, D.L. (1997) *Focus Groups as Qualitative Research*. 2nd ed. California: Thousand Oaks, p. 3.

13. Stewart, D.W. and Shamdasani, P. N. (1990) *Focus Groups: Theory and Practice*. California: Sage, p. 15.

14. Ibid., p. 12.

15. De Chernatony, L. and McDonald, M. (1998) *Creating Powerful Brands*. 2$^{nd}$ ed. Oxford: Butterworth Heinemann, p. 78.

16. Palmer, A.J. (1996) 'Integrating brand development and relationship marketing', *Journal of Retailing and Consumer Services* 3(4): 251–7.

17. Gilbert, D., op. cit., p. 190.

18. De Kare-Silver, M. (1998) *e-Shock: The Electronic Shopping Revolution: Strategies for Retailers and Manufacturers*. London: Macmillan Press, p. 222.

19. Ryals, L. (2002) Are your customers worth more than money? *Journal of Retailing and Consumer Services* 9(5): 241–51.

20. *Publishing News* is available from *http://www.publishingnews.co.uk*.

21. Thorpe, V. (2004) *Book giants 'buying their way on to shelves'*. Available from *http://books.guardian.co.uk/news/articles/0,6109,1212776,00.html* [Accessed 1 May, 2004].

22. Publishing News Online (2005) 'Three-for-twos attacked', Available from: *http://www.publishing news.co.uk/pnarchive* [Accessed 19 May 2005].

23. Ross, A. (2002) 'Store wars: the case for the independents', *Logos* 13(2): 78–83.

24. Anderson, W. (2002) 'Independent vs corporate bookselling: A British view', *Logos* 13(3): 145–50.

25. Phillips, H. (2003) 'Selling ourselves short', *The Bookseller* 5074: 22–4.

26. Gilbert, D., op. cit., p. 40.

27. Gardiner, J. (2002) 'Reformulating the reader: internet bookselling and its impact on the construction of reading practices', *Changing English*, 9(2): 161–8.

28. Manguel, A. (1996) *A History of Reading*. London: HarperCollins.

29. Ibid., pp. 116–9.

30. Ong, W.J. (1982) *Orality and Literacy: The Technologizing of the World*. p. London: Methuen, p. 115.

31. Miller, L.J. (1999) 'Shopping for community: the transformation of the bookstore into a vital community institution', *Media, Culture and Society*, 21(3): 385–407.

32. Sanderson, C. (1999) 'Doing the Grounds', *The Bookseller* 4904: 24–6.

33. Kreitzman, L. (1999) *The 24 Hour Society*. London: Profile Books.

34. Oldenburg, R. (1997) *The Great Good Place*. 2nd ed. New York: Marlowe and co.

35. Nozzi, D. *What is a 'third place' and why are they important?* Available from: *http://user.gru.net/domz/third.htm* [Accessed 12 Nov 2004].

36. Satterthwaite, A. (2001) *Going Shopping*. London: Yale University Press, p. 234.

37. Stallard, P. (1999) *Consumption and Identity in the World of the Book*. Sheffield: PhD thesis, Sheffield University.

38. McCabe, D. (1998) 'How to sell the bookish life', *The Bookseller* 4802: 45–6.

39. Kreitzman, L., op. cit., p. 36.

40. Cartwright, H. (2001) *Change in Store? An investigation into the impact of the book superstore environment on use, perceptions and expectations of the public library as a space, place and experience.* MA Thesis. University of Sheffield. Available from: *http://www.dagda.shef.ac.uk/dissertation/2000-01/cartwright.pdf* [Accessed 16 July 2003], p. 23.

41. Przybys, J. (2000) *Bookstores expanding role as community centers.* Available from: *http://www.reviewjournal.com* [Accessed 28 July 2003].

42. Anon., (2002) WHSmith is putting £1.5m into a community programme. *Marketing* 21st February, p. 4.

43. Smith, K. (1999) 'The Bookshop as community space', *The Bookseller* 4892: 31.

44. Underhill, P. (1999) *Why we buy: The Science of Shopping.* London: Orion Business.

45. Shields, R. (1992) Spaces for the subject of consumption. In *Lifestyle Shopping; The Subject of Consumption*, ed. Rob Shields. London: Routledge, p. 15.

46. Cartwright, H., op. cit., pp. 68–76.

47. Sennett, R. (1992) *The Fall of Public Man.* New York: W.W. Norton.

# 9

# Diversity, or is it all the same?
## Book consumption on the Internet in Sweden

*Ann Steiner*

# Introduction

Modern media society has stimulated a new behaviour among readers and book buyers and patterns of book consumption have changed with the expansion of the Internet, as bookstores in cyberspace have had an effect on the general book trade, globally as well as locally. The Internet bookstores have been highly successful in Sweden, and in this article I will address how they have influenced the book trade and consumption of literature in general. One of the more interesting issues is whether these bookstores provide readers with a more diverse selection of literature, or if the Internet is only illusory in its claim to promote diversity. What book consumers are really offered might be more or less the same as always – a few blockbusters read all over the globe.

Juliet Gardiner's concept of 'the consuming reader' has brought attention to the fact that marketing today identifies the needs of consumers. The production and sale of books centres around creating consumer identities, which are then employed in the promotion of new books.[1] Publishers try, Gardiner says, to create groups of consumers, for example with a special interest in particular subgenres, like young males devoted to fantasy, or urban, single woman readers. In the Internet store, previously bought books identify the consumer. Accordingly, the identity of the consumer is implicated and reinforced by the decision to buy a certain book. The bookstore knows what the reader bought before and provides information about other books that will confirm this constructed identity. Buying a book on the Internet brings the individual into a communal reading experience, or at least shopping experience. As Gardiner claims: 'Reader-identity is established on purchase and thus commodified.[2] The trend of commodified reading, she asserts, can be regarded as a social practice.

The notion of reading as a social practice was introduced by the French historian Michel de Certeau. He maintains that reading erodes: when we read we forget what we have read before. According to de Certeau, the only way for a reader to protect himself against this erosion is to buy the book, although the possession of the book is no more than a substitute for lost readings.[3] Reading is, according to de Certeau, also a form of consumption. This process is initiated already at the moment of purchase by the desire for the book. The almost physical longing to possess an object is connected to the ambition to become a better and more interesting person. These feelings are to a large extent promoted by the subtle product marketing staged by international agents on the book market.

Can this desire for a book also be created in the Internet shopping moment? An important part of traditional shopping is based on sensory experiences. An interesting example of this is the fieldwork study by Paco Underhill that shows that it is common for people to experience a book in a sensory way before buying it; for example, smelling it. A visit to the bookstore is thus so much more than looking at a cover and reading the blurb. It is an experience that engages all senses.[4] On the Internet, however, sensual practices like touching and smelling are excluded and will have to be substituted. This replacement is provided by a strong feeling of belonging to a communal experience. Buying the same book as others provides a sense of belonging to a global community.

A strengthened relationship between the social practices of reading and shopping can be discerned in the last thirty years of the Swedish book trade. Readers have been transformed into book consumers. Reader identity is claimed through the consumption of particular books, and, also, through the places of purchase. In Sweden, an important reason for the rapid expansion of sales on the Internet can be found in the tradition of buying books outside the regular bookstores. The Internet stores can, consequently, be regarded as a development of pre-existing structures.

# Book sales in Sweden from a historical perspective

Even if regular bookstores enjoyed high cultural prestige in Sweden, there were always other types of commercial enterprises, selling cheap paperback fiction as well as alternative literature. The Internet bookstores in Sweden appear to have inherited many distinctive features from these enterprises, such as the combination of commercialism and avant-garde culture.

The history of the Swedish book trade has generally been an account of traditional bookstores connected to the prestigious publishing houses. In 1843, the trade was divided into different market segments with the foundation of the Publishers' Guild. This organization saw a need for better control of the booksellers, and enforced strict regulations regarding who should be allowed to sell their books. It resulted in a division between an established circuit for book sales and the large unregulated general trade. The bookstores connected to the Publishers' Guild had at their very best a fifty per cent share of the market. Most of the time, however, they only represented around thirty per cent of retail sales.[5] Different forms of distribution, like door-to-door sales, book clubs, subscriptions, and news-stands, as well as sales to libraries, schools, and other government institutions, constituted the rest of the trade. This 'other' trade consisted of a mixture of cheap paperback editions, maps, calendars, canonical classics in inexpensive editions, religious pamphlets, and political propaganda.

In 1970 the balance that had characterised the market for more than a hundred years changed, when the government deregulated the trade and banned fixed book prices. The deregulation also included the abolition of strict control regarding the opening of bookstores. As a result, the close ties between certain publishers and bookstores were dissolved, and the old system, where these stores had to stock all new books from the organised publishers, was abandoned. Suddenly the bookstores could choose what to sell, and the publishers could distribute their titles in any way they wished.

The deregulated book market gave rise to controversies, and many people in the trade wanted the old system back. Most highbrow commentators, for example critics and authors, deplored the state of the trade. The strongest reactions concerned the large number of subscription book clubs that were introduced in the 1970s. By 1980, these clubs had taken over thirty per cent of the market, and had also come to influence contemporary literature. Critics generally resented the poor literary quality of the books sold in clubs. In retrospect there was, however, no real difference between the titles sold in book clubs and in the regular bookstores.[6]

Nevertheless, and partly as a result of the emergence of book clubs, the regular bookstores lost a large share of the market during the 1970s. Many individual shops had to close down while others joined bookstore chains. The loss of sales to libraries and schools of course also contributed to this development. During the 1970s, a company owned by the public libraries had successfully campaigned to take over library distribution from the bookstores. Additionally, in 1972 new regulations permitted municipal schools to buy books directly from the publishing houses, thus causing severe losses of profit for the bookstores.

A common opinion has been that all this resulted in an increased commercialisation of publishing and bookselling. If the developments are seen in light of a more international context, different conclusions can, however, be drawn. Even if the developments in Sweden in some ways were unique, similar transitions can be noticed in other countries during this time. A trade conference in Zurich in 1971 actually reported problems of the same kind in the book trade in a large part of Western Europe as well. Fluctuations on the market after the affluent sixties had led to a general decline in book sales.[7]

The Swedish book trade in the 1970s can best be described in terms of concentration and polarisation. Concentration meant that mergers, buy-outs, and closures haunted publishing. This in turn led to polarisation, which provided a niche for small businesses, co-ops, and all sorts of private initiatives. Some of these were indeed small, but others turned out to be quite important for the contemporary literature.

A similar pattern can a decade later be seen affecting the retail sector of the trade. In the 1970s, bookstores were paralysed, but in the 1980s they 'counterattacked' (according to their own rhetoric). The strategy was to create chains of bookstores and use marketing schemes similar to the book clubs. As a result, critics debated the 'new Moguls' of the book trade – that is, the people who decided which books the large book clubs and the bookstore chains should offer. Bookstores and book clubs consequently became one and the same, one critic said, as they sold the same titles to the same advantageous prices. The book clubs and the chain stores, he claimed, were thus the new gatekeepers.[8]

If the 1970s was a time of transition in the Swedish book trade, the 1980s was a decade of consolidation and the establishing of a new division in the book market. The large bookstore-chains and the book clubs were on one side, and all sorts of different systems of distribution and sales on the other. Bookstores and clubs had only half of the total market in the 1980s, while the other half – paperback crime fiction, textbooks, exclusive poetry editions, books on military history, and *Harlequin*-novels – were sold outside the regular bookstore.

# The impact of the Internet in the 1990s

A new time of transition arrived with the introduction of the Internet in the 1990s. In 1995, Amazon launched its site, and in 1997 the first Swedish Internet bookstore, Bokus, opened. And they were both followed by a wide range of similar ventures. The rapid development of broadband, combined with political high-tech ambitions in Sweden, soon led to the highest percentage of Internet users per capita in Europe.[9] Shopping on the Net skyrocketed, and numerous Internet bookstores of various sizes opened. During the first few years of the twenty-first century, Internet bookstores in Sweden have grown into popular sites for everybody. The main reason for their success can almost certainly be found in the traditional Swedish way of buying books outside the regular bookstores. Sales figures indicate that most of the Internet trading comes from precisely 'the other half' of the market, that is, from the book clubs, subscriptions, and supermarkets. Regular bookstores have only suffered marginal losses.

The official estimation of Internet sales in Sweden today is 8 per cent of the 'official' market. This number does, however, not include small sites, publications from smaller publishing houses, or foreign sales, through Amazon for example. The sales of books on the Internet in Sweden are thus in reality more likely to be somewhere between 10 to 15 per cent. Even though the sales figures in other countries probably also are incomplete, there seem to be national differences. According to a recent survey, figures for France and Italy show that the market share for Internet bookstores is as low as 1 per cent, while the United Kingdom supposedly has 17 per cent, and Germany an estimated 4 to 5 per cent.[10] Another factor that is not yet discussed is the used books trade, which has expanded in the wake of the Internet. Very little, however, is known about the real proportions of this kind of book sales.

In the 1990s, the Internet bookstores opened up the trade of international books to an unseen scale. This success was at first closely linked to the sales of books in English and to certain kinds of customers, e.g. academics and fans. Scholars and students knew exactly which titles they wanted, and bought mainly books in English. The fans were generally interested in a specific genre – often crime fiction, fantasy, or science fiction. Both these groups were well acquainted with their fields and highly aware of what to look for. Additionally, they bought books that are rarely translated into Swedish, in relation to the size of academic publishing and this kind of popular fiction books.

Both the domestic Internet stores and the foreign sites, like Amazon, have thus sold well to Swedish customers. Until 2001, Sweden had a twenty-five per cent VAT on books, but this could be avoided if you bought books from Amazon.[11] As a direct result, the governmentally-implemented VAT was lowered to six per cent. During the first six years of Internet operation, it was impossible for Swedish bookstores to compete with Internet stores such as Amazon regarding books in English. Today the two main Swedish operators have between one and two million titles listed. Most of these are in English.

The principal agents in the global book trade are the multinational corporations, and one can wonder, as American musicologist Gage Averill has done, what effect globalization will have on cultural diversity in the world?[12] What happens to literature published in a minor language when it has to compete with books in other languages, or, in reality, with books in English? Are books in foreign languages a threat to the national language and literature of Sweden? It might possibly be so in the long run, but so far no statistics have proved that this is the case. Book sales in Swedish are definitely not declining.

According to the Internet bestseller lists of Swedish language literature, most of the titles are domestic publications, as opposed to translations from foreign languages. Bestselling lists from the three largest Swedish Internet bookstores in June 2005 disclose that about fifty per cent of the titles were Swedish originals and thirty per cent translations from English.[13] The English figures are fairly low, which indicates that books in English are to a greater extent than before consumed in the original language. Translations from English, consequently, have difficulties in upholding their position as compared to ten years ago. Swedish publishers are concerned about the sales of books in the original language. The fact that the English version of *Harry Potter and the Half-blood Prince* (2005) already by September 2005 had sold in 115,000 copies in Sweden, will have consequences for future translations of English books (probably not for Harry Potter no. 7, though).

In 1975, Sweden had the highest production of books per capita in the world, but this is no longer the case.[14] The financial boom of the last thirty years has not had the same effects on the Swedish book trade as it has had in other countries. Book publishing has not diminished, however. It has just not expanded. A steady amount of books originally written in Swedish are still being published, but as previously stated, more Swedes today read books in English than in the 1970s. This means that the number of titles accessible to most Swedes in fact is substantially higher now in 2005, than it was in 1975.

# The access to international publishing

There is a dream of a globally accessible culture for everyone, independent of censorship, money, education, and class, through the Internet. At the same time there is a great fear in many countries of the gradual Americanisation of literature. The relative hegemony of Anglo-Saxon culture has created many counter-movements in order to protect national literature, language, and specificity, most visibly in countries such as France and Iceland. There is a risk that 'global' will only mean 'English', and that national cultures will decline. The freedom to buy the same books everywhere might not sound as good if it means that we all buy the same ten books from the bestseller lists on Amazon. There is an ongoing debate whether the international book trade is becoming increasingly concentrated, thus leaving operational space only for a few multinational corporations. Nevertheless, the prospects might prove to be the very opposite. The diversity created through the Internet may finally provide space for counterculture. The Internet book trade does provide the opportunities for distribution of a wider range of books. *The long tail*, as outlined by Chris Anderson in *Wired* magazine, suggests that a new and diverse book trade is the future.

The long tail, Anderson explains, is the large number of titles sold and rented in very small numbers on sites like Amazon, iTunes Music Store, and Netflix. Anderson notes that successful businesses on the Internet offer a wide range of titles, each to a limited number of customers. Thus, they offer much more diversity than the regular bookstores, music stores, and rental spots, as these provide only the most popular titles. Anderson argues that Amazon proved that there was a rising demand for obscure books and that there was money to be made from them. If all the sales of low sellers are combined, these will constitute a much larger market than the one provided by the bestsellers. Popularity, accordingly, no longer has monopoly on profitability. Anderson even suggests that while the twentieth century entertainment industry was about 'hits', the twenty-first century might give equal status to 'misses'.[15]

At the very far end of the long tail you can find anything, says Anderson. People do find all sorts of odd books, mainly through a system of recommendations. This technique was developed by Amazon and was soon adopted by others, including the two main Swedish Internet bookstores. A few clicks will take you from the top selling titles down the tail. For example, on 30 May 2005 the Swedish bookstore Adlibris displayed six illustrated book covers on their homepage. The most striking was a book on the sexual lives of animals by science journalist Olivia Judson.[16] A click takes us to suggestions for reading by Swedish contemporary authors (Anna-Karin Palm and Otto Fagerstedt), both of whom could be regarded as mid-list although critically acclaimed. Another click or two and we enter an expanding world of Swedish and international literature, a mixture of fact and fiction (Monika Fagerholm, Alice Munroe, Annie Proulx, Trezza Azzopardi).

But, says Anderson, creating a long tail-business is not that easy. You have to help the customer to find the tail through recommendations, but you also have to make the customers enter and stay on your site long enough. The hits and the bestsellers will perform this job, and, therefore, internationally bestselling authors like Dan Brown, Paolo Coelho, and Alexander McCall Smith can be found on the front pages of Amazon as well as on the Swedish Internet stores.

The astonishing reality of the long tail is the fact that it contradicts the axiom that we have bestsellers because that is what people want. Book buying on the Internet indicates that the regular bookstores have not stocked what readers really desire. The unlimited selections in the Internet stores further reveal that people do want titles that are *not* bestsellers. Our taste is, then, not as mainstream as we have been made to believe. It is even likely that many of our assumptions about popular culture and taste have been based on a poor distribution system.

Amazon has gone very far in treating the consumer as an individual. The Swedish Internet bookstores are still rather unsophisticated in their recommendations, and in their ways of leading people down the long tail, but this is slowly changing. One of the Swedish stores in particular, Adlibris, claims to be a long tail-business. In 2004, the 1000 best selling titles made up only twenty-five per cent of their annual sales. We do not live on the bestsellers, but on the backlist, says Adlibris, and forty per cent of their sales are titles that do not exist in regular bookstores. Most of the two million titles offered by Adlibris are yet unsold, but the company reckons that this is where they can increase their sales.[17] This implies that the growth of the Internet bookstores comes from ground so far untouched – that is, by the sales of books that rarely found on a store bookshelf.

What the Internet bookstores have really done in Sweden is to conform to an old tradition of selling books outside regular bookstores. An important similarity between the Internet stores and the, by now, ancient forms of book sales, is the tendency to treat all genres in the same way. The shopping tour in cyberspace makes no distinction between Jeanette Winterson, Michael Connelly, J.M. Coetzee, and Barbara Cartland. Although the Internet stores have changed the way in which we buy books, it can be argued that this is merely a development of previous practices.

# The price of a book

Dutch economists Marcel Canoy, Jan van Ours, and Frederick van der Ploeg have pointed out that the value of a book is associated with social cohesion, national identity, the institution of criticism and personal experience. These crucial factors are, however, not reflected in the price. The total economic value of a book might in reality be higher, or indeed, lower, than the price paid.[10]

It has already been mentioned that the Internet stores indirectly lowered the VAT on books in Sweden, but they have also had a major impact on book prices in general. It is, however, not clear what the price of a book is today. A governmental survey on book prices was conducted in Sweden between 2001 and 2005, but in the final report there was nothing on the average price of a book.[18] Depending on which store you go to, if you have a membership card, if you buy it on the Internet, or if you buy other books at the same time, the price you pay can vary substantially.

In the present debate over fixed book prices in some European countries, the Internet sales have been a source of controversy. Fixed book prices, some say, severely limit the Internet stores, as they cannot compete with low prices. Frederick van der Ploeg claims that the technological development has created 'a real democratization of culture' as it allows for the publication and distribution of niche books.[19] As fixed book prices were abolished in Sweden already in 1970, this has not been an obstacle for the Internet stores in the mid-1990s. From a consumer perspective, the effects of Internet stores in Sweden have been generally positive. The Internet lowered the prices on books and has not really constituted a threat to Swedish language literature. The main setback is that the English dominance of language and literature has been strengthened, at the expense, of, say, the Germanic or the Francophone.

## Conclusion

Umberto Eco claims that '[b]ooks are menaced by books. Any excess of information produces silence. [...] Bookstores are so crowded with books they can only afford to keep the most recent ones.'[20] Others have seen the flow of books as an important means of creating greater interest in reading.[21] It is, however, clear that regular bookstores with their limited shelf space, somewhat paradoxically, can become a threat to the book as a medium of cultural diversity, as they put so much emphasis on recent hits, regarding anything older than a year as obsolete. Perhaps it is the ability of the Internet bookstore to treat all books equally that is our greatest hope for diversity, choice, and availability in the book trade.

It might seem overoptimistic to believe that the large media conglomerates will not be able to control the distribution of literature on the Internet, but it is clear that there are new ways of making money in the global economy. Selling a large variety of different kinds of books might look like a prosperous path to take. One strong argument for such a claim is that many of the large operators in the book trade seem to be interested in including small publishers and printers. And seen from the perspective of a minor European country the Internet does provide a far more diverse trade than has ever existed before in Sweden.

## Notes

1. Gardiner, J. (2002) 'Reformulating the Reader: Internet bookselling and its impact on the construction of reading practices', *Changing English* 9: 161–8.
2. Ibid., p. 167.
3. de Certeau, M. (1984) *The Practice of Everyday Life*, trans. by

Steven Rendell. Berkeley: University of California Press, p. xxi.

4. Underhill, P. (1999) *Why We Buy. The Science of Shopping*. New York: Simon and Schuster.

5. In 1930 the organised bookstores had a 30 per cent market share, in 1970 34 per cent and in 1996 40 per cent (Johan Svedjedal, Bokens samhälle: Svenska Bokförläggareföreningen och svensk bokmarknad 1887–1943 (Stockholm: Svenska bokförläggareföreningen, 1993), p. 493, En bok om böcker (Stockholm: SOU 1972:80, 1972), p. 72, Boken i tiden, (Stockholm: SOU 1997:141, 1997, p. 98).

6. I discuss this in detail in a study of the Swedish book trade during the 1970s and the rise of book clubs; I litteraturens mittfåra. Månadens bok och svensk bokmarknad under 1970-talet (Stockholm: Makadam, 2006) ['In the Literary Mainstream: The Book-of-the-Month Club and the Swedish Book Trade during the 1970s'].

7. Helms, A. (1971) 'Bokens domedag', *Svensk Bokhandel* 12: pp. 330–6.

8. Stefan Mählqvist, 'Bokmarknadens nya moguler', in Litteratursociologi, ed. by Lars Furuland and Johan Svedjedal (Lund: Studentlitteratur, 1997), pp. 472–489.

9. In 2002 63 per cent of the Swedish population used the Internet regularly. This was at the time the highest percentage in Europe. (MedieSverige 2004, ed. by Ulla Carlsson and Ulrika Facht, (Göteborg: Nordicom-Sverige, 2004), p. 226).

10. Canoy, M., van Ours, J.C. and van der Ploeg, F. The Economics of Books. Unpublished manuscript in the forthcoming *Handbook of the Economics of Art and Culture*, eds V. Ginsburg and D. Throsby, section 2.3.

11. Avoiding the high VAT could be done through buying books from Internet stores within the European union, from 1998 the British and German sites and in 2000 the French site. Books bought from the US site were, however, generally taxed by customs.

12. Averill, G. (1996) Global Imaginings. In *Making and Selling Culture* ed. R. Ohmann. Hanover: Wesleyan University Press, pp. 203–23.

13. Comparison between the bestseller lists in the three major Internet stores in June 2005, Adlibris, Bokus and Akademibokhandeln, both hardback list and paperback list. Fifty-three per cent in Swedish, 33 per cent in English and 14 per cent in another language.

14. In 1975 the figure for Sweden was 110 published titles per 100,000

inhabitants, in 1999 it was 141. This should be compared with the United Kingdom that had 63 published books per 100,000 inhabitants in 1975 and 188 in 1999, or Spain that went from 66 in 1975 to 148 in 1999. (Canoy, van Ours and van der Ploeg, table 5)

15.  Anderson, C. (2004) The Long Tail. *Wired* 12.10, available from *http://www.wired.com/wired/archive/12.10/tail.html* (accessed 26 September 2005).

16.  Judson, O. (2002) *Dr. Tatiana's Sex Advice to All Creation.* London and New York: Metropolitan Books.

17.  Schmidt, L. (2005) 'Bokhandeln med längst svan vinner kunderna', *Svensk Bokhandel* 8: 28–9.

18.  Bokpriskommissionens slutrapport (2005) Det skall vara billigt att köpa böcker och tidskrifter. SOU 2005: 12, Stockholm.

19.  van der Ploeg, F. (2004) 'Beyond the Dogma of the Fixed Book Price Agreement', *Journal of Cultural Economics* 28: 1–20.

20.  Eco, U. (1994) The Future of Literacy. In *Apocalypse Postponed,* ed. R. Lumley. Bloomington: Indiana University Press, pp. 64–71.

21.  Schultz Nybacka, P. (2005) Människans väg till boken: En studie om böcker och läsande efter momssämnkningen. Dissertation draft, p. 112.

# 10

# New voices in the new millennium

*David Lynn*

Although I have lived in Great Britain a number of times over the past thirty years, my particular expertise is with the literary scene in the United States. Nevertheless, I believe that much of what I will suggest here also applies to publishing around the world.

This is a time of enormous change and uncertainty in US publishing, among both commercial and independent presses. The full implications are a separate topic from what I have been asked to write on here, but they are connected. The fact is, however, that this is also a period of significant opportunity for writers from minority communities. Indeed, they are being published in greater numbers and to greater acclaim than ever before. This has led, naturally enough, to a greater variety, vitality, and creativity for American literature as a whole.

Let me offer first a very specific historical case. Discovering 'new voices' and presenting them side by side with the established and great authors of the moment has been part of the proud mission of *The Kenyon Review* since it was founded by the poet and critic John Crowe Ransom in 1939. But it has been really only in the last fifteen years, first under Marilyn Hacker and then, since 1994, myself, that we have deliberately sought out new authors from those very communities that lacked the opportunity to be heard or given voice in earlier generations.

Although I am quite proud of what we have done at *KR* – and I believe we have played a leadership role in this endeavour – it is not unique. Of the more than 600 literary journals published in the US (and there is a burgeoning number of electronic publications as well), most welcome contributions from diverse communities. And significantly, not only are writers from minority backgrounds finding much easier access into print, but many journals and presses have been specifically created to publish work of hitherto disenfranchised voices. For example, *Callalloo*, one of the most ambitious, impressive, and esteemed journals in the US, is only one of many principally concerned with African American authors and topics.

It is also true that authors from minority backgrounds now play a much larger role in publications from commercial New York publishers. Toni Morrison, Jamaica Kincaid, Rita Dove, Caryl Phillips, Michael Ondaatje, Charles Johnson, Maxine Hong Kingston, Scott Momaday, Louise Erdrich, are names just plucked off the top of my head as writers who have no trouble getting their books into print, and whose books sell across the country and across cultural divides. They are well represented on the best-seller lists. Their works are widely required in school and university curricula.

If younger writers of colour have more trouble catching a break with a New York publisher, I am willing to bet that it's not because of the colour of their skin or their accent, but because they are unknowns with equally unknown profit potentials. Just like younger writers of Anglo-European heritage.

This is because with only one or two exceptions, all the old New York publishing houses have been bought and consolidated by enormous international conglomerates, mostly from Europe. These famous houses – Scribner's & Sons, Knopf, Random House – originally existed to publish good and successful books. They certainly sought profits, but they were in the book business.

Corporate conglomerates, however, aren't in the book business because they love literature. Far from it. They are driven by the bottom line and seek the largest return on their capital. Literature, per se, is far less remunerative than cookbooks, dieting books, and self-help books. If a novel is purchased for publication (most of the major houses won't even consider poetry anymore), it will be coordinated with the distributors and the movie production companies, which are also owned by the same conglomerates. Each publisher desperately seeks blockbusters and markets lavishly and accordingly. The old and distinguished 'mid list' is now a curse, dooming an author to insignificance.

Many of these publishing houses do, of course, still publish literature. But they are able to do so, to satisfy their corporate masters, only if they have enough blockbusters or self-help manuals to essentially underwrite the costs of literary risk.

In fact, a talented younger writer of colour or from a disadvantaged community may hold a slight advantage over an Anglo-European American, as the New York publishers are always on the hunt from something *new*, some exciting discovery. First novels by *anyone*, as a matter of fact, are much easier to place these days than second or third ones, even though these later works may be more mature, even 'better' fiction.

Does this lead to a commodification of the exotic? Are writers from less familiar backgrounds published not because of the talent and skill they bring to bear in their art? Well, perhaps. But this is a tricky and interesting question. I will give you an example, not from the commercial world but, again, from my personal experience. As you may imagine, I get hundreds and thousands of perfectly well written stories across my desk, many polished to a very fine lustre at MFA workshops. Many are about moving but familiar topics – the death of a loved one by cancer, the anguish of watching a parent suffer through Alzheimer's or other dementia, the painful discovery that first love may not be final love. Well, in truth, I don't have much patience for these subjects, precisely because they are so familiar. Unless the stories have some startling insight, are unexpectedly moving, or are written with a surpassing skill and grace, I spend little time on them and will send them back without comment.

On the other hand … A few years ago I received an unsolicited essay called 'If You Are What You Eat, Then What Am I?' It was written by a young woman who had emigrated from India with her parents and was now living in Pittsburgh. The title pretty much speaks for itself. The piece was about this woman's attempts to navigate the transition from a more traditional identity as still maintained by her parents, and her own desire to develop her own sense of self as someone from an Indian background but now educated and living in the United States with her non-Indian husband. Ingeniously, she employed the language of food as a rich metaphor for her journey and struggle. Ultimately, then, the essay was far deeper and richer than the merely gustatory. It had to do with personal identity, the struggle to understand ourselves and the question of how far we control who we are and who we become. It had to do with family and loyalty and love and free choice.

From the start I loved it. But initially it was also deeply flawed. There were problems of organization and of logic. The argument was a little fuzzy. The author didn't bring out the strengths of the essay to their greatest advantage. So I wrote back to her suggesting some changes for revision. Indeed – and this is very rare for me – we went back and forth several times before we were both convinced the piece had come as far as it could. I published it happily, and I'm also happy to say that it won some significant awards.

But was I commodifying the exotic? I don't think so. What this writer brought to me was a fresh subject, a new perspective, some insights that are rare and particular and pressing in our modern world. And that is true of so many of the fine authors from less traditional backgrounds. Precisely because these communities have lacked public voice, at least through traditional modes of publication in the past, what they bring now is vitality, discovery, and freshness.

They more easily accomplish what I frequently say is necessary to all successful art: their poetry and prose are full of delight and surprise. But that too is a slightly separate topic ...

What does all of this mean for and about the American 'mainstream'. Well, for much of our history what we've meant by mainstream has been literature written by and for middle and upper-middle class whites. (Not entirely: from Walt Whitman and Frederick Douglass on, there have been authors who wrote against the grain and were nevertheless able to publish.) What I think we are seeing today, however, is the transformation of that flowing river so that we better understand how it is made up of so many different currents and channels, sources of life and story and poetry.

As a result, and this may be the greatest benefit of all, we are in the process of coming to new recognitions about the nature of identity itself so that, no longer trapped or categorised simply by colour or speech, we may better understand how each of us has an identity that is fluid, or indeed, that we all embrace multiple identities, depending on the context of the moment. Whether we consider ourselves white, black, yellow, or red, male or female or transgendered, gay or straight, rich or poor, Jewish, Muslim, Christian, Hindu, or pagan, the stories we tell are richer for the textures of this growing awareness and cultural collaboration.

# 11

# Reviving the oral tradition
## The evolution of audiobooks

*Jennifer Cavender and Lisa Stuchell*

# Dear readers[1]

I'd like to tell you a story. As we were conducting research for this paper, I asked an audio reference librarian if she listened to many books on tape. She replied, 'No. I still *read* books.' Many critics debate the relevance of an audio medium. Are audiobooks really books? The question plagues critics in the *New York Times* and other popular periodicals to such an extent that they can't seem to push past the argument into the realm of true debate. Audio debate exists in a vacuum in the academic world, as we found only two academic papers on the subject. We think the problem is evident. Whether or not we as scholars agree that audiobooks are books, and that reading books is better than listening to audiobooks, is irrelevant. People listen. In fact, Amy Harmon records in the *New York Times* that fewer people are reading today, but almost a third more are listening to audiobooks.[2] The fact that so many people listen and the numbers will likely continue to rise shows that audiobooks are relevant sources of textual information. Therefore, we as scholars have an urgent need to study the implications of transposing written text to an oral medium.

As parents, we read to our children to increase their auditory skills and to encourage their interest in books. And as children, many of us enjoyed hearing a story play out for us nightly. Yet, many scholars and readers frown upon the oral medium (past the age of ten or twelve) as an avenue for obtaining knowledge and information; they seem to believe that the activity of listening is less active than actually reading a text.

Admittedly, listening to a text discourages the action of skimming over sections, moving backwards or forwards in the work, and of course, prevents marginalia. Yet, the activity of listening requires more concentration and patience. As Walter Ong points out in *Orality and Literacy*, orality requires some understanding of literacy.[3] When people speak, we unconsciously attempt to recall the letters and formations of words. We are able to see the sentences in our minds. When we listen to audiobooks, we piece together the words, the sentences, the paragraphs, the meanings, and the entire book in our minds. Listening is a terribly active procedure and one that gets overlooked with the studying of texts and literature.

We believe that one of the main causes for debate concerning the relevance of audiobooks is the difference between unabridged and abridged versions of texts. James Shokoff, in 'What is an Audiobook,' argues that in the future audiobooks will have their own genre much like movies today.[4] Audiobooks will be classified not just by their story, but by how they are told: unabridged or abridged. We view audiobooks in the editorial theory perspective as a version of the text and work. With abridged versions of texts, however, the text changes so much from the original work that it becomes an adaptation of the book. As Jerome McGann explains in *A Critique of Modern Textual Criticism*, versions occur when 'authors demonstrated a number of different wishes and intentions about what text they wanted to be presented to the public, and that these differences reflect accommodations to changed circumstances and sometimes to changed publics'.[5] In other words, authors can have different authorial intentions based upon their intended audience. Editorial theory determines the author's intention of the text, specifically the placement of words and punctuation on the page. Variants of the text would inevitably prove an alternative intention by the author. Meaning, therefore, is derived out of these versions of texts. As one word changes, the meaning also changes. With abridged versions, sections and words and characters can be deleted and/or changed. Because these texts are so manipulated, they become adaptations. Unabridged audiobooks for the most part remain true to the printed text, causing them to be an alternative version of the work.

Even if we view abridged audiobooks as adaptations, editors still need to take great care in transforming them into the oral medium as abridged audiobooks transform the meaning of the text. In *Conversations on the Writing Life*[6] Julia Cameron describes a problem with editorial fallacy in the audio production of *The Right to Write*.[7,8] The editor deleted all of the passages about writing and transcribed only the passages pertaining to relationships. Cameron's intention to write a book about writing changed as her editor focused on just one aspect of Cameron's work. While the creation process for both writer and editor is based on what McGann refers to as the 'sociality of texts,' meaning people are influenced by their social surroundings when interpreting the meaning of a text, it stands to reason that editors are also influenced by the market, the audience, and even their own personal agendas.[9] Therefore, the production of the abridged adaptation of Cameron's work neglects her intention. The public never heard this adaptation as Cameron vetoed the abridgement and insisted the editor include writing passages. We know this adaptation exists because of Cameron's discussion in *Conversations on the Writing Life*. While contemporary authors have the power to veto bad adaptations, obviously, deceased writers have no control over the reprinting or the creation of audiobooks. Authors' intentions are changed then to 'accommodate the modern reader,' or listener as the case may be, as many classic works are drastically shortened into abridged adaptations.[10] From this, the text has transformed into another entity, and the meaning behind the words has been forever altered.

Staying true to the text and the author's intentions can be a difficult process for editors. The audio version of Toni Morrison's *Jazz*, for example, does not reflect the author's original meaning because of the effects of the audio medium. Morrison writes:

> But I can't say that aloud; I can't tell anyone that I have been waiting for this all my life and that being chosen to wait is the reason I can. If I were able I'd say it. Say make me, remake me. You are free to do it and I am free to let you because look, look. Look where your hands are. Now.[11]

As readers, we give voice to the text as we interpret meaning, and as Ong points out 'Written texts all have to be related somehow, directly or indirectly, to the world of sound ... "Reading" a text means converting to sound aloud or in the imagination'.[12] The reader provides the voice for the narration, and as reception theory explains, reading is not a straightforward linear movement. We understand what the narrator is asking us to do because we are prepared as readers to act, and we have the free will to make the text have meaning. Our hands physically hold the book, and we actively interpret the text. Listeners of Morrison's work, however, do not hold the book and cannot truly participate in the making of the book. They may be driving a car, cleaning house, or even working. They do not have the power to remake the book like readers do. Thus, the audio version changes Morrison's meaning. Listeners also will notice that the first line of this quote contradicts itself: 'But I can't say that aloud.' 'But,' the performer acting as the narrator has said it aloud through the audio format making the words that follow confusing to understand. The performer has done the work and has remade the text. Listeners are not part of the creation process that Morrison urges and expects her readers to participate in.

While Toni Morrison's primary authorial intention in *Jazz* differs from the abridged audio version, Morrison's secondary authorial intention prevails as she performs the audiobook[13] herself. In John Young's article 'Toni Morrison, Oprah Winfrey, and Postmodern Popular Audiences,' he discusses the impact Morrison's narration has upon the listening audience: '… with Morrison reading these passages, the lines between book and author are reblurred'.[14,15] Listeners cannot distinguish between the author as writer of the book and the narrator as speaker of the book; they merge into one and the same, allowing the audiobook medium a chance to have 'a greater sense of intimacy between audience and author'.[16] Audiobooks performed by the author immediately persuade listeners to trust the authors; the authors' voices, therefore, help in preserving authorial intentions.

In the audio version of *The Joy Luck Club*,[17] Amy Tan carves the 12-page story 'Two Kinds' down into a two and a half page transcription; thereby, she creates two diverse authorial intentions, one for her listening audience and one for her reading audience. The audio character Jing-Mei Woo, like her printed counterpart, does not become a prodigy, but audio listeners are led to believe that Jing-Mei Woo empowers herself by putting a stop to her mother's demands. The audio listener is unaware that in the printed text Jing-Mei Woo's mother signs her up for piano lessons as the audio narration ends before the piano exists. In the printed text, Jing-Mei Woo's feeling of empowerment comes from her refusal to do her best. Thus, Tan has inevitably created two different characters as seen between these two different mediums. Jing-Mei Woo's mother tells us in 'Two Kinds,' 'Only two kinds of daughters … Those who are obedient and those who follow their own mind'.[18] In the printed text, we have a character who is both obedient and has her own mind. By following her mother's orders by practising piano, Jing-Mei is the 'obedient daughter,' but by playing badly, not putting her whole heart into it, Jing-Mei 'follow[s] her own mind.' In the audio version, Jing-Mei is only the second kind of daughter, the one who solely 'follow[s] her own mind.' Tan also 'follow[s] her own mind' and reinvents the character

Jing-Mei Woo in this abridged audiobook adaptation, ironically displaying 'two kinds' of authorial intentions for her two differing audiences.

Likewise, issues concerning authorial intention with audiobooks become even more evident with texts that call for the readers to act or react. Charlotte Bronte writes in *Jane Eyre*, 'Reader, though I look comfortably accommodated, I am not very tranquil in my mind'.[19] Who is the reader? The answer is obvious in the textual version, the person physically holding the book. In the audio version, then, the reader is the performer, not the actual audience. In this case, Jane Eyre speaks to a specific reader, 'the performer,' omitting all the listeners. A simple change to 'listener' would draw the audience into the novel, something Charlotte Bronte intended, but is not authenticated in the audio version.[20] By changing the word 'reader' to 'listener,' however, the audio version would not comply with Bronte's text. Editorial theorists would question this change because it does not reflect the author's original work. But, 'listener' would appeal to the audiobook audience and would promote what Bronte intended: to grab her audience and to make them a part of her story. Because people know *Jane Eyre* first existed in print form as a novel, listeners are able to suspend their disbelief and pretend that they are 'readers.' With contemporary literature, however, listeners may be less able to suspend this disbelief as the audiobook first existed to them in the audio medium and not as a textual publication. With audiobooks, there is no easy way to resolve these problems. Editors must consider what the audience needs to hear and what the author means to say in order to produce a successful audio version of a text.

The audiobook industry can provide writers with even greater opportunities to express their intentions by exposing lost drafts and work prior to the publishing and editing process. As McGann mentions in *The Textual Condition*, variants are lost forever due to deleting words and thoughts from the computer screen.[21] Writers lose their own work as they type, and then again their work is revised during editing where more of the author's original work is removed or changed.[22] In *A Conversation on the Writing Life*, recorded in 1999, Natalie Goldberg reads an excerpt from her forthcoming book *Thunder and Lightning*,[23] published in hardcover in August 2000. She had just completed writing the book three weeks before the taping of this session. Thus, we have Goldberg's draft before editing. On tape, Goldberg begins her narrative with, 'But I do think audiobooks could be dangerous. I'll tell you why.' The book editor eliminates this introduction, and 'catapults' the reader directly into the story. Only after Goldberg describes how engrossed she was in Cormac McCarthy's *The Crossing* does she exclaim, 'So if you're like me, it's probably better not to be driving as you listen – it could be dangerous'.[24] This line is identical to the version Goldberg reads in the *Conversation* recording, but by eliminating the introduction, this line minimises the danger of audiobooks. They are only dangerous if (1) you're like Natalie Goldberg, and (2) if you listen while driving.

Recorded conversations, workshops, and readings offer us an invaluable reference by providing us with alternate versions of texts or drafts, as well as supplemental textual information. In 2004, Random House released *The Voice of the Poet*,[25] a CD and supplemental text of Allen Ginsberg's poetry. By reading his poetry on the CD, Ginsberg provides us with his tonal inflections and pauses not evident on the textual page. The published edition of the supplemental book of poems includes a footnote, explaining that the text in the book may differ from Ginsberg's reading, preserving the different drafts of the editing process. In the readings, Ginsberg often introduces his poetry with biographical information. Ginsberg wrote 'My Sad Self,' for example, 'in an attempt to imitate the style of Frank O'Hara's Lunch poems' (*Voice*). While the astute reader may glean the information from the textual publication if he has read Frank O'Hara's poetry, the audio listener does not have to rely on his prior knowledge. Before reading 'White Shroud,' Ginsberg informs the audience that his inspiration for the poem came from a supernatural visit with his dead mother (*Voice*). In addition to the biographical information, the CD preserves Ginsberg's initial intention of a musical and poetic performance similar to when he first performed 'White Shroud' at the Neropa Institute in Boulder, Colorado. In the audio version, Steven Taylor provides musical accompaniment on the strings. The musicality aspect of the poem is not represented on the textual page, nor does the editor of the supplemental text provide a footnote mentioning the music in the performing version. Likewise, Ginsberg's 'Personals Ad' illustrates how the author's initial intended audience transforms the text, and with it the meaning. In her audio workshop *Writing the Landscape of Your Mind*, Natalie Goldberg reads the original version of Ginsberg's 'Personals Ad,' a poem first published in *Harper's Magazine* in June 1990 featuring Ginsberg's address at the end of the poem. The supplemental text in *The Voice of the Poet* does not include the address, nor does Ginsberg's recording. Goldberg, a personal friend of the poet, enlightens us through her workshop on what many of Ginsberg's initial audience didn't get – the fact that the poet's inclusion of his address transforms the poem into what it represents, a personal ad. According to Goldberg, Ginsberg received only two or three replies, and she quotes him as saying, 'I guess they didn't think it was real'.[26] He did, however, meet someone through the poem, a fact which would be lost on the modern audience, the one who is subjected to the later publications of the poem in both oral and written form.

With *State of Fear*, Michael Crichton's personal and political statement about the public's irrational fear of global warming becomes lost on the audio audience. In the printed text's preface, he writes, 'References to real people, institutions and organizations that are documented in footnotes are accurate. Footnotes are real.' And as Jasper Gerard tells us in an interview with the author, 'If you doubt Crichton's research, he offers enough footnotes citing scientific journals to fill a hefty volume of their own'.[27] But, no footnotes exist in the audio version,[28] which results in Crichton's personal and political statement being diluted into a fictional story. In addition to the footnotes and list of references, the text provides editors with the challenge of converting a multi-genre work with graphs and pictures into an audio format. Again, we see an absence in the representation. There is no way to represent pictures without detracting from the story. In the published version, Crichton provides us with a memo in which certain words have been deleted.[29] The reader can look at the memo and guess as to the missing words, gleaning some type of meaning from the picture. The listener, however, can glean no such meaning as the performer of the audiobook version fills in the missing words with 'deleted word' or 'deleted passage' or 'deleted.' The performer does not describe the graphs or pictures. The dialogue tells us 'as is represented by this graph,' but the listener has no idea that the graph actually exists on the page, or if it is just an imaginary graph alluded to by the character. As we continue to see more multi-genre books, and more and more multi-genre books are released in an audio format, the need to take advantage of multi-media as supplemental texts will emerge.

Supplemental texts could also enhance the listener's understanding of dramatic works. The most authentic production of *Hamlet* would obviously be on stage, where Shakespeare intended his actors to be. After that, a production of *Hamlet* in an audio format where different performers, or even one performer, is able to vary the voices, creates a version that *sounds* authentic. The audio version provides us with a fluid narrative – we can hear the voices, but we are blinded from the stage. Listeners must imagine the way the characters look, the scene changes, and the setting of the story without any indication of what they should imagine. Readers, however, have the most textual information and create images in their minds through the stage cues and setting descriptions provided by the editors. By keeping up with the language, the stage directions, the running narrative, and the characters' actions, readers can become trapped by so many visual representations of the words. In essence, readers have too much visual information, and listeners do not have enough. Audiobook publishers in the future will bridge this paradox and strengthen our understanding of Shakespeare and the like by creating audio versions of texts and including the supplemental written form. Listeners will be able to follow along and read the cues, so they can form a more accurate picture of where the action takes place and what the characters are doing. Supplemental texts with audiobooks, as seen currently with many poetry works, will continue to improve the audiobook industry and to expand the audience.

As audiobooks become part of mainstream publishing and more people want to listen to books, we have spiralled into what Ong refers to as 'secondary orality,' which 'refers to those familiar with writing'.[30] The audio version of *Beowulf*[31] falls within this form of orality, as it was once primary orality, meaning preliterate generations passed the epic down orally until the formation of the written language and then the epic became a written and published text. The written Old English text translated by Seamus Heaney serves as the basis for the audio version. In this sense, *Beowulf* has transformed itself into a piece of secondary orality, since as listeners we hear the oral epic and can imagine the visual representation of the words in a way the original listeners could not.

From secondary orality, the future of audiobooks will one day include an alternative approach to writing and listening: postliterate orality. In these cases, there will no longer be a written published text as a source for the audio version. In some cases, writers will become speakers, and the audience will once again be listeners without any written material to refer to. The audio industry will also change to accommodate the modern listener who has a voracious appetite to consume literature, in both the written and audio format. This revival and reinvention of the oral tradition will play to an audience that resembles the traditional audience, yet the modern audience will still be a reading audience. Unlike performances from the past, technology works like a photograph, capturing a fixed performance in which the words, tonal inflections, pauses, and accents will remain the same every time the listener presses play. And, as the rise in audio sales suggests, the modern audience will continue to press play because people love stories no matter what the form. So all you readers, listen up.

# Works consulted

Eagleton, Terry (1996) *Literary Theory*. Minneapolis, Minnesota: University of Minnesota Press.

Gaskell, Philip (1985) Night and Day: The Development of a Play Text. *Textual Criticism and Literary Interpretation*. (McGann, Jerome, Ed.). Chicago: University of Chicago Press, pp. 162–79.

Kozloff, Sarah (1995) 'Audio books in a visual culture', *Journal of American Culture* 18.4: 83–96.

# Notes

1.  In the conference presentation, we substituted the word 'listeners' for 'readers' since we addressed a listening audience. In the published version, our audience is a reading audience, which necessitates a slight change in wording.

2.  Harmon, Amy (2005) Loud, Proud, Unabridged: It is Too Reading! *New York Times* 26 May 2005: G1–G2.

3.  Ong, Walter (2002) *Orality and Literacy*. New York: Routledge, p. 10.

4.  Shokoff, James (2001) 'What is an audio book?', *Journal of Popular Culture* 34.4: 179.

5.  McGann, Jerome (1983) *A Critique of Modern Textual Criticism*. Charlottesville, Virginia: UP of Virginia, p. 32.

6.  Cameron, Julia and Goldberg, Natalie (1999) *A Conversation on the Writing Life*. Audiobook. Boulder, Colorado: Sounds True.

7.  Cameron, Julia (1998) *The Right to Write*. New York: Putnam.

8.  Cameron, Julia (1998) *The Right to Write*. Audiobook. Read by Julia Cameron. New York: Audio Renaissance.

9.  McGann (1983), op. cit., p. 75.

10. Spisak, James W., ed. (1983) Introduction and Notes. *Caxton's Malory*. By Sir Thomas Malory. Berkeley: University of California Press, Vol. 2, p. 629.

11. Morrison, Toni (1992) *Jazz*. New York: Knopf, p. 229.

12. Ong, op. cit., p. 8.

13. Morrison, Toni (1992) *Jazz*. Audiobook. Read by Toni Morrison. New York: Random House.

14. Young, John. (2001) 'Toni Morrison, Oprah Winfrey, and

postmodern popular audiences', *African American Review* 35.2: 181–204.

15. Young's article provides further analysis of Toni Morrison's *Jazz* and the effects of her narration upon the listening public as well as African-American oral tradition.

16. Young, op. cit., p. 199.

17. Tan, Amy (1989) *The Joy Luck Club*. Audiobook. Read by Amy Tan. Stow, Ohio: Dove Audio.

18. Tan, Amy (1989) *The Joy Luck Club*. New York: G.P. Putnam's Sons, p. 142.

19. Bronte, Charlotte (1994) *Jane Eyre*. London: Puffin Books, 1994 edn, p. 126.

20. Bronte, Charlotte (1980) *Jane Eyre*. Audiobook. Unabridged read by Flo Gibson. Charlotte Hall, Maryland: Recorded Books, 1980 edn.

21. McGann, Jerome (1991) *The Textual Condition*. Princeton, New Jersey: Princeton UP, p. 91.

22. Ibid., pp. 91–2.

23. Goldberg, Natalie (2000) *Thunder and Lightning*. New York: Bantam.

24. Cameron, Julia and Goldberg, Natalie, op. cit., p 24.

25. McClatchy, J. D. ed. (2004) *The Voice of the Poet: Allen Ginsberg*. Audiobook. Read by Allen Ginsberg. New York: Random House.

26. Goldberg, Natalie (1993) *Writing the Landscape of Your Mind*. Audiobook. Minnetonka, Minnesota: Writer's AudioShop.

27. Gerard, Jasper. (2005) Interview: Jasper Gerard meets Michael Crichton. *TIMES ONLINE* 02 Jan. 2005. 01 Sept. 2005 available from *http://www.timesonline.co.uk/0,,1-525-1422283-525,00.html*.

28. Crichton. Michael (2004) *State of Fear*. Audiobook. Unabridged read by George Wilson. New York: Harper Audio.

29. Crichton, Michael (2004) *State of Fear*. New York: Harper Collins.

30. Ong, op. cit., p. 6.

31. Heaney, Seamus (2000) *Beowulf*. Audiobook. Read by Seamus Heaney. Minneapolis, Minnesota: Highbridge Audio.

# 12

# Are you being served?
## Librarianship past, present, and future

*Maureen Brunsdale and Jennifer Hootman*

## Introduction

At the American Library Association conference for librarians in San Francisco in October 1891, Samuel Swett Green, librarian of the Free Public Library, Worcester, Massachusetts, delivered a grand speech on the librarian, libraries, and library schools.[1] In that speech Green asserted:

> The function of a library is to serve its users. It is the duty of a public library to serve the public. A good librarian . . . will keep constantly in mind, of giving as much pleasure as possible to users of the library, and of exerting as widespread and elevating an educational influence as circumstances will allow. The chief purpose of a library is to stimulate and encourage persons of all ages, learned and unlearned, to make investigations and read good books, and to help them cordially and persistently in finding answers to their inquiries and in getting at books of standard value adapted to supply their special needs.[2]

From the first time the word 'reference' was used with the word 'library,' there has been a well-noted underlying element of instruction in the interchanges between patron and librarian. This article will examine the conjoined aspects of reference and instruction in librarianship during three pivotal times throughout modern American history: when librarians were first formally instructed in their profession and reference departments were established; at the dawn of library automation; and today, a time of the 'Information Age' when the amount of information being accessed from nearly everywhere is exponentially growing and the need for critically identifying and analysing the information has never been more essential. Looking at librarians, libraries, and library schools past and present, this article will not only examine where reference and instruction intersect but also will attempt to identify – or at least question – the paths that point to the future of the information-seeking reference and instruction library professionals.

# Origin of instructional reference services

In early nineteenth century America, a public library was considered little more than a storehouse of literature. Furthermore, until the latter portion of the nineteenth century, librarianship in the United States was perhaps little more than an occupation largely concerned with the maintenance and preservation of a small, limited collection rather than encouraging and supporting reading and scholarship.[3] It was not until the period between the start of the Civil War (1860) and First World War (1914) that there was a 'transfiguration experienced by most American libraries.'[4] During this era of 'transfiguration' there began a 'redefinition of American libraries and American librarianship' and a 'general restructuring of American institutions and intellectual life, and a change directly related to similar developments in education, scholarship, government, and science – as well as in the American publishing industry.'[5]

To gain a better understanding it is important to examine the mid-century just prior to this period of transfiguration in libraries and librarianship. In the 1850s there were few American libraries being used as research institutions. The public library was in its early stages. College libraries and historical societies, too, had collections that were lacking to the point that they could scarcely be considered for scholarly research. Even the largest government library in the country, the Library of Congress, cared for a collection that may have boasted a large medical and theological collection, but greatly suffered in many other areas such as the humanities, arts, and social sciences. It was an uneven collection at best. Though collections of the majority of public American libraries were anaemic and insufficient for research, the private libraries of east coast financially influential men such as George Bancroft, George Ticknor, and Francis

Parkman were not. It was these immense, purposeful, strategic personal collections that launched what is commonly considered the public library movement between 1850 and 1854.[6]

The public library movement originated with the establishment of the Boston Public Library in the early 1850s. Reasons and motivations behind the public library movement varied from city to city and township to township. Regardless of these differing motivations there was a general underlying commitment to the education of the populace and creating more educational opportunities.[7] For instance, George Ticknor, whose private library helped to build the Boston Public Library's collection, thought that this institution was the perfect complement to Boston's well-liked public education system and that it also could serve as 'an apparatus that shall carry this taste for reading as deep as possible into society.'[8] Edward Everett, another initial donor to the Boston Public Library, thought the new library should be 'a quiet retreat for persons of both sexes who desire earnestly to improve their minds.'[9] The emphasis of the library's mission, however, still remained to accumulate and preserve.

New York City's Astor Library opened the same year as the Boston Public Library: 1854. What followed was the growth of public libraries sweeping from New England to the Midwest. By 1876 there were 188 public libraries financially supported through taxes. One hundred and twenty-seven of them were located in Massachusetts, 14 in Illinois, 13 in New Hampshire, and 9 in Ohio. Between 1854 and 1876 a number of cities had established free municipal libraries such as Cincinnati (1856), Detroit and St. Louis (1865), Cleveland (1869), Louisville (1871), Indianapolis (1872), and Chicago (1873).[10] During this era of great public library growth and focus on accumulation and preservation of materials, librarians mainly considered themselves to be 'cultural custodians and concentrated their efforts on the careful selection of books that would properly educate the patrons of the library; the accessibility and use of a collection was of less importance than its steady and careful accumulation.'[11]

Two distinct yet nearly simultaneous forces that worked to redefine the purpose and mission of American libraries and librarianship were Andrew Carnegie and Melvil Dewey. Carnegie carried on a philanthropic tradition in America to which all its public libraries find their roots. Contributing over 41 million dollars to build over 1,600 libraries primarily in the West and Midwest, each community constructing a Carnegie library was required to build and maintain the collection, supported through their taxes. Carnegie viewed these libraries to be 'democratic institutions' promoting community progress and self-improvement.[12]

As these Carnegie libraries grew, so did their services. An educational role added new reference assistance for their patrons. In many states, this educational role also included 'Americanization' programs for immigrants and special programs for children. Interestingly, the college library lagged behind the public library in both collections and services, finally beginning to develop these aspects in the 1870s.[13]

A symbolic date in this age of redefinition and transfiguration of American libraries and librarianship is October 1876, the founding of the American Library Association (ALA) spearheaded by Melvil Dewey. With the establishment of ALA, the era when librarians solely concentrated their efforts on accumulation and preservation came to an end. The new focus became the efficient use of collections. This professional association was a bit different than many other professional associations established at that time. For instance, librarians were considered the middlemen caring for and making accessible the collections for the benefit of the public, students of higher education, and other professional associations. Librarians at this time were not subject specialists. This had its advantages and disadvantages working in the academic world.[14]

In addition to working to establish ALA, Dewey also was responsible for creating the first graduate school for librarians at New York's Columbia College in 1887. In a memorable 1886 speech delivered to an association of college women Melvil Dewey stated that

> Librarianship to-day means quite a different thing from what it meant twenty years ago. The old library was passive, asleep, a reservoir or cistern, getting in but not giving out. . . . The new library is active . . . a living fountain of good influences . . . and the librarian occupies a field of active usefulness second to none.[15]

As he articulated a new role in librarianship, Dewey was responsible for recruiting seventeen well-educated women into the new School of Library Economy situated at Columbia College. On January 5, 1887, they assembled for the first day of class.[16]

Though Dewey was forced to leave Columbia because of integrating female students into an all-male campus, his targeted recruiting efforts and the willingness of women to participate in formal training is what led to the possibility of creating the first library training program. One of the reasons behind female students is clear. There simply were not enough male students to populate one class. Since the 1850s, women have been working as librarians in US public libraries and participating nationally at American Library Association conferences since 1876. But it is interesting to note that, up until the first class of female library school graduates, library leadership had often been the purview of male librarians.[17]

These new library school graduates entered the profession at a time when the US was undergoing changes spurred by educational reform efforts, the aforementioned Carnegie philanthropy, and the women's club movement which were part of a number of dramatic societal changes leading to such a rapid growth in public libraries. In a less than fifty-year span from 1876 to 1923, the total number of American libraries grew from 2,637 to 4,167. In addition to this growth in new libraries, existing libraries expanded to include branches and new departments such as extension services, children's work, and reference services. Due to this growth the number of library positions more than tripled from 1900 to 1920. By 1920 women accounted for over 88 per cent of the total number of librarians at 15,297.[18] During the Progressive Era (1890–1913), the

> 'modern' public library was expected to provide resources for an informed citizenry complementing the work of the schools, serving business people and labourers, offering a means of 'wholesome' recreation to rich and poor, and spreading cultural enrichment to the whole community.[19]

Libraries and librarianship were beginning to reflect a more democratic society engaged with its educational, vocational, and cultural improvement.

With a growing concern for greater accessibility, librarians were beginning to emphasise cataloguing and classification during the last twenty-five years of the nineteenth century. Dewey viewed the value of any collection to be dependent on the classification, cataloguing and indexing functions. He believed that if a patron cannot find what is needed then the collection is rendered useless. This push for greater accessibility spurred a dramatic shift in all services including extending library hours, developing interlibrary loan systems, and opening the stacks to patrons.[20] With *use* as the focus of librarians' work instructional reference assistance was beginning to become more formalised largely through the efforts of Dewey. As early as 1876 at the first ALA conference, Dewey stated that

> The time *was* when a library was very like a museum, and a librarian was a mouser in musty books, and visitors looked with curious eyes at ancient tomes and manuscripts. The time *is* when

the library is a school, and the librarian is in the highest sense a teacher, and the visitor is a reader among the books as a workman among his tools.[21]

Though librarians were offering greater instructional reference assistance to their patrons in the public libraries and Dewey was asserting the role of the library as a school and librarian as a teacher well before the turn of the century, it nonetheless took another twenty-five years to become accepted practice in the academic libraries.[22]

Academic libraries were still consumed with building their collections until after 1900. Furthermore, many academic librarians were so committed to their catalogues and access issues that many felt the reader needed no further assistance. Added to that view was the fact that many scholars were insulted by anyone thinking that they needed any kind of assistance. Even following the development of departmental libraries, specialised reference assistance was not accepted by either party the librarian or the patron. At this time, in the early twentieth century, the professional librarian specializing in a particular subject was still a rare combination.[23] Once again, however, as Chief Librarian at Columbia, Dewey was vocal in his concern that 'With the limited time at the command of students and investigators, and the immense amount of material with which the individual must often deal, the aid of someone fully acquainted with the resources of the library…and at hand to impart the desired help, becomes imperatively necessary.'[24] That same year, in 1884, he established a reference department. As academic libraries became more specialised so eventually did the librarians. After 1900, Dewey expressed that as academic libraries became more specialised reference librarians should too specialise in specific subject areas to provide a greater degree of subject-specific reference assistance. This kind of reference assistance which initially swept through public libraries in the later portion of the nineteenth century eventually found its way into academic libraries, specialised libraries, and finally the Library of Congress itself as late as the 1910s.[25]

## Automation and instructional reference services

From the late nineteenth and early twentieth century (days of Dewey) until the automation of the library (1970s), instructional reference services remained somewhat stagnate, providing the same kind of assistance and service as they had since the era of redefinition and transfiguration of American libraries and librarianship. This is not to diminish the fact that there were a great many debates over librarianship from the 1920s through the 1960s. Topics of these debates included: what traits or characteristics were necessary for the successful librarian; what the reference librarian should be taught in library schools; what determines a professional librarian from a clerical or paraprofessional in the library; how much information the librarian should impart to the reader during the reference interview; what the difference is between a subject specialist and general reference librarian; and what the main purpose or role is of the reference librarian regardless of the type of library.[26]

Even today, these debates continue and garner a great deal of attention in the library profession. With regard to the relationship between the reader or patron and the librarian, however, there has always been some hint of an instructional component in the act of reference assistance. Though reference assistance was slow to develop in academic libraries particularly, the reference librarian (either general or a subject specialist) has been considered an educator to some degree. For instance, the mid-nineteenth century Victorian ideology cast the librarian as educator who 'creates and stimulates a desire for knowledge and who directs its use' and '...stimulating public thought, moulding public opinion, educating to all of the higher possibilities of human thought and action; to become a means for enriching, beautifying and making fruitful the barren places of in human life.'[27] While this saviour-educator role of the reference librarian in mid-century Victorian American life did not carry through to the twentieth century, the educator aspect of the role certainly did, although slightly diminished in its importance. The fifty-year stretch from the 1920s through the 1960s saw library schools and textbooks offering various approaches to the teaching of reference to aspiring librarians, but there was a consistent emphasis placed on approachability, service focused on the patron needs, patience, courtesy, open-mindedness, answering the patron's questions satisfactorily, and teaching the patron how to serve him or herself. This emphasis on teaching the patron to serve him or herself and become self-sufficient remained the instructional component of reference assistance during that period of time. It was not until the automation of the library in the 1970s that the instructional component became a movement in the library world.[28]

Library automation, in the form of computer databases and online catalogues, revolutionised accessibility and collection maintenance. At this time the patron may have become more aware of the expertise required for reference assistance, but the instructional component of that interaction remained somewhat passive. To explain further, the reference librarian waits for the patrons to seek assistance rather than being proactive and anticipating their needs.[29] With automation, the library schools in the 1970s began to recognise the need to change their approach to the teaching of reference work due to the changing library environment for reference librarians. Three new subjects sprouted in many library schools that were closely related to reference work. One such course was 'computer-based reference service' which was referred to as 'online services.' Another course developed during this time period was 'community information services' or 'urban information services' also known as 'information and referral services.' A third new course offered by many library schools was known as 'bibliographic instruction' or 'library use instruction.' Though there had always been an instructional component in librarianship, there was a noticeable increase in this type of instruction as early as 1967. This increase in instruction-specific services in the libraries and the push for separate instruction courses in the library schools since the late 1960s has been dubbed 'the bibliographic instruction (BI) movement.' Numbers of individuals identifying themselves as 'library instruction librarians' grew in number and voice.[30]

Though reference work spawned three new components during the late 1960s and 1970s, the central purpose of the reference librarian seemed to remain relatively the same while 'library instruction librarians' took a greater role in anticipating and proactively addressing the needs of patrons. Today, there are reference librarians that specialise in 'online or electronic services,' 'referral services,' and 'library instruction.' Interestingly, despite the fact that these new facets of librarianship became distinct areas of specialization, the role of the reference librarian (general or subject specialist) still maintains an instructional component.

# Virtual environments and instructional reference services

As American libraries and librarianship reached the 1990s it could be effectively argued that nothing has impacted the profession more than the advent of virtual environments hosted on the Internet. Tools leading up to the present – paper indexes, bibliographies, fee-based services such as DIALOG, and even databases on tape or CDs – were not as universally available at academic institutional libraries as web-based tools, or the free Internet, are now. Of course, this technology did not magically appear one day, but has been growing rapidly over time. Librarians have been partnered in this growth, adapting quickly as well.

It might be helpful to document here some of the typical tools being used today in an academic library (knowing that 'typical' is a generalization and generalizations are dangerous to espouse). Online catalogues and databases, the Internet, hardcopy and virtual reference collections along with their requisite hardware, provide the basics of support for reference personnel to offer service at the desk, over the phone, or over the Internet via chat or e-mail. Networked personal computers, printers, datashow technologies, and screens are pivotal for instructional purposes in the classroom.

Librarians have always been and are still service providers in the classic sense. Listening to patrons, asking questions of them to determine their needs, searching for the requested information, and retrieving the same remains at the heart of what occurs during an in-person reference interaction. Yet perhaps, as Elmborg maintains, academic librarians are currently in the position of quickly supplying answers without instructing our patrons of the methodology utilised to get them.

If librarians have steered away from the instructional element of reference, as Elmborg suggests, perhaps a causal agent might be the so-called 'virtual reference,' meaning e-mail and chat reference services. These services support rapid responses by both parties. The person with the query puts it forth in a shortened fashion, sometimes lacking important elements. The librarian, without the benefit of the non-visual cues and complete information tries to assess the question, get more information from the patron, and provide an accurate and rapid answer. Knowing patrons can often 'virtually' visit other places to get help (Ask.com, etc.), the librarian tries to assist as quickly and effectively as possible.

Elmborg suggests that a librarian's responsibility is 'to participate in discourse, to engage our students with meaningful talk about their research, to help them develop a language of inquiry that will allow them to articulate to themselves how to proceed with present and future research challenges.'[31] While providing rapid-fire answers to questions posed the same way, it is conceivable that some librarians may have neglected to instruct at times. And, it should be stated that not every question always has an instructional component. Thinking of directional or hours-types of queries here supplies types of questions for which short and quick answers are appropriate.

Participating and engaging students can best be accomplished in person. However, the Association of Research Libraries statistics 'show a 30 per cent drop in reference transactions from a high in 1997 ... to 2002.'[32] Interestingly, gate counts are similarly suffering. Therefore, a concept that is once again showing itself in library professional literature is an old one, almost as old as reference itself: Roving reference. Samuel Swett Green of the Worcester, Massachusetts Free Public Library supported the idea of a professional being seen in the library so that she could be easily diverted and asked for assistance. Smith and Pietraszewski detail the testing of a roving reference program at Texas A & M University at College Station. In this program the two librarian/authors donned scrub coats in their University colour (maroon) so as to be easily identifiable and carried tablet PCs so that they could roam throughout the library and answer questions at the point-of-need. Their findings suggest an unsurprising need for further study, but they also ponder 'we may have illustrated very clearly that the demand for face-to-face reference interactions is *not* [our italic] our future.'[33]

While the numbers of quick- or ready-reference type of questions may be decreasing, it seems as if the more involved reference questions remain. Added to this, is the perceived increase in the instructional component of reference. What is meant here, more specifically, is the need to educate the patron on how to evaluate what is found. With so much information readily available at the fingertips, the need to instruct the patron becomes vitally important. Establishing the veracity of the websource is the key. Librarians are the best equipped to assist university constituents in this way. But, are our patrons ready to ask these kinds of questions, or to expect a new vantage on reference service?

'People not only need a range of resources and services, they want those resources and services to be *quick* and *cheap* (or, better still, *free*) and easy to use and access and – perhaps most importantly – *good enough*.'[34] As indicated in his piece, 'Academic Reference: Playing to Our Strengths,' Janes recognises that this is a natural human tendency. People do want to get things like information quickly and easily, often paying less heed to accuracy or quality.

Chat reference and e-mail reference have joined the ranks of traditional reference services in most academic libraries. The reasons behind this are simple to extrapolate. Students, an academic librarian's largest demographic constituency, are more used to looking online for help and they do not want to traverse the campus (or cannot, if for example they are enrolled in distance education programs) to get to the library. Put differently, students want 'to settle for information that meets the 'three

Fs' requirement: first, fastest, and full-text.'[35] Take this together with the fact that the reference personnel strive to meet patrons at their point-of-need, the trend towards electronic reference comes even more into focus. So, what about the future of reference and its vital instructional component?

# Future of instructional reference services

There is no way to accurately predict the future of reference service. But there are definite certainties. Technology will continue to play a significant role in the library profession. As electronic advances continue, the speed with which people want to access desired information will likely also increase. And the personality traits of a reference librarian's largest constituency – the students – will draw them to those aforementioned Fs (first, fastest, and full text).

The tools used to do reference will – and should – change to include new technologies as well as the traditional ones. Librarians will need to reach out to patrons with the tools they so readily adapt. They have, by and large, done this thus far with virtual reference and phone reference. What about Instant Messaging, text-messaging, blogging, kiosk reference, and wikis? It seems likely that these 'gadget reference' tools used for quick- or ready-reference will be embraced by forward thinking libraries looking to offer an integrated service environment.

For in-depth research questions a paradigm shift may be needed.

Study after study has shown that students struggle with search strategies; they often do not distinguish between information found on the open Web, library online catalogues, and subscription databases; and that their selection of information is often based on the expectations of their professors' course assignments rather than on their critical, analytical abilities to sort through, compare, and eventually find the precise evaluative information that they need.[36]

Perhaps librarians need to actively change the student's 'take and run' reference scenario to more of a 'stop and think' one. Providing this kind of instructional reference-on-demand service would help increase the numbers of information literate.

Getting this kind of scenario into the minds of patrons may at first be perplexing, but not impossible. As a group, librarians are poised to take on this challenge. Moving away from the library – for example, having office hours in academic departments and kiosk service in the dormitories – to meet our patron's at their point-of-need would assist both in demonstrating our pivotal role in the Information World. Perhaps too marketing or promoting library services to the highest levels of faculty could trickle down to the students.

Thompson[37] draws attention to the fact that librarians have done an inordinate amount of research on the reference interview but relatively little 'on persuading people to get to the reference department so that they can have a reference interview.'[38] This is something that should also be studied. The results could prove to be immensely illustrative for the library profession.

Undeniably, reference statistics have gone down. However, 'Is it possible that successful information-literacy programs are the reason that fewer questions are asked at the reference desk?'[39] This indeed is not only a point to ponder, but one to further research.

# Conclusion

Today, the bond between reference and instruction has never been stronger. This relationship, however, took over a century to develop. Dewey's mere establishment of a reference department at Columbia was itself a groundbreaking achievement. As reference services evolved the instructional component grew, too, to become a more defined, acknowledged and expected service. Whether the reference librarian (general or subject specialist) is working with a student one-on-one or conducting an instructional session for a class of thirty or more students, instruction has become an inherent element of this type of librarianship. As American libraries push into the twenty-first century the reference librarian is faced with new instructional challenges. The overabundance of information readily available at the fingertips demands that librarians teach assessment/evaluation of that information; that they teach patrons how to construct effective research queries so that they can obtain the specific data that they need. Stated differently, the instructional component of reference services continues to grow and evolve as the tools with which librarians work have demanded that they need to act more quickly to remind patrons of the value added to their information transaction.

Reference librarians must also work to expand the instructional, point-of-need service to the virtual or real places, wherever it is needed most, and utilise the necessary technologies to forge ahead into the frontier of librarianship.

## Works consulted

Abram, Stephen and Judy Luther (2004) 'Born with the chip', *Library Journal* 129,8: 34–7.

Atlas, Michel C. (2005) 'Library anxiety in the electronic era, or why won't anybody talk to me anymore', *Reference & User Services Quarterly* 44, (4) 314–9.

Crowe, Kathryn M. (2003) 'Collaborative leadership: A model for reference services', *The Reference Librarian* 81: 59–69.

Duckett, Bob (2004) 'From reference library to information service: services in danger', *Library Review* 53,6: 301–8.

Ferguson, Chris. (2000) 'Shaking the Conceptual Foundations' Too: Integrating Research and Technology Support for the Next Generation of Information Service', *College & Research Libraries* 61: 300–11.

Kyrillidou, Martha and Mark Young (2005) ARL Statistics 2001-2002: Research Library Trends. Available from *http://www.arl.org/stats/arlstat/02pub/intro02.html* (accessed April 11, 2005)

Woodward, Jeannette (2005) *Creating the Customer-driven Library: Building on the Bookstore Model.* Chicago: American Library Association.

## Notes

1. Green, Samuel Swett (1891) Address of the President. Conference of Librarians, San Francisco, October 12–16. *Library Journal* 16 (Conference Issue): 1.
2. Ibid., p. 1–3.
3. Maack, Mary Niles (1998) Gender, Culture, and the Transformations of American Librarianship, 1890–1920. *Libraries and Culture* 33(1): 51.
4. Cole, John Y. (1979) Storehouses and Workshops: American

Libraries and the Uses of Knowledge. In *The Organization of Knowledge in Modern America, 1860–1920* eds Alexandra Oleson and John Voss. Baltimore, MD: Johns Hopkins University Press, pp 364–85.

5.  Ibid., p. 364.
6.  Ibid., pp. 364–5.
7.  Ibid., p. 365.
8.  Quoted in ibid., p. 366.
9.  Quoted in ibid., p. 366.
10. Ibid., p. 366.
11. Ibid., p. 368.
12. Ibid., p. 369.
13. Ibid., pp. 369–70.
14. Ibid., pp. 370–2.
15. Maack, op. cit., 51.
16. Ibid., 51.
17. Ibid., 51–2.
18. Ibid., 52. Today, just shy of a century later women remarkably hold approximately 84.4 per cent of the total number of library positions (US Department of Commerce, Bureau of the Census. Employed Civilians by Occupation, Sex, Race, and Hispanic Origin: 2003. Statistical Abstract of the United States: 2004–2005, Washington, DC.)
19. Ibid., 53.
20. Cole, op. cit., p. 373.
21. Quoted in ibid., p. 374.
22. Ibid., p. 375.
23. Ibid., p. 375.
24. Quoted in ibid., p. 376.
25. Ibid., pp. 376–77, 382.
26. Genz, Marcella D. (1998) 'Working the reference desk', *Library Trends* 46(3): 505–25.
27. Quoted in ibid, 507–8.
28. Ibid., 506–20.
29. Ibid., 517–18.
30. Samuel Rothstein's research is indispensable for studying the history of reference in libraries. Rothstein, Samuel (1989) The Making of a Reference Librarian. *The Reference Librarian* 25/26: 332–3.
31. Elmborg, James K. (2002) 'Teaching at the desk: toward a reference pedagogy', *Portal: Libraries and the Academy* 2(3): 461.

32. Smith, Michael M. and Pietraszewski, Barbara A. (2004) 'Enabling the roving reference librarian: wireless access with tablet PCs', *Reference Services Review* 32(3): 249.
33. Ibid., 254.
34. Janes, Joseph (2004) 'Academic reference: Playing to our strengths', *Portal: Libraries and the Academy* 4(4): 535.
35. MacWhinnie, Laurie A. (2003) 'The information commons: The academic library of the future', *Portal: Libraries and the Academy* 3(2): 245.
36. Rockman, Ilene F. (2003) 'Thinking deeply about the future', *Reference Services Review* 31(1): 2.
37. Thompson, W.A. (2004) 'Recessional: The future of the reference department', *Illinois Libraries* 65(2): 26–40.
38. Ibid, 33.
39. Jackson, Michael Gordon. (2003) 'The great reference debate continued – with a manifesto', *American Libraries* 34(5): 51.

# 13

# Access, convergence and print on demand:
## The library dimension

*John Feather*

## Introduction

The convergence of information and communication media and technologies was a characteristic of the last few years of the twentieth century. It was facilitated and to some extent driven by the use of common digital technologies. Both cable-based and wireless digital systems can deliver television, voice communications and interactive computing, as well as ancillary systems such as teletext and viewdata. The impact of convergence can be seen at every level. Globally, the great multi-national corporations which control much of the media, communications and entertainment industries make commercial sense because of the interchangeability of digital data files. Companies like Time Warner or News Corp have interests which cover print-on-paper publishing of books, newspapers and magazines, movie production for both theatre and home use, satellite and cable television distribution networks and production, and music production and distribution. The intellectual property rights in digital content can be manipulated to produce a multiplicity of formats and outputs, each serving its own market both demographically and geographically. This has had an impact across the whole of the information industry and for all information service providers. At institutional level, many academic libraries have been brought under joint management with computing and other media services since the mid-1990s.[1-4] Convergence, however, has been more than a fashion in university management. It has also brought about a new 'interoperability' of people. The common technologies have a common skill base in which the ability to design, implement and use electronic digital information systems is breaking down the traditional barriers between different branches of the information professions, and between public service providers and private sector suppliers.[5]

The rapid advance of both technological and structural convergence raises a number of issues and concerns. Essentially these fall under three broad headings

- technology;

- content;

- cost.

Convergence, however, is also driving another, arguably more complex and certainly more subtle, change. This change is in the relationship between key stakeholders. In the publishing sector, much of the thinking around this issue has focussed on three groups:

- academic authors and readers;

- academic librarians;

- publishers.

We shall consider each of these in turn, but there is also another stakeholder group, less often featured in discussions of the changing direction of information provision: the public libraries and their users. What are the political, economic and social implications of convergence for all of these people and organizations?

## Technology – the easy questions

Digital technologies have four characteristics which underpin convergence. In summary, the technologies are:

- universal;

- compatible;

- interoperable;

- future-proofed.

In practice, all of these need some qualification, but they essentially describe the position. The first three are intimately connected. Differences between systems can lead to incompatibility, but the digital data itself, at its most basic level, can normally be adapted to run on any system. Even where systems are not wholly compatible and unlimited interoperability is not possible, the underlying binary data remains as an integrating factor. The real problem is future-proofing, and it is in this respect that some key stakeholders have had their greatest concerns. The issues are genuinely difficult, but they are not primarily technical. Ensuring that each new generation of software can deal with files created by its predecessors is now the normal practice of the IT industry. Files themselves can be preserved by copying, by independent storage of multiple copies, and by regular refreshment. A document such as a paper in a scientific journal which is complete before it goes into the public domain can be preserved in its authentic form for as long as it is needed. It is not a free good in financial terms – an issue to which we shall return – but unrestricted access is not a technical problem.

Another way of expressing this it to say that digital data files have many of the characteristics of printed documents. They have a universal and well-understood format. Having learned to use such a document, the skill can be applied, with comparatively minor adaptations, to using any other document. It is possible to use two or more documents from different sources, although not necessarily simultaneously. And there is a reasonable expectation that the document can be stored in a way which will make it available throughout its useful lifetime. Moreover, technology adds value to digital documents by offering facilities which are either unavailable or more difficult to obtain with their print-on-paper equivalents. Among the more obvious are de facto instantaneous access, desk-top delivery, searchability, and the capacity to store the document locally and perhaps the ability to manipulate its content. In practical terms, this means that the users of scientific journals (to take an example from the domain where electronic publishing is currently most widely used) can access the specific paper which is being sought directly from their own desk-top PCs, read it, print it, download and store it, and perhaps have click-on access to relevant datasets or the bibliographical references provided by the author. The coming generation of technology, advancing rapidly, will make the process even more flexible and personal through the use of genuinely portable devices with wireless access to networked services.

Technical simplicity, however, is only one dimension of a more complex picture. Access is worthwhile only if the content is worthwhile; and content presents far more difficult problems.

# Content – the difficult questions

Content is the *raison d'être* of any published document. The process of publication, whatever the format or medium, puts content through three processes: creation, transmission and use. This is not, however, a simple linear relationship, as older models of communication might suggest.[6] The variable which has to be introduced into a valid model is the role of the user. The 'user' may indeed be simply an end-user, a passive consumer. The reader of a novel or a textbook might be argued to be typically in that position, although even that proposition could be challenged. In a more sophisticated model, however, there has to be space to recognise that any given user may, on another occasion, be a creator or even an intermediary (Figure 13.1).

The three participants in this interactive model of knowledge creation, distribution and consumption all have their own perspectives on the process in which they are engaged.

The knowledge *creator* – for this purpose the author – wishes to make the content available to its intended audience. This might be the millions of readers of a popular novel; it might be the handful of readers of scientific research paper. To reach this audience however, the author typically uses an intermediary. The knowledge *distributor* – the publisher – has historically been the provider of risk capital as well as the provider of technical and commercial structures. Electronic knowledge distribution can, in principle, eliminate the intermediary, although even if there is no intellectual or commercial intervention between author and reader, there is still necessarily some kind of managed system. The author who puts

**Figure 13.1** Knowledge cycle.

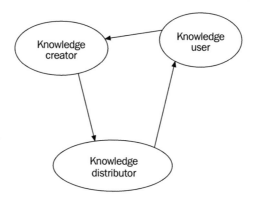

a piece on his own Website is using systems and a network provided by others, to which a financial cost is typically attached. The distributor may have lost the key publishing function of editorial intervention and hence of quality control, but the intermediary role remains.

The knowledge *user* may indeed be merely a passive recipient. In practice, however, knowledge is normally acquired and used for a purpose. The purpose may be social, personal, cultural or professional, but in each case the acquisition of knowledge typically has a purpose beyond the act of acquisition itself, even if that purpose is only personal pleasure or gratification of desire. In the most complex cases, knowledge acquisition is the basis for the generation of additional knowledge. The scientist reads a scientific paper and incorporates its contents into his own knowledge and understanding of the subject. If the reader is an active researcher, the newly acquired knowledge may be incorporated into further research which will generate additional knowledge which is then put into public domain in its turn. The user thus becomes a creator, and the creator is also a user. The processes of creation, transmission and use are thus in an interactive relationship rather than being a linear continuum.

The practical aspect of these theoretical considerations is that the perspectives of individual players in the process may change according to the role which they happen to be playing at the time. The creator wants to put newly generated knowledge into public domain, and the user wants access to it. But creators also want to protect some aspects of what they have created; they want to be given credit for their creations, and they want to protect them from inappropriate use or misrepresentation. They may even seek some financial gain from the work which they have done. The balance between the rights of creators and the interests of users is the conflict which is regulated by the law of intellectual property, whose future is one of many aspects of the management of information in the public sphere which is being called into question by the consequences of technological change.[7]

# Paying for it all – the *really* difficult questions

The familiar business models of traditional publishing are comparatively simple. In the case of the typical scientific journal or academic monograph the author writes, the publisher publishes, the librarian buys and the user reads. In general trade publishing, the user may buy as well as read, or the book may be bought as a gift, but these and multitudes of other minor variations do not change the fundamental business process. Historically, the publisher was the provider of the capital and the expertise which sustained the publishing process. The input may have varied in the extent of the publisher's control of content (from almost absolute for general trade non-fiction, to almost none for a scientific journal), but the principles involved were essentially unchanged. The difficulty is that this business model is conceptually closer to a simple linear model than it is to the interactive model of knowledge creation and transfer which was proposed earlier (Figure 13.2). This creates a further difficulty. If interactivity more accurately represents what happens in electronic publishing, then the e-publishing business models need to articulate more closely with current reality.

New business models are, of course, being developed. Publishers of electronic journals are now typically offering packages rather than simple

**Figure 13.2**    Linear knowledge transfer.

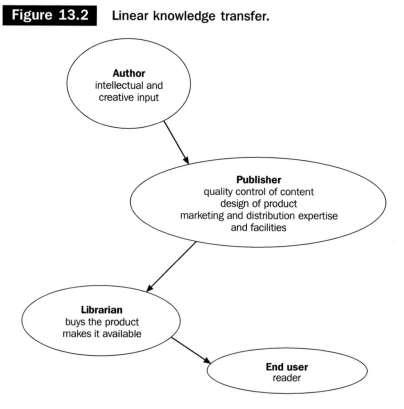

subscriptions. The largest is a dual subscription to hard copy and online access, but it can be as little as buying access to individual articles on a pay-per-view basis. Access may be confined to a single site or be licensed for distribution across a whole campus or institution, or even to members of the institution when they are off-site.[8] This is a very different world from that of the traditional serials agent chasing missing issues for librarians!

A recent study undertaken on behalf of the Joint Information Services Committee (JISC) of the higher education funding bodies in the UK found that librarians and publishers had very different perspectives on both the problem and the solution. Put crudely, the librarians wanted to maximise access, while the publishers wanted to maximise profits. The consultants proposed a whole series of theoretical models, some of which are already being used by publishers. The key question, however, remains whether the publishers can continue to provide the research community with the journals it wants at a price which it can afford. Solutions which appeal to the academic sector and its financially hard-pressed librarians include the idea of national licences for universities and colleges to access particular serials, and the so-called 'core + peripheral' approach in which the publisher offers an institution a bundle of core titles, with access to others on a pay-per-view basis. Publishers naturally favour packages which maximise their income, which means subscribing to large numbers of titles, or paying high access fees.[9] This however perpetuates the long-standing problem of buying content of which only a small proportion will ever be consulted in any given library. Solutions can be modelled, but we are some way away from wholly satisfactory and generally acceptable schemes. Indeed, it seems unlikely that there will be a unique answer to the question. One size will never fit all. The world-class research university and the smaller specialised institution will always have very different needs. The former may well be able to use their collective financial muscle to work in consortia to obtain the best possible deals from publishers. Smaller or less wealthy institutions have a very different problem, and may gradually find themselves excluded from the research community for this reason alone.

# The forgotten stakeholders: academic authors and readers

The attempt to adapt traditional subscription models to electronic journals accessed online is only one approach. The alternative is the more radical concept of open access, in which – to a greater or lesser extent – the producer community and the user community overlap and even begin to merge. Consortia of universities, research funding bodies and learned societies can actually manage the whole process of funding, researching, peer reviewing and dissemination without any intervention from a publisher. Consortia and cooperatives are a *de facto* recognition of the near-impossibility of distinguishing between the author and user communities for specialised research journals. For these researchers there are only two requirements of a publication system: that they have access as both readers and contributors, and that they can rely on the quality of the content. Researcher-driven consortia facilitate this. Moreover, there is a clear historical precedent. Despite differences in terminology, learned societies have been doing precisely this since the middle of the nineteenth century. This is hardly surprising as such societies are membership organizations. It is no accident that it was scientific societies such as the Royal Society of Chemistry and the Institute of Physics which were among the pioneers of electronic journal publishing, reflecting the wishes and needs of their members.[10]

It has been argued that new virtual communities have emerged among researchers because of their collaboration in producing their own electronic journal literature.[11] It is also the case that new business models are being developed which revolve around authors or research-led organizations. A new model for the traditional learned society journal is perhaps to be found in the *New Journal of Physics*, published jointly by the Institute of Physics in the UK and the Deutsche Physikalische Gesselschaft in Germany. The research community itself – through these two prestigious societies – determined that its preferred business model was that authors should pay a fee of US$500 for the publication of their peer-reviewed papers. This effectively allowed the two societies to eliminate commercial publishers from the process. Physicists as authors thus took control of the publication of their work. Physicists as readers, meanwhile, had the advantage of instantaneous online access, including immediate publication of accepted papers.[12] The 'author pays' model, although adapted from established page-charging process which prevailed for print-on-paper journals in some scientific disciplines, is really a new way of funding journal publication which takes account of the realities of open access and of the imperative to publish. It has become widespread in the biosciences, and is rapidly spreading through other research communities[13].

New business models which involve publication by third parties, such as learned societies or consortia of researchers and publishers, have been devised, and are broadly acceptable to the research community. This, however, is only one aspect of what is happening. Genuinely open-access electronic archives have existed since the 1990s, exemplified by ArXiv, an e-print archive developed by the physics community which has been operational since 1991. While it has not fundamentally changed how the literature is used, it has greatly facilitated use, and has become a critical element in the international system of communication in the discipline.[14] The most recent development is that of the institutional repository. The principle is simple: authors of published papers deposit an electronic copy in the repository of the institution by which they are employed. The repository itself is open access. There has been considerable political pressure behind this idea, to the extent that the UK research councils are now insisting on deposit, with the support of the British government.[15] The system is rapidly being adopted in the United States.[16] Publishers are less comfortable than scholars with this rapid progress. They have been deploying a number of arguments including the alleged difficulties of access. Their underlying concern, however, is that open access and digital repositories are destabilising the business model of the publication system[17] while at same time creating additional problems about intellectual property rights[18] and possibly about long-term preservation and access.[19]

# The not-quite-forgotten stakeholders: librarians

The development of new business models to support open access to electronic resources has largely been driven by the demands of the almost indistinguishable communities of knowledge creators and knowledge users in the research domain. The reduction in the role of the commercial intermediaries – the publishers, booksellers, distributors and agents – is obvious. But other changes are also taking place. The other non-commercial intermediaries – the librarians and information officers – are also facing radical change. The university library is no longer the only point of access to the research literature. Indeed, in most universities in the industrialised world, desk-top Internet access is now the norm. Researchers barely need to leave their offices in order to access the literature. This is not only true of secondary literature. Primary research data in many fields is also available online, including data sets and primary research resources. This is not only true in the sciences. Social data is available electronically from government departments, international organizations and independent bodies. The are full-text databases of sources as diverse as the works of Shakespeare and the US Census. The library could become no more than a book storage depot and a working-space for students.

The positive approach is that the library remains at the centre of the university's information resource provision, but it offers access points and network management rather than materials and physical access. Indeed, librarians have been at the forefront of many of the developments in the scientific publication system, bringing their professional expertise in information management to bear on key issues such as retrieval systems. The library is typically the manager of the institutional repository, and thus takes on the role of publisher as well as information provider. In practice, libraries in universities and other research institutions are now information providers, access points and quasi-publishers all bundled into one set of activities. It is another consequence of technology-driven change in the process of scholarly communication.

# The *really* forgotten stakeholders: readers and public libraries

Public libraries, at least in the English-speaking world, have always had a dual role as providers of both information and entertainment. While not catering for highly specialised scientific or scholarly users – seeing that as the business of university and research libraries – they have always tried to provide for a wide range of interests and to offer a multiplicity of resources. For more than thirty years, this has included diversification into each generation of new media. There is substantial evidence to suggest that those libraries which pioneered innovative services have been among the most successful in the sector.[20,21] The public demand is there. Moreover, there has historically been some overlap between the literature sought by the general public and that used by scholars and scientists. General trade publishers are familiar with works – particularly in disciplines like history – which attract a significant market but are also used for learning and research purposes in higher education. Even some scientific journals – *Nature*, or *Scientific American* – fall into this overlap category.

The potential loss of public access to the overlap literature must be a matter of serious social concern.[22] Journals with large circulations are not, of course, at risk, and the highly specialised small-circulation journals are not those for which there is a wider demand. But it remains the case that as the scientific community in particular, and the scholarly research community in general, takes greater control of its own communications systems, the effect is, albeit unintentionally, to create zones of exclusion. At a time when the UK research councils, and many of their equivalents in other countries, are increasingly concerned to demonstrate the public benefit derived from publicly-funded research, this has significant political implications.

## An inconclusive conclusion

There are no easy answers. New systems of information dissemination, whether through online access to databases or by using new variations of older technologies such as on-demand printing, have changed the relationships between those involved in the processes. In the research community, the recognition of the close convergence of interest between authors and readers is diminishing or fundamentally changing the roles of the traditional intermediaries, the publishers and the librarians. In the wider public sector, the issues have barely begun to be considered. Pioneering public provision of new services and new media has proved to be immensely popular, but it has often been achieved (for financial reasons) at the expense of the provision of traditional services which are still highly valued by the public at large. The revolution in scientific communications has largely been achieved by the scientists themselves. Perhaps the user community – the taxpayers – will be the drivers of policy in public libraries as they too adapt to a new world of communication and information.

## Notes

1.  Foster, A. (1995) 'The emergence of convergence', *Library Manager* 11: 12–3.
2.  Brewer, G. (2003) 'Convergence for the right reasons', *Multimedia Information and Technology* 29(4): 107–9.

3. Pugh, L. (1997) *Convergence in Academic Support Services*. London: The British Library Research and Innovation Report, 54.

4. Field, C. D. (2001) 'Theory and practice: reflections on convergence in United Kingdom universities', *Liber Quarterly* 11(3): 267–89.

5. Andrews, A. M. and Ellis, D. (2005) 'The changing nature of work in library and information services in the UK: an analysis', *Education for Information* 23(1,2): 57–77.

6. Shannon, C. E. and Weaver, W. (1949) *The Mathematical Theory of Communication*. Illinois: University of Illinois Press.

7. Clausen, H. (2004) 'Intellectual property, the Internet and libraries', *New Library World* 105(11,12): 417–22.

8. Boissy, R. W. (2005) 'Business models for scholarly serials', *Serials Review* 31(3): 185–6.

9. Look, H., Sparks, S. and Henderson, H. (2005) 'Business models for e-journals: reconciling library and publisher requirements', *Serials* 18(2): 157–61.

10. Welham, R. (1990) 'Why I publish – a learned society', *Serials* 3(2): 34–7.

11. Warr, W. A. (1998) 'Communication and communities of chemists', *Journal of Chemical Information and Computer Sciences* 38(6): 966–75.

12. Haynes, J. (1999) 'New Journal of Physics: a web-based and author funded journal', *Learned Publishing* 12(4): 265–9.

13. Willinsky, J. (2006) *The Access Principle. The case for open access to research and scholarship*. The MIT Press, p. 214.

14. Brown, C. (2001) 'The e-volution of preprints in the scholarly communication of physicists and astronomers', *Journal of the American Society for Information Science* 53(2): 187–200.

15. Oppenheim, C. (2005) 'Open access and the UK Science and Technology Select Committee report Free for All?', *Journal of Librarianship and Information Science* 37(1): 3–6.

16. Lynch, C. and Lippincott, J. K. (2005) 'Institutional repository deployment in the United States as of early 2005', *D-Lib Magazine* 11(9).

17. Richardson, M. (2005) 'Post-print archives: parasite or symbiont', *Learned Publishing* 18(3): 221–3.

18. Greig, M. (2005) 'Repositories and copyright?: experiences from the DAEDALUS project', *ALISS Quarterly* 1(1): 24–7.

19. Takeuchi, H. (2005) 'Institutional repositories and preservation of digital resources', *Journal of Information Processing and Management* 48(7): 462–4.

20. Batt, C. (1999) 'I have seen the future and IT works', *Library Review* 48(1,2): 11–17.
21. Patterson, T. (2001) '"Ideas Stores": London's new libraries', *Library Journal* 126(8): 48–9.
22. Willinsky, op. cit.

# 14

# New text technologies, globalization and the future of the book

*Bill Cope and Mary Kalantzis*

## The changing business of manufacturing words

Of all second millennium inventions, it is the book that has most defined the shape of the modern world. The creation of the first printed book in 1450 by a jeweller in Mainz, Germany, Johannes Gutenberg, became the basis of modern mass literacy, and thus the basis of modern education, modern democracy, modern science and a modern consciousness and general awareness of peoples and places well beyond the immediate and the local.

This is the common view, and although occasionally contested (was not the invention of the compass more important? asks the renowned historian, Fernand Braudel), it does not seem too much of an exaggeration. However, writing was not itself invented at that moment, nor even books. Before that time, an elaborate written culture had developed around scribed books.

Actually, the world-defining thing that Gutenberg did was not to invent the book in its modern form, so much as to invent two fundamental aspects of modern manufacturing (and thus, in another perhaps more important but less immediately recognizable way, the modern world). The first was the idea that you could tackle complexity by modularisation. Rather than having to make whole things by hand – a hand carved wood-block to be printed, for instance, or the page of a scribed book –

it was possible to mass manufacture and assemble the component parts. In the case of Gutenberg's first press, he put his jeweller's craft skills to work making moulds from which he could produce the characters of the alphabet, thus defining the character, for the most practical of reasons, as the modular unit of the technology of manufactured writing for the next five hundred years.

Gutenberg's second great manufacturing idea was mass production. There was an extraordinarily high cost to producing the first printed book of a run compared to the one-off copy of a hand-crafted book. However, this would be offset by the minimal per unit cost of the rest of a run, and the longer the run, the lower the per unit cost. Gutenberg's was the first of all modern mass production systems, and as its corollary came mass consumption. It was not just a matter of manufacturing lots of books for an ever-broadening reading public, but, necessarily, lots of the same books. Put simply, the more of the same, the better. The impact of this technology was immediate. Within fifty years, there were print shops in every sizeable town in Europe, and eight million books had been printed.[1]

Now, five hundred and fifty years later, we are in the midst of another technological revolution, the digital revolution. And once again, people are saying that the computer and the Internet are defining technologies – technologies that will change the world. Indeed, the more optimistic among us are making claims about the personal computer, increasingly interconnected through the worldwide networking of the Internet, which sound very much like the claims made for the printing press. Digital technologies are another impetus to the spread of literacy; they will make education more accessible through online learning resources and online delivery; they are a new agent of democracy; they are tools for the advancement of the modern scientific community; they are an invention that makes our consciousness truly global. Again, this common view may not be too much of an exaggeration.

But, in one sense, the digital revolution only does many things that have been done before. It is not so revolutionary at all. For instance, the Internet does much of what books have already been doing for a long time. Books are extended texts built with writing sometimes aided by visuals, and as such can be defined by their structural devices. A book needs to be defined, not as a product, but as an information architecture. This exceptionally complex architecture can include a number of characteristic elements – the book title, author attribution, contents, chapters, headings and subheadings, references and an index. Importantly, too, a book does not begin and end at is covers, despite the deceptive appearances of its physical manifestation. It sits in a precise place in the world of other books, either literally, in the case of libraries, driven by sophisticated subject cataloguing systems, or more profoundly in the form of the apparatuses of attribution (referencing) and subject definition (contents and indexes). Books have elaborate ways of bursting out of their covers, of always referring to the world outside their covers, including to other books. This relationship to other writing and other books comes to be regulated by the laws, conventions and ethics of copyright, plagiarism, quotation, citation, attribution and fair use.

The texts of the Internet may not, by and large, be as long as books (although many are) However, the Internet adds nothing of significance to the structural devices of the book, nor to the protocols developed throughout the history of the book to interlink a particular book with the world to which it refers (subject, contents, index) and to other books (quotations, references, acknowledgment of sources). For all the hype in hypertext, it only does what books have always done, which is to point to connections outside of a particular text. And the search function only does what indexes and tables of contents have always done. Moreover, the idea that books are linear and the Internet is lateral is based on the assumption that readers of books necessarily read in a linear way. In fact, the devices of contents, indexing and referencing were designed precisely for lateral readings, hypertextual readings, if you like. And the idea that the book is a text with a neat beginning and a neat end, unlike the Internet, which is an endless, seamless web of cross-linkages, is to judge the book by its cover. See beyond the deceptive appearance of those covers, and the world of books and libraries is as seamlessly cross-linked as the Web. As for the hyperbole of the 'virtual', this revolution has long-since become commonplace, beginning in fact with the book itself as a communication technology, and one by means of which during the course of the second half of the last millennium people were brought so strangely close to distant and exotic places though the representation of those places in the words and images on the printed page. So vivid, indeed, was the representation that you could be excused for thinking you were virtually there.

Certainly, some things are different about the Internet in this regard. Clicking a hypertext link is faster and easier than leafing through cross-referenced pages or dashing to the library to find a reference. But this difference is a matter of degree, not a qualitative difference. In fact, the Internet sorely needs some of the skills of the old book trade. Compared to a library catalogue and a good book index, even the best of search engines seems rudimentary. The Internet is also a place where the quality of texts is at best uneven because copyright questions have been poorly resolved and the practices of editing and publishing have not yet been developed to the extent they have for the printed book. So, for all its dazzle, the Internet is not really that different to a book, and mostly still, not even as smart as a book.

However, if there is something very new about the digital environment, it is its ability to overturn the two fundamentals of Gutenberg's revolution. If Gutenberg's first revolution in the manufacture of written and visual meanings was in the areas of modularisation and mass production, we are now on the edge of a second revolution. The full shape and consequences of this revolution are as yet barely visible. And paradoxically (as we argue in this book), it is a revolution that may well breathe new life into the book, not only as an information architecture, but even its printed manifestation.

The first revolutionary thing about the Gutenberg invention was its modularisation of text as a manufacturing technique, and in this process, the creation of the character as the elementary modular unit. The consequence was that the meanings on the page of a book were very much bound into written language, and mostly the one, standardised national form of a written language at that. For technological reasons, images and text did not sit easily on the same page. This was the beginning of the dramatic rise to dominance of language – and the written word in particular – in modern societies. The burgeoning world of books, created, as Eisenstein argues, a shift from an image culture to word culture.[2] Gunther Kress argues that our focus on language and writing is a peculiarly modern thing.[3] With their graphic representations of Biblical stories, Catholic and Orthodox churches reflected the dominance of the visual in the pre-literate world. By contrast, the enthusiastically modernising Protestant 'people of The Word' removed all 'graven images' from their places of worship, and the focus of religious experience became a personal encounter with the written text. Gutenberg's modularisation of meaning to the written character, was one of the things that made the world a word-driven place, or at the very least, made our fetish for writing and word-centredness practicable.

The personal computer and the Internet change this entirely. The elementary modular manufacturing unit is the bit, equally capable of creating characters or images, all by placing pixels (picture elements) somewhere – on a screen, or on a page – pixel by pixel to render a character, and pixel by pixel to render an image. This revolution began in the third quarter of the twentieth century, with the mix of early digitization and the photo-engraving processes linked to offset print, both of which made it much easier than ever to put images and text on the same page. Before this, because visuals and text were best manufactured separately, they were mostly bound in different sections of a book. And so, we begin a journey in which visual culture is revived, albeit in very new forms, and written-textual culture itself is more closely integrated with visual culture.

Meanwhile, the very manufacturing process means that text no longer needs to be bound, by virtue of the elementary unit of modularisation, to the character set of a particular national language. The pixels can just as easily be arranged in any font, from any language. Indeed, the emerging international character set, Unicode, mixes ideographs and characters as though they were interchangeable – the ninety-odd characters of Roman upper and lower case and punctuation, pale into insignificance amongst the 94,000 characters representing most human symbologies, including every Chinese character as well as the international symbol-language which includes modern pictograms such as 'no entry' and 'recycled product'.

The other radical shift away from Gutenberg technology is the end that the digital era puts to the manufacturing logic of mass production. Take the fully digital printing process. Every page can be different to the preceding page, and every book different to the previous book, and at no greater cost than identical consecutive books and pages. Economies of scale are flat. The first copy off the press costs the same to manufacture as the thousandth. This makes digital printing a fundamentally different technology in its commercial and cultural logic, to all preceding technologies for manufacturing words and images. There is no difference in cost between running 5,000 copies of the same book, 100 copies of each of 50 different books, or even one copy of 5,000 different books. The consequences for book printing, and culture, are enormous.

Here is a bold commercial hypothesis: the total number of books produced in the 3,000 plus run-length range (what is normally considered the lower limit for economical production of traditionally printed books) may well be equalled by the pent-up supply of, and demand for, books in the 1 to 3,000 range. The number of titles may expand by a factor of hundreds or even thousands (and that is no more challenging in terms of information explosion than the number of books currently in print – the trick will still be to search and select and cross-reference effectively). These new titles, we are hypothesising, may add up to as many or more than the total number of printed books produced today.

As for cultural logic, the consequences may be just as extraordinary. Instead of a world where success (cultural and commercial) is measured according to the formula many times the same, success will arise just as easily through multiplying many by different. Small cultures, expert knowledge communities, bizarre interests and obscure languages will all thrive.

At least, this is what digital technology such as fully digital printing promise in theory. In practice, economies of scale are not flat because there are procedures required to get the book run-of-one on to the digital press (dealing with the customer, taking the disc and plugging it in, running the book on the machine, invoicing and dispatching the book). Flat economies of scale will only be achieved with automated file and production flow, from the creator to the consumer. Only then will the process, from a commercial and technological point of view, be friction-free. Only then will the advantages of mass customisation be realised and niche markets served in a way that fully realises the potential of the new technologies.

So here is a scenario completely within sight in terms of today's technologies. A consumer enters an online bookstore (or a bookstore proprietor, on a consumer's prompting, comes into a publisher's online warehouse), and orders a single book. The bookstore/warehouse is in fact a repository of book files, created through the online interaction of author and publisher/editor. This triggers a print order for a book printer to print, bind, pack, and dispatch the book to the delivery address. The process is totally automated, as individual books are automatically batched and queued. On dispatch, payments are made according to an agreement created as part of the online author/publisher relationship, including royalties and payments to the printer and the publisher. The whole costly, inefficient and fundamentally unsatisfactory infrastructure of long run printing, warehousing, distribution and retailing has been done away with. And, from a production and distribution point of view, it makes no difference in terms of per unit production cost whether a title sells one copy or a hundred thousand (so long as, somehow or other, whether its by selling one title or a hundred thousand different titles, a hundred thousand copies are sold, to cover the cost of the infrastructure).

Of course, from the author and publisher's points of view, there will always economies of scale, and these relate to the author's and the publisher's time. But authors and publishing communities' motivations are not always simply commercial. They have things to say in the world (political or poetic), or the commercial benefits may be secondary (an academic career or the instruction manual for a large and complex one-off product). And, even with primarily commercial aims in which the parties might well want to cost the author's and publisher's time into the cost of the run, the new technologies remove all other risk, thus allowing riskier ventures and rewarding small commercial successes (the $40 book which ends up selling 500 copies). In fact, with the author and (to a lesser extent, in terms of total time input) the publisher now being the primary risk takers, their rewards will surely be greater.

The book was instrumental in the creation of the modern world, in the development of its systems of production, as well as capably documenting its own cultural effects. With the Internet and electronic text, the pundits say, the book is dead. However, the paradox is that the book is a lead product once again, and in ways which would have been unimaginable even a decade ago. Apart from software and hardware (and we can leave these out, as here the technological medium are the commercial product), books are the lead product on the Internet. The aptly named Amazon.com is the world's largest online retailer, and it began with books. This is because books are such a highly niched product: a market that is, so the expression goes, an inch deep and a mile wide. The mix of technological developments involved in digital book production have the potential to make the market so wide and so thin that there is no depth and the width can barely be measured. This is the quintessential market of the future, where every product is niched and every service customised.

# Globalization's new potentials

The word 'globalization' describes many of the contradictory forces driving change at the beginning of the twenty-first century. Some of these forces are socially and economically objective; others are highly emotive and political. The more objective forces of globalization are palpable, and their rapid rise can be measured by:

- the increasing proportion of total production which daily and yearly crosses borders;

- the proportion of local capital which is not locally owned;

- the increasing amount of human movement in the form of international travel;

- the sheer scale of labour and refugee migrations which have created multicultural societies around the world;

- the rapid increase in direct, person-to-person international communication in the form of mail, telephone calls and electronic communications; and

- the movement of cultural products and ideas across borders through the media and publishing industries.

Globalization also manifests itself as a highly emotive force, and in this form it has become part of an undeniably political reality. The emotive force of globalization is no less real, even if it is not so clearly measurable. We can count how many international phone calls are made in a day, or the number of books imported and exported. But it is not so easy to measure people's level of wellbeing or anxiety around the ideas and realities of globalization, even though the political effects of the anxieties are very real.

In technological and economic terms, some people see globalization as a harbinger of progress: as a source of investment; as a carrier of new technologies which improve people's work and home lives; and as a force which gradually improves the lot of the poor even though it seems to improve the lot of the rich more rapidly. However, others see these technological and economic forces as regressive – as the root cause of foreign domination and the diminishing of local self-governance and democracy; as a displacer of local skills and technologies; and as a force that only serves to exacerbate disparities of wealth and privilege.

In cultural terms, the argument is no less heated. Some believe the cultural forces of globalization help create open, cosmopolitan, multicultural societies, and a sense of citizenship built on a world-consciousness capable of handling issues which cannot or will not be tackled adequately by nation-states – environmental sustainability, human rights and fair trade. However, others believe that the cultural forces of globalization ride roughshod over local cultures and languages, even to the point of destroying them.

The publishing and communications industries find themselves at the heart of the processes of globalization, torn between alternative interpretations of its meaning and significance. This is an area where we may well ask the question of whether global technology drivers enable, or whether they make things more difficult for local industries. In a world economy and a competitive local economy, there is often little alternative but to invest in the best and latest tools, and in a small countries these are almost entirely imported. But this very act of importing technology has immediate consequences. It means that an importing country has no particular technological edge over the source countries and other countries who have imported the same technologies, whilst at the same time being disadvantaged in relation to low labour cost countries, whether they choose to invest in the latest technologies or not. Also, the technologies are often highly loaded in cultural terms, and one example of this discussed in this book is the dominance of roman scripts and the English language through the ASCII (American Standard Code for Information Interchange) character framework, which is still the basis of most computing and text manufacturing technologies. Technology, all too easily, becomes an ally of the cultural drivers of globalization that often seem to do enormous damage to local cultural and linguistic diversity. This technology also seems to work in concert with commercial drivers. Publishing is increasingly dominated by global companies whose interest is in bottom lines more than it is local creators, and whose investment decisions are often made in the capitals of the Anglophone publishing world: New York and London.

The remainder of this chapter sets out to argue two things: first, that the technological, commercial and cultural forces of globalization are moving into a very complex phase in which the effects on the publishing industry may be in some senses counter-intuitive, and certainly not those predicted in many of the more emotive and political responses of recent times. The forces of globalization need not fortify and extend the technological, commercial and cultural domination of multinational corporations, the United States and the English language. Or, at the very least, they might not only do this. Equally, they could be agents that foster increasing cultural diversity, greater local commercial autonomy, and the revival of local and ancestral languages and cultures. In this book, we illustrate this latter possibility with one small example – the evolution of multilingual text creation technologies during the most recent phase of globalization.

# Globalization and language

English, the supporters and opponents of globalization argue with equal vehemence, is becoming a world language, a lingua mundi, as well as a common language, a lingua franca, of global communications and commerce. An estimated one billion of the world's population now speaks English, the majority as a second language. Meanwhile, the world's language diversity is dramatically decreasing. It is estimated that one and a half indigenous Australian languages disappear every year, as the last speakers of those languages die. At the current rate, between 60 and 90 per cent of the world's 6,000 languages will disappear by the end of this century.

Yet here is a paradox: recent developments in information and communications technologies may reverse this trend. Just as English appears to be becoming more important, there are signs that it may become less important. The proportion of the world's websites in English has been in permanent decline since the invention of the Internet as an almost English-only place. The proportion of the books published in English is reducing as demand for books slowly grows in rough proportion to population growth in English speaking markets, whilst at the same time massively unmet needs are gradually satisfied in rapidly growing and modernising non-English language markets, such as those of Asia.

More importantly, however, new technologies make language difference a less important factor in social communication and multilingualism the norm. We will illustrate this with one simple example: e-commerce enabled banking using a variety of machine interfaces – the automatic teller machine (ATM), Internet banking or automated telephone banking using computer-generated audio. Banking is a complex modern form of social communication. I have money, I give it to the bank to keep, and when I ask for some of it back, I make a formal application, and, if approved, the bank says so and gives it to me. This is a kind of conversational structure, carried out in the traditional shopfront bank by a complex array of written documentation, supported by actual conversations which frame the details of the transaction and give context to the written documentation. In the world of banking before electronic commerce, this was a heavily language bound activity. You had to fill out a withdrawal slip that was almost invariably only available in the 'national' language of the bank, and then speak to a teller in that language. Occasionally, in deference to multiculturalism and to make a mark on niche markets, banks would make sure there were some bilingual tellers, in order to conduct transactions with Japanese tourists, or to serve immigrant languages heavily represented in a local neighbourhood. But there were practical limits to this, the principal of which is the number of languages that can be practically serviced by a local bank.

e-Commerce enabled banking – the ATM, online banking, and automated phone banking – changes all of that. Various highly routine and predictable conversations, such as the 'I want some of my money' conversation, or the 'I want to know how much money I have left' conversation, do not really (despite appearances) happen in English. They happen through a translation of the routine operation of withdrawing funds, or seeking an account balance, into a series of computer-generated prompts. The way these prompts are realised in a particular language is arbitrary. There is nothing particular about the language of the conversation. Semantics and grammar, or meaning and information structure, are everything. The logic of the communicative exchange now operates above the level of language. Various 'banking conversations' are constructed as a universal, transnational, translinguistic code (actually, computer code, because the customer is talking to the bank's computer), in which the language manifestation of that code is, in a communicative sense, trivial. You can choose any language you like at the beginning of the online banking session and the visible 'tags' describing the effect of pressing alternative buttons will be translated into your language of choice. There is nothing to stop this being in any script; or the screen swapping its directionality if you were to choose Arabic; or non-written and non-visual interfaces, such as Braille, or interfaces translating audio to text. The ATM and telephone 'phone banking' do the same thing, working off the same e-commerce abstracted text. The rendering of the meaning and even the words of the text can be different; but the meaning-structure and semantics are the same. The business of making the banking service available in another language is as simple as translating the tags – a few hundred words at the most, and putting them into the system as writing or recording computer-generated speech for telephone banking. Once, the grammar of language was the entry point into the grammar of banking – if the customer and the bank were not able to operate competently in the same conversational, written and thus cultural world, there could be no transaction. Banking was a language-specific game, no less and no more, and the prescribed language or languages were a non-negotiable precondition for playing the banking game. However, in the world of e-commerce, the grammar of banking is created first, and this grammar can be realised in any language. Not only is this a completely different way of doing business; it is also a totally new way of thinking about communication and, even more importantly, making communication work.

Coming back to the big-picture questions of globalization, this example captures something quite contradictory. On the one hand, billions of people have been drawn into the culture of ATMs since they were introduced in the last quarter of the twentieth century. To use a term defined and developed by the linguist Jim Gee, they have become proficient speakers of a 'social language',[4] which we might call 'global ATM' or 'electronic banking'. The particular language-form in which this social discourse is realised for a particular transaction is, measured in terms of human action and social meaning, an arbitrary and trivial accident of birth. Yes, the culture of electronic commerce and modern banking is taking over the world, making the world the same, and doing it multilingually might be seen as a kind of ploy. But this move does meet one of the accusations of the forces opposing globalization – it improves access for outsiders. And, at least for this kind of communication, it has become less necessary to learn the dominant language. Now you can play the global banking game, but you don't have to homogenise to be in it. You can be in a country where your language is not spoken in banks, and it doesn't matter because you can go to an ATM or ring telephone banking and deal with computer-audio, or, if needs be, a live operator in a call centre somewhere in the world who speaks your language. This is just one small and symptomatic example of the way in which new communications technologies will support language diversity, and make it less important in many settings to know a lingua franca such as English.

The first generation of digital technologies emerged in a close fit with monolingual publishing. They were based on ASCII rendering of the Roman alphabet. If translation were to occur, it would be through another publisher who purchases rights for a different market and who republishes the work there. And the rendering technology – the printed book with its heavy upfront costs and economies of scale – favoured large languages and affluent markets.

Second-generation digital technologies change much of this dynamic in five areas:

- The development of new font rendering systems.

- The convergence of linguistic and visual text creation tools.

- Text discovery and text structuring systems based on multilingual metadata.

- Machine translation and machine-mediated human translation.

- Flat economies of scale in digital text rendering.

## 1.  New font rendering systems

The ASCII framework consists of 94 characters – upper and lower case in the English alphabet, numerals and punctuation marks. An 8-bit character encoding system is capable of storing each of these letters as a unique pattern of up to eight zeros and ones. A whole character in a simple character set like those used for English normally 'costs' the space in memory of 1 byte, the basic unit for measuring memory and file sizes on a computer. These characters can be rendered to screen or to print as a series of dots (pixels), the number of dots depending on the image clarity required. An 8 bit (1 byte) encoding system, however, cannot represent more than a theoretical 256 characters. To represent languages with larger character sets, such as those of languages whose writing system is ideographic, specialised 2 byte systems were created. However, these remained, for all intents and purposes, separate, and designed for localised country and language use. Extensions to the ASCII 1 byte framework were created to include characters and diacritica from languages other than English whose base character set was Roman. But non-Roman scripting systems remained in their own 2 byte world. As the relationship between each character and the pattern of zeros and ones is arbitrary, and as the various systems were not necessarily created to talk to each other, different computer systems were often incompatible with each other.

For a second generation of digital technologies, a universal character system has been created called 'Unicode' in which every character and symbol in every human language is represented in a consolidated 2 byte system (*http://www.unicode.org*). The 8 zeros and ones which represent the 26 lower case letters of the Roman alphabet are now embedded in a new sixteen-bit character encoding, and are now a mere 26 characters amongst the 94,140 characters of Unicode 3.1. These Unicode characters not only capture every character in every human language, they also capture archaic languages – Linear B, a precursor to Greek found on clay tablets in Crete, has recently been added. It also captures panoply mathematical and scientific symbols. It captures geometric shapes often used in typesetting (squares, circles, dots and the like), and it captures pictographs, ranging from arrows, to international symbols such as the recycling symbol, to something so seemingly obscure as the 15 Japanese dentistry symbols.

The potential with Unicode is for every computer and every printer in the world to render text in any and every language and symbol system, and perhaps most significantly for a multilingual world, to render different scripts and symbologies on the same screen or the same page. The shift from a 1 byte to a 2 byte system increases the computer's memory requirements and decreases its speed proportionally, but measured against the pace of hardware developments in these areas, this shift is not important.

## 2.  *The visual and the textual*

The elemental modular unit for representing written language in the Gutenberg system was the character, and until the digitization of text at the end of the twentieth century, this remained the elemental unit. Types were cast as separate characters and then assembled into words and lines on formes. And the elementary modular unit for representing visuals was the whole image – originally a hand engraving, and most recently, a photoengraving. These technologies and processes for manufacturing printed words and images were entirely different. In fact, as argued in Book 1, until offset printing, it made a lot of practical sense to keep words and images separate. In the case of a book, for instance, this was achieved by printing the text and the plates in separate sections.

Digital technologies make it remarkably easy to put the images and words together, and this is in part because text and images are built on the same elemental modular unit. The elemental unit of computer-rendered text is an abstraction in computer code made up of perhaps eight (e.g. ASCII) or sixteen (e.g. Unicode) bits. This is then rendered visually through the mechanised arrangement of dots, or pixels (picture elements) – a smallish number of dots rendering the particular design of the letter 'A' in 12 point Helvetica to a screen, and many more dots when rendering the same letter to a laser printer. Images are rendered in precisely the same way, as a series of dots in a particular combination differentiated range of halftones and colours. Whether they are text or images, the raw materials of digital design and rendering are all bits and pixels.

Thinking of the consequences of this change narrowly, in terms of the tools of the text creation trade, typesetting no longer even happens by itself. It has been replaced by desktop publishing in which textual and visual design happen on the same page for rendering on the same page. Even typing tools, such as Microsoft Word, have sophisticated methods for creating (drawing) and combining images.

More broadly, this convergence of linguistic and visual text creation tools facilitates and supports a shift in our communications environment which has been characterised by Gunther Kress as a movement towards visual representation and away from language.[3] We are living in a world that is becoming less reliant on words, or more precisely, a world in which words have to stand on their own, as though they are merely visual prompts. Sometimes the communication has become purely visual – it is possible to navigate an airport using the international pictographs. Other times, the visual and the linguistic are powerfully interwoven in a common communicative framework.[5]

Moving away from language, or moving away from language alone, is one aspect of globalization and multilingualism. Such a shift is a practical response to globalization in the case of airport signage where it is simply impossible to operate in the language of every traveller. It also reduces language to a less important part of the communications equation. The real meaning of a technical manual is in its structure and diagrams; and if the design of the manual text is kept to a minimum, it is a relatively inexpensive task to translate labels and text and insert this into the digitised pages. The real meaning (and most of the design work) in an architectural glossy is in the images, the plans and the technical data. Introductions, captions and other text are easily translated and inserted into the source file. Communications, in other words, are built on linguistically open visual templates, in which the text is no more than a secondary component.

Ron Scollon speaks of an emerging 'visual holophrastic language'. He derives the term 'holophrastic' from research on young children's language in which an enormous load is put on a word such as 'some' which can only be interpreted by a caregiver in a context of visual, spatial and experiential association. In today's globalised world, brand logos and brand names (to what language does the word 'SONY' belong? he asks), form an internationalised visual language. A visual holophrastic symbol brings with it a whole pile of visual, spatial and experiential associations, and these are designed to cross language barriers.[6]

## 3. Multilingual metadata

Metadata schemas use 'tagging' frameworks to describe the content of documents. In the case of documents locatable on the Internet, Dublin Core is one of the principal emerging standards (*http://dublincore.org*), and is typical of others. It contains a number of elements: title, creator, subject, description, publisher, contributor, date, resource type, format, resource identifier, source, language, relation, coverage and rights. The schema is designed to function as a kind of 'catalogue card' for the Internet, so that it becomes possible, for instance, to search for Benjamin Disraeli as an author (creator) because you want to locate one of his novels, as opposed to writings about Benjamin Disraeli as a British Prime Minister (subject) because you have an interest in British parliamentary history. The intention of Dublin Core is to develop resource discovery tools more sophisticated than the current search tools, which can do little more than search indiscriminately for words and combinations of words.

This kind of a framework supports multilingualism in several ways. Firstly, it does not assume ('naturally') that the data will be in any particular language, presumably the language of point of search and entry. Even if you are working through an English language searching and cataloguing framework and the data happens to be in English, English will be specified. Data in any language sits within a common, multilingual resource description framework. Second, the tags are progressively being translated into a variety of languages. Although this may seem a small move in a practical sense, merely involving the translation of a few dozen terms for each additional language, conceptually it is a huge move. In fact, it turns a linguistically expressed term into a mere 'token' of a core concept that exists above and beyond any particular language. To achieve this, thesauri of terms are created in parallel across multiple languages in order to stabilise language tokens for each of the core concepts. This means that the metadata qualifier for locating an author is not really 'creator' at all, but the concept of creator which has been translated into however many languages, and is always marked by the same word from each of these languages.

The same potential exists for physical books. The online information transfer language, ONIX, is being developed to create a common platform for B-2-B and B-2-C e-commerce transactions for publishers and booksellers. However, being an initiative of the US and UK Publishing Associations, this is as yet an English-only framework. Creating one world for e-commerce in books is a matter of translating the ONIX tags.

The most advanced of contemporary dedicated book creation tools, such as DocBook, build text around the book as a structural architecture, rather than the book as a physical product whose structure is merely seen in the visual rendering. They also radically blur the distinction between data and metadata. 'Creator' is not only a metadata concept; it is possibly an instruction to render the creator's name on the title page of the book. Metadata does not only sit outside of the data; it creates rules that automate the manufacture of alternative renderings. The printed book will be rendered in one way, the html text another, the e-book for a reading tablet another, the talking-book another. But the creator will always be the creator and the rendering will always make it clear that this particular set of words does, in fact, represent the name of the creator. DocBook supports Unicode characters within the data. The revolutionary step (and technically quite straightforward) will occur when the tags that structure the text – title, chapter heading, subheading, table of contents and so on – are available in multiple languages and scripts, and the translation of these tags is stabilised by convention. Then it will be possible to write a book in any language or script in the world, and print it on any printer.

In a globalised and multilingual world, Ron Scollon argues, social languages or discourses are more similar across languages than within languages.[6] The way academics write in English and Japanese is very similar in terms of the structure of their texts and the ways those texts describe the world. A DocBook framework for structuring academic text, which may include elaborate referencing, keyword, indexing and abstracting apparatuses, will work across languages if the tags are translated, and this is because the most important thing about the discourse, and the final document, does not sit inside a particular language. Text structured and rendered using tools such as DocBook is a perfect platform for multilingual, multi-script publishing in communities more and more defined by discourse (what they want to do in the world, as expressed in peculiar ways of communicating about the world) than by the accident of mother tongue.

## 4. Machine translation

Into this environment, more than fortuitously, steps machine translation. Despite the enormous complexities of human language, machine translation tools can now provide the gist of the meaning of a written text. Some of these, such as AltaVista's Babelfish, offer instantaneous online translations free. The Babelfish service is powered by Systran, one of the founding companies in the machine translation field, and offers nineteen language pairs (*http://babel.altavista.com*). Machine translation is getting progressively better, even though it may never equal human translation.

The gist of a text might be sufficient to justify a decision to pay for human translation. Systran, for instance, offers an online human translation service in alliance with Berlitz Globalnet in which any document below 2000 words will be translated and e-mailed back within twenty-four hours. Machine translation also makes the job quicker, particularly when it is linked to texts which have been deliberately designed for multilingual delivery, using such methods as controlled vocabularies, based on the translation of technical terms peculiar to a particular field.

The range of language pairs available in online human translation services is still limited. The potential, though is enormous. A researcher working on frogs in a rainforest in Laos wants to make a comparison with a similar tree frog in a Brazil. Using a resource discovery framework which operates multilingually, this researcher locates a chapter of a book about the Brazilian frog in Portuguese, decides from a machine translation of gist that this is an important reference, then finds a Portuguese-Laotian translator amongst the thousands of registered translators representing every imaginable language pair. The publisher then captures this translation forever.

Highly structured text frameworks for capturing data and metadata, along the lines of DocBook, will also help in the machine translation process, as well as, even more simply, making text of printed books available online in a format in which it is possible to undertake machine translation faithful to the text's structure and form.

## 5. Economies of scale in digital text rendering

Finally, the flat economies of scale in the new world of digital print and e-text convergence discussed in Book 2.1, make it possible for small languages and small cultures to express themselves through the book form. With the kinds of mass customisation systems envisaged in Book 2.3, the per unit cost of a digitally printed book is constant regardless of the run length. There is no effective distinction between long run and short run, niche markets and mass markets. If there is only a small market for a book of Chinese diasporic poetry, the cost of manufacture and publishing will no longer be an inhibitor to that book's production. The text creation process will occur online in an environment in which all the tagging and mark-up required to render the book to print and other formats can be seen in Chinese, in which the text itself can be written using Unicode, and in which the book, once published will be available in any online bookstore in the world.

To take another example of how this may provide opportunities and access for small cultures and small languages, East Timor faces a daunting challenge to replace Indonesian as the language of instruction in schools. The cost of producing textbooks is prohibitive. But a teacher with a single computer with metadata maker and structured text framework translated into Tetum, one of the main local languages, will be able to produce precisely the number of books needed, printed cheaply using digital print technology. It is these kinds of technologies, these kinds of possibilities, which might breathe new life into small and declining languages.

# Notes

1. Eisenstein, Elizabeth L. (1979) *The Printing Press as an Agent of Change: Communications and Cultural Transformation in Early-Modern Europe*. Cambridge: Cambridge University Press, p. 44.

2. Ibid., p. 67.

3. Kress, Gunther (2001) Issues for a Working Agenda in Literacy. In *Transformations in Language and Learning: Perspectives on Multiliteracies* eds M. Kalantzis and B. Cope. Melbourne: theLearner.com/Common Ground Publishing.

4. Gee, James P. (1996) *Social Linguistics and Literacies: Ideology in Discourses*. 2nd Edition. London: Taylor & Francis.

5. Cope, Bill, and Kalantzis, Mary, eds (2000) *Multiliteracies: Literacy Learning and the Design of Social Futures*. London: Routledge.

6. Scollon, Ron (1999) Multilingualism and Intellectual Property: Visual Holophrastic Discourse and the Commodity/Sign. Paper presented at GURT 1999.

# 15

# A whiff of tobacco smoke on the page
## Primary sources in the cold new world – evidence, imagination and experience

*Mark Woodhouse*

Quarry Farm, on East Hill outside Elmira, New York, was the home of Susan and Theodore Crane, and it was here that the Cranes' famous brother-in-law Samuel Clemens – Mark Twain – summered with his wife and daughters for twenty years. In a small octagonal study built for him by Susan Crane on the top of the hill above the farm, he produced some of his best-known works. While staying with the Cranes, Clemens read from the books in the library at the farm, and made notes in the margins of books belonging to Susan and Theodore.

Quarry Farm along with its contents was given to Elmira College in 1982 and eventually the books containing Twain's marginalia were brought to the Gannett-Tripp library for safekeeping and for the use of scholars. One such scholar, examining William Hartpole Lecky's *History of European Morals*, a favourite of Twain's, had the page open to a particularly interesting bit of marginalia and suddenly, wide eyed, he thrust the book up close to my nose.

'Do you smell that?' he said – 'Tobacco smoke! And look – 'he said pointing to a small brown fleck tucked down in the gutter – 'Tobacco!'

His enthusiasm forced me to admit that I did indeed smell something and that the little brown fleck was almost certainly tobacco and more than likely, I conceded, the tobacco of Clemens himself.

Maybe, maybe not. Yet, such was the power of being in the presence of the book, seeing Clemens own hand and seeing the page, much as

Clemens himself had seen it, that the researcher was transported in a very real sense back in time.

This is probably not an unusual experience for anyone involved with rare books and special collections. In addition to the Mark Twain collection, other items in the Special Collections of Elmira College elicit similar responses. One class of advanced placement High School students, for example, came visibly alive when they were allowed to put on white gloves and examine the music manuscripts of composer Charles Tomlinson Griffes.

In another instance, an original copy of Blake's proofs for *The Book of Job* was used in a presentation to a liberal studies class. Alongside the original was a volume of reproductions and they were allowed to come up close to both books as the pages were turned. Many of them had never heard of Blake but they were mesmerised by the clarity of the original images compared to the reproductions and by the presence of Blake that permeates the 1826 original.

It is not uncommon for the response to such materials to be one of a certain reverence and wonder and, beyond that, in many cases, one of heightened insight. Joseph Janes, describing a visit to the Library of Congress Rare Books Room says that it is the 'very tangibility that fascinates and spellbinds,'[1] and Nicholas Basbanes notes in writing about Umberto Eco that 'Eco is inspired to produce his most insightful commentary when he is able to handle authentic documents, not surrogate copies in facsimile or microfilm.'[2]

In Gregory Corso's poem 'I Held A Shelley Manuscript' he describes an experience in the Houghton Library at Harvard.

My hands did numb to beauty
As they reached into Death and tightened!

Quickly, my eyes moved quickly,
Sought for smell for dust for lace
For dry hair![3]

Virginie Greene, trying to understand Corso's experience goes to the Houghton and while looking for the piece that affected him, examines instead a different poem in Shelley's notebook.

'On this page written in Shelley's hand, no matter how many words I missed, I could decipher his fear of death and the sea. I could also recognise my own twin fears of emptiness and fullness. – nobody around seemed to realise how dangerous it is to hold a Shelley manuscript in the reading room of the Houghton Library.'[4]

Part of this intensity of experience can be attributed to encountering the original in approximately the way that it was originally seen in terms of the ink, the texture of the paper, flaws, subtle shadings and so forth. Of course the original shows its age. It doesn't actually look as it would have looked when new so, why doesn't a good clean reproduction that is a faithful facsimile elicit the same sort of response?

For one thing, 'Visual processes are cognitively impenetrable'[5] to borrow a phrase from the visual arts, or, in other words, perception operates within a complex system that draws inferences from a far greater variety of sources than are immediately obvious. That would account for some subliminal effect beyond the obvious physical characteristics, however, it seems that another unseen source has something to do with the intangible and lingering essence of the persons and events associated with the object.

According to Walter Benjamin, 'the authenticity of a thing is the essence of all that is transmissible from its beginning, ranging from its substantive duration to its testimony to the history which it has experienced. – What is really jeopardised when the historical testimony is affected is the authority of the object – one might subsume the eliminated element in the term "aura" and go on to say: that which withers in the age of mechanical reproduction is the aura of the work of art.'[6]

Or, as Hillel Schwartz notes 'consider the modern potter who insists, like Karen Kames of Vermont that "only a [unique] piece thrown by hand has the particular quality of transmission of spirit from maker to receiver."'[7]

Whether we impose this quality – investing the artefact with a talismanic significance – or whether the quality exists in the object as a real but intangible trace would be difficult to prove. But, the reality of the perception, the fact that we discern a qualitative difference between the actual thing and a representation, seems clear.

Yet, the current state of things suggests that we are being pulled further and further from an appreciation of the real, in no small part due to the pervasive presence of the virtual in popular culture. Some, like Morris Berman, see this as nothing less than the beginning of the end of culture. 'The rise of the new microchip technology – also contributes to the dumbing down of America.' he writes, 'The experience of sitting with a book enables the reader to sink into a private world and ultimately discover who he or she is. [The Internet] works against depth and self-reflection, and the net effect (no pun intended) is a diffuse self, an identity that is forged by a kind of meaningless infotainment. There is no context here.'[8]

In contrast to that view, in his recent book *Everything Bad is Good for You* Steven Johnson puts forth the argument that the prevalent pastimes of popular culture, primarily computer games and television shows, are, contrary to the general view, making us smarter rather than the opposite.

Johnson goes beyond the common concessions to enhanced motor skills and the technical facility observable among devotees of computer games. Citing, among other things, the complex structure of television shows such as *24* and *Alias* that require greater viewer attention and involvement than shows of the past, the cognitive complexity of video games and the steady increase in IQ among the general population he makes a case for popular culture as a positive influence on intellectual development.

He claims that we are becoming sharper slowly and inexorably because of exposure to popular culture and calls this phenomenon the 'Sleeper Curve, after the classic sequence from Woody Allen's film where a team of scientists from 2173 are astonished that twentieth century society failed to grasp the nutritional merits of cream pies and hot fudge.'[9] He is well aware of the objections to his premise and late in his argument he addresses the concerns of critics who complain that, on the whole, people are reading less.

'The fact that we are spending so much time online gets to the other, more crucial objection: yes, we're spending less time reading literary fiction, but that's because we're spending less time doing *everything* we used to do before. – We're buying fewer CDs, we're going out to the movies less regularly – because about a dozen new activities have become bona fide mainstream pursuits in the past few years: the Web, e-mail, games, DVDs, cable on demand, text chat. [but] as long as reading books remains *part* of our cultural diet, and as long as the new popular forms continue to offer their own cognitive rewards, we're not likely to descend into a culture of mental atrophy anytime soon.'[10]

Johnson's overall argument is frequently compelling and the evidence is clear as far as it goes, but his criteria still point to largely quantitative, analytical and, in some cases, mechanical skills. The fact that we may be getting heretofore overlooked benefits from our seemingly unavoidable immersion in popular media doesn't speak to the possibility that the development that is occurring is lop sided; that the left hemisphere of the brain is experiencing a greater work-out than the right or that our easy familiarity with the virtual comes at the expense of an appreciation for the authentic. That is, it never addresses, or appears to even recognise, how we might be losing touch with Benjamin's 'aura' or, for lack of a better term, the soul of things.

As Schwartz comments, ' the more adroit we are at carbon copies the more confused we are about the unique, the original, the Real McCoy.'[11] As librarians and archivists we have become quite adroit indeed. Our concern for the preservation of cultural artefacts has led to a reliance on the strategic use of surrogates. The great strides of the past decade in terms of digitization have literally eliminated the barriers of space and time that confronted researchers seeking access to a vast wealth of material. The value of that can't be denied. But, at the same time we seem to be witnessing an undesirable by-product, a blurring of the virtual and the real into a sort of indiscriminate equivalency that indicates a larger problem, one that goes beyond the traditional debates over artefactual versus informational value.

For example, a fourth grade teacher, writing in *Instructor* magazine about her use of a 1622 Pilgrim's Journal commonly referred to as *Mount's Relation* says that 'One of the most exciting ways for kids to connect with the past is with primary sources. When these voices, images, and artefacts of the past are before them, children have an easier time imagining faraway times and people as real.'[12] True enough. But, later on in the article she explains that 'Many versions of *Mount's Relation* are available both online and in print. – For the first session, I make copies of the first few pages of the journal for each of my students. (They're combined onto one page for you to use as a reproducible.) I then enlarge one copy to chart size (you could use this as an overhead), and I model how I would translate the excerpt into modern English.'[13]

While the lesson being described is valuable and in some ways innovative, the description of a chart sized blow up of a photocopy of a print out from a scan residing on a website as an example of putting the artefact before them seems less than perfectly accurate.

Of course, no one would suggest that the actual Pilgrim's Journal of 1622, were the teacher so fortunate as to have one in her possession, should be subjected to close and repeated examination and handling by a class of nine year olds. But, neither should it be desirable to allow the concept of primary research to succumb too easily to processes that are demonstrably qualitatively different than that afforded by exposure to the real thing.

Steven Johnson, even while making his case in defence of new media is forced to concede that 'popular culture is not doing a good job at training our minds to follow a sustained textual argument or narrative that doesn't involve genuine interaction – you can convey attitude and connection in the online world with ease; But it is harder to transmit a fully-fledged worldview. The good news, he goes on to say, is that kids aren't being educated exclusively by the media, 'we still have schools and parents to teach wisdom that the popular culture fails to impart.'[14]

So when it comes to wisdom, as opposed to all of the varieties of raw information we're taking in, the challenge rests with educators to figure out how to convey important lessons in the midst of a culture competing quite loudly and persistently for the attention of the young. One important way for libraries to help transmit these lessons for young and old alike, it seems, would be to reacquaint them with the genuine.

Particularly in these times when library collections are becoming homogenous and libraries are struggling to reassert their purpose and viability in a networked world that increasingly sees them as superfluous, unique and important collections afford an opportunity to fill an important role. They can give users an enhanced and unique educational experience that provides a needed balance and intimacy with the real for which our largely unreal world hungers.

Describing the manifestation of this hunger, Paul Ray, a market researcher and sociologist, has identified an American subculture that displays what he calls an 'angry demand for authenticity.' This group, now commonly called by Ray's label 'cultural creatives' represent 26 per cent of the American population, according to his research, and are characterised by their advocacy of voluntary simplicity, spiritual self-discovery, public service and by their demand for authenticity. And Ray says 'they have clout.'[15]

Interestingly, there appear to be those who feel threatened by an undue emphasis on the real. Reporting in the *New York Times Magazine* in October of 2004 Ron Suskind quotes from a 'senior advisor' to George W. Bush who explains that reporters like Suskind have become irrelevant. They 'belong to the "reality based community"', which he defined as people who 'believe that solutions emerge from judicious study of discernible reality. – That's not the way the world really works anymore. – We're an Empire now, and when we act, we create our own reality.'[16]

If those who rule have an investment in the exploitation of confusion such that a phrase as innocuous as 'reality based community' can become a dismissive expression of thinly veiled contempt then perhaps that's a clear enough signal that we need to pay closer attention to our grasp on what is real and what isn't. Uneasiness with the current state of things often returns to questions of authenticity which, in the final analysis, have to do with questions of truth. These are questions that strike at the spiritual health of societies.

Libraries, in tandem with their growing ability to provide greater amounts of information from a greater variety of sources than ever before, have an obligation to find ways of addressing the needs at the heart of these questions. One great tool at their disposal rests in Special Collections – the real thing, the genuine article, the Real McCoy.

Whether or not our researcher was catching a whiff of Sam Clemens' tobacco or not he was getting a good dose of something real. And as Clemens himself said: ' I don't care anything about being humorous, or poetical or eloquent or anything of the kind – the end and aim of my ambition is to be authentic – is to be considered authentic.'[17]

# Notes

1. Janes, Joseph (2003) 'The web that was', *American Libraries* Apr: 90.
2. Basbanes, Nicholas A. (2003) *A Splendor of Letters: the Permanence of Books in an Impermanent World*. New York: Harper Collins, p. 7.
3. Corso, Gregory (1960) *The Happy Birthday of Death*. New York: New Directions, p. 22.
4. Greene, Virginie (2005) 'Three approaches to poetry', *PMLA*. 120 (1): 233.
5. Danto, Arthur C. (2001) 'Seeing and showing', *The Journal of Aesthetics and Art Criticism*. 59,1: 8.
6. Benjamin, Walter (1968) The Work of Art in the Age of Mechanical Reproduction. In *Illuminations*, trans, H. Zohn. New York: Harcourt, Brace & World, p. 223.
7. Schwartz, Hillel (1996) *The Culture of the Copy: Striking Likenesses, Unreasonable Facsimiles*. New York: Zone Books, p. 257.
8. Berman, Morris (2000) *The Twilight of American Culture*. New York: W.W. Norton, p. 49.
9. Johnson, Steven (2005) *Everything Bad is Good for You:How Today's Popular Culture is Actually Making Us Smarter*. New York: Riverhead Books, p. xiv.
10. Ibid., p. 183.
11. Schwartz, op. cit., p. 11.

12. Edinger, Monica (2001) 'Time travel with primary sources', *Instructor*. 111(4): 1.
13. Ibid., 2.
14. Johnson, op. cit., p. 187.
15. Madison, Cathy (1997) 'Reality hunger', *Utne Reade* Jul/Aug: 55.
16. Suskind, Ron (2004) 'What makes Bush's presidency so radical even to some republicans is his preternatural, faith-infused certainty in uncertain times', *New York Times Magazine* October 17, p44.
17. Rasmussen, Kent (1997) *The Quotable Mark Twain: His Essential Aphorisms, Witticisms, and Concise Opinions.* Chicago: Contemporary Books.

# Index